HEAVY TIMBER STRUCTURES

Creating Comfort in Public Spaces

HEAVY TIMBER STRUCTURES

Creating Comfort in Public Spaces

Anthony F. Zaya & Tim Diener

Schiffer Publishing Ltd
4880 Lower Valley Road • Atglen, PA 19310

We dedicate this book to our parents,
Anthony F. and Yolanda M. Zaya,
and Paul W. and Shirley Ann Diener.

Other Schiffer Books
by Tim Diener and Anthony Zaya:
Timber Frame Hybrids: Enduring Traditions, Boundless Possibilities, ISBN 978-0-7643-2894-7

Other Schiffer Books
on Related Subjects:
Artisan Crafted Timber Frame Homes,
by Tina Skinner, ISBN 978-0-7643-2486-4
Log & Timber Frame Homes,
by Tina Skinner, ISBN 978-0-7643-1754-5

Library of Congress Control Number: 2017935602

Designed by Matthew Goodman
Type set in Brandon Text

ISBN: 978-0-7643-5420-5
Printed in China

Published by Schiffer Publishing, Ltd.
4880 Lower Valley Road
Atglen, PA 19310
Phone: (610) 593-1777; Fax: (610) 593-2002
E-mail: Info@schifferbooks.com
Web: www.schifferbooks.com

“ . . . although they could not be seen . . . the oversize beams made themselves felt, almost like something alive there in the dark.”

—Eric Sloane, *An Age of Barns*

Contents

Preface

At Lancaster County Timber Frames, Inc., we make custom designed, handcrafted timber frames. The company has designed, carved, and erected timber frames in twenty states—from Florida to Vermont, and Massachusetts to New Mexico. Our work has received numerous local, state, national, and international awards, and has been featured on the covers of a dozen magazines. One of our projects was selected by HGTV for its season-long *Dream House* series and broadcast during the 2008 season. In 2007, and again in 2009, Lancaster County Timber Frames was named to the *Inc.* 5000 list of the fastest-growing private companies in America.

The projects in this volume represent a cross section of the commercial projects we have completed over the years. They were selected to illustrate the variety and range of heavy timber use in buildings. Some of the projects are very modest; others not so much.

In some cases only traditional mortise and tenon joinery was employed; other projects involved steel—either exposed or embedded. In other structures all of these methods of joining were utilized.

Some of the pictures show solid timbers, some show glulams, and still others show peeled logs. Some have an oil finish while others are whitewashed or stained.

The structures are used as retail spaces, gathering areas, or places to eat. Some are houses of worship or reflection; others are for rehabilitation or healing. Some link back to the past; some push toward the future. All of them celebrate the wondrous material that is wood.

—www.lancotf.com

Introduction

A Few Words about Wood in General and Heavy Timbers in Particular

There is something about wood in the built environment that is quite unlike any other material.

To begin with, in the history of building, no other material has been replicated, emulated, or just outright faked as much as wood. None even comes close. Conversely, it's one of the few materials that is rarely used to mimic others. For thousands of years, we have tried to transfer the look and texture of wood to other materials—first to stone, then to plaster and concrete, then to aluminum and plastics. The immortal forms of classical Greek temples are known to derive from the timber materials from which those temples were originally built.[1] The fluted columns evoke the rough-hewn tree trunk colonnade; the triglyphs recall the checked end-grain of roof beams; even the capitals—later the site of the most ornate embellishments—may have originally been but a utilitarian contrivance to restrain the timber columns' natural tendency to split.

At the opposite end of the historical and aesthetic spectrum, we have all witnessed the transcendent fatuousness of wood-grained vinyl siding. Not far removed from this, perhaps, but often exalted

St. Joseph Adoration Chapel at Belmont Abbey College, Charlotte, North Carolina.

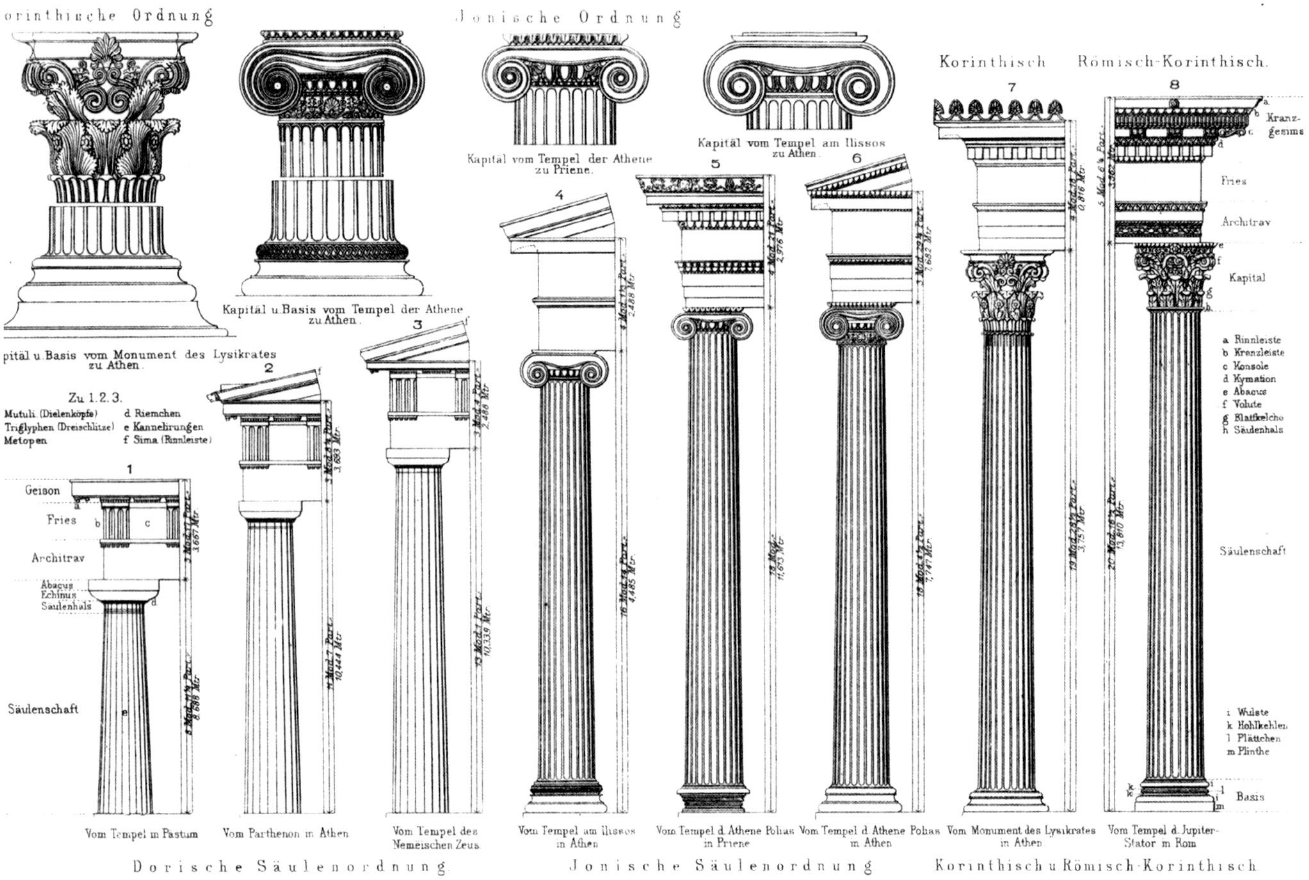

Vitruvius maintained that the forms of classical Greek architecture derived from and referred to earlier wooden structures.

by discursive irony, are brutal masses of concrete formed and imprinted with rough wooden boards. (Of course, this may be but a sly wink, implicitly acknowledging that in no manner could such shallow impressions transmute the underlying materials, or perhaps even confer on them a tinge of the absent nobility.) A stroll through a big box home improvement store will turn up faux wood ceramic tile, vinyl flooring, venetian blind slats, ceiling fan blades, tool handles, flower pots, fiber-cement siding, decking, interior and exterior trim—the list is seemingly endless. Likewise, big box home furnishing businesses do a brisk trade in faux wood tables, chairs, desks, shelves, and the like.

And so has it ever gone with the materials from which we choose to construct our dwellings and public structures. Yet while our buildings often pay lip service to wood, we have never really succeeded in imbuing those counterfeit materials with the spirit of wood. Why, in spite of this failure, have we so doggedly persisted? What has made the simulacrum of wood as prevalent as its model?

The original impulse may be haptic. People seem to feel a need to touch wood, to move their hands across the surface of a timber. They can't help it. Not so, however, with steel, concrete, stone, or glass—except maybe, in the case of glass, a toddler with sticky fingers. Masonry materials—stone, brick, even concrete—have great intrinsic beauty and radiate a sense of mass and strength, but they are abrasive and cold, both figuratively and literally. Glass and steel are visually and viscerally seductive, too, but while neither is abrasive, both are cold—well below the temperature of the human body.

So, again: what is it about wood? What is it about wood that pulls us in, that grabs us, that makes us want to touch it, maybe even caress it?

For one thing, wood is a sumptuous feast for the senses. Who wouldn't stare in rapt fascination at the riotous intricacies of a burl-veneered tabletop? Run one's hand over the volutes of a railing polished by the hands of generations of men, women, and children? Draw in a lung-full of air scented by a Spanish cedar cigar box, a sandalwood trifle, a stand of eucalyptus trees, even the shavings in a pencil sharpener? We seem to be endowed with an innate intuitive appreciation of the acoustic properties of wood. We'll rap our knuckles on the body of a guitar just to delight in its resonances, but so will we test the thickness or hardness or soundness of a wall, a box, a tree in the same way. Taste? Think of a filet of salmon broiled on a cedar plank, meats smoked with hickory or mesquite wood chips. Sure, we do some of these things with other materials, too, but it is predominantly wood that most reliably beckons to all five of the traditionally defined senses. Even some of the non-traditional senses (our vestibular and kinesthetic senses, for example) summon most readily the aid of a prop made, ideally, of wood—a crutch, a cane, a walking stick.

Sensory experience, it is now understood, is a dynamically active perceptual process. We perceive a thing and our mind acts to interpret it and initiate a response, often at or above the threshold of consciousness. Yet even while our senses seek out and delight in the many forms of wood in our built environment, wood materials are equally capable of engaging us subliminally, evoking memories, emotions, and even spiritual associations that often lie deep below the level of explicit consciousness.

A Tinkertoy set transports one into the dim past: the hardness and weight and perfect fist-full of the basswood spools, the connecting rods' brittle slotted ends, the warm resinous smell of the wood wafting up out of the cardboard tube they were shipped in—all a more serviceable time machine than anything H. G. Wells ever dreamt up. The family's hunting cabin in the woods, in all likelihood a veritable cocoon of wood, conjures some of our most elemental positive emotions—security and reassurance, comfort and warmth. The sight of some exquisitely handcrafted object—a musical instrument, a piece of furniture, a sculpture—summons the emotions of respect, admiration, or even envy; in our minds the master craftsman in wood possesses virtues of character surpassing most of the distinctions modern workaday life can bestow upon us.

Wood objects and structures figure prominently in the spiritual life of many cultures and creeds. Is it not fitting that the True Cross—one of the most venerated relics in Christendom, fragments of which are claimed to reside in hundreds of churches across Europe—was of wood, and that a spirited debate on its species and provenance has been carried on since the early centuries of Christianity? Both of the world's oldest and, until quite recently, largest wooden structures are religious: the pagoda at Hōryū-ji and the Great Buddha Hall at Tōdai-ji, both in Nara Prefecture, Japan. In some remote recess of our minds, we certainly grasp that all wood was once a living thing, and that, like we humans, it is infinite in its variety. Wood is so inextricably linked with our genetic memory, and has been such a crucial component of our built environment for so long, that our associations with wood appear to be all but hardwired. It is the character of this "hardwiring" that has, in recent years, become an object of study for a branch of the field known as environmental psychology.

Environmental psychology is a broad interdisciplinary field that studies the interactions between individuals or groups and their environments. The breadth of the field derives, in part, from the many possible definitions of environments; there is, of course, the natural environment, but there are also social, learning, built, and even informational environments, among many others; and then there are subsets, and subsets of subsets, of these. For our purposes, the interplay between the human response to the natural and built environments are of the most interest.

Early environmental psychology studies paid a great deal of attention to the negative impact of a given environment on the individual; specifically, to the adverse effects of the urban environment—crowding, noise, pollution. An implicit assumption

Ceramic tile with faux grain pattern and hand-scraped texture.

Makassar ebony-veneered cigar humidor.

Handcrafted cherry flag case with inlaid walnut corner splines.

underlying these early studies was that the "natural" environment was the ideal in relation to which all other environments should be judged. Ultimately, this assumption itself was problematized, leading to efforts to refine our understanding of what constitutes an ideal human environment, and to studies of the positive effects of those ideal surroundings on the human psyche. In the literature of the 1980s, these ideal surroundings came to be identified as restorative environments, defined as those that held the greatest potential for psychophysiological stress recovery, and virtually always coterminous with natural settings.

As it happens, most of us don't spend very much time in nature[2]. According to the US Environmental Protection Agency, the average American spends ninety-three percent of his or her life indoors. Of that, six percent is spent in vehicles, and the remainder inside a structure of some sort—a home, workplace, or store, for example. That leaves about seven percent of our time to be spent outdoors, in nature. That's more than it sounds like actually, a little more than an hour and a half a day, but, evidently, still not enough. This may help to explain the premium many of us place on a view in our homes and workplaces. In fact, a number of early studies in the field of environmental psychology purported to show that the recovery experiences of post-operative patients differed according to whether their hospital rooms had a view. Those placed in rooms without a view tended to take longer to recover and required more pain medication than patients whose rooms looked out on a park.

The Hall of the Great Buddha at Tōdai-ji, Nara, Japan.

A view of a natural setting thus affords at least a share of the restorative benefit of actually being in nature itself. The mind, in all its triumphant plasticity and eagerness to supplement reality, finds a way to derive some advantage from the mere suggestion of nature. So it should not surprise us that the common drive to bring nature indoors finds further expression in the ubiquity of plants in the home and now, frequently, the workplace. Here again, studies have sought to examine and quantify the effects that indoor plants have on our behavior and emotional states. One such study claims that their presence actually raised the test subjects' pain threshold; another study demonstrated improved performance on creative tasks when undertaken in interior environments furnished with plants. Indeed, there is a profusion of recent and current studies on the effects of indoor plants on their occupants, claiming salutary effects as various as:

- Increased productivity; enhanced employee attitudes and disposition;
- Decreased blood pressure; decreased sympathetic nervous system (SNS) activation (the primary

function of the SNS is to stimulate the body's flight-or-flight response);

- An almost immediate lessening of stress, some of which may be the result of reductions in office noise levels as a direct consequence of strategic placement of plants;
- Reduced employee absenteeism; a mean reduction in the occurrence of an array of common ailments such as cough, dry skin, fatigue, headache, sore throat, etc.;
- Heightened perceived value of the interior spaces;
- Better overall indoor air quality; more effective maintenance of indoor air humidity levels within the ideal human comfort zone of thirty to sixty percent; lowered heating and cooling costs; reduced levels of airborne toxins from indoor pollutants such as benzene, xlyene, trichloroethylene, and formaldehyde;
- Truly astonishing hypothetical levels of business and industry savings from reductions in "sick building syndrome"—related illnesses and associated losses in worker performance.

The study of the effects of plants in interior environments is still very much a dynamic field of inquiry, with university institutes, government agencies, private and industry groups, and international organizations all actively engaged. If such explorations can indeed demonstrate measurable stress

The Room of the Poor in the Hôtel-Dieu in Beaune, France. This institution was founded as a hospital for the poor in 1443. In addition to the berths along the outer walls, originally there was also a double row of sick berths running down the middle of the 16-meter-wide-by-50-meter-long space. The sick berths were richly paneled in solid wood.

reduction and other beneficial effects of bringing natural elements into the built environment in the form of plants, how then do humans respond to the presence of other natural objects and materials, notably wood, in the built environment? In the last twenty to twenty-five years, this very question has begun to attract the attention of researchers across a broad spectrum of disciplines and geographic areas, from university forestry programs and wood industry trade groups to cognitive studies and architecture programs, from Japan and New Zealand to Canada, Denmark, Norway, and beyond.

Academic and industry researchers in Japan, for example, conducted a number of the earliest studies to determine that exposure to wood in interior environments had a measurable beneficial effect on blood pressure, heart rate, and mood. Subsequent research in Japan has shown that stress, as indicated by glucocorticoid levels in the blood (glucocorticoids are hormones synthesized in the adrenal glands in response to stress stimuli), was reduced in hospital rooms into which wood paneling was introduced.

More recently, research at a forestry studies program at a Canadian university found that sympathetic nervous system activation and skin conductance levels were substantially lower in office environments with wood than in comparable environments without wood. (As mentioned previously, the sympathetic nervous system is the neural network associated with humans' fight-or-flight response; skin conductance is a common indicator of stress level.)

Yet another, year-long study of high school classrooms in Austria found that heart rate variability—an indication of parasympathetic nervous system activation—increased in students being instructed in classrooms outfitted with materials that looked like wood. (The parasympathetic nervous system is the neural network associated with stress reduction and the promotion of healing and recovery; in other words, with counterbalancing the sympathetic nervous system.) Olfactory system-mediated responses to alpha-pinenes in wood have also been found to lower heart rate and blood pressure, and electromyography studies have established enhanced concentration and relaxation functions in environments furnished with materials that look like wood (paneling and/or furniture). Improvements in memory and sleep functions have been similarly documented.

What these and many similar studies have in common is their reliance on measurable psychophysiological responses to wood in interior settings. But environmental psychology research into the nexus

The entry lobby of the Ambrosia Treatment Center in Medford, New Jersey.

The entry lobby of the Lebanon Veterans Administration Behavioral Health Building.

of wood and health has not been confined to studies of precognitive psychophysiological effects. Indeed, if anything, the research into the subjective dimensions of our responses to wood in interior environments has been even more far-reaching. Such research often makes use of surveys, interviews, and a technique referred to as Q-sorting, or Q-methodology. (At the risk of over-simplification, this method of factor analysis looks for correlations between subject responses across a sampling of variables, e.g., varying responses to differing extents of decorative wood elements in a photograph of an interior.) Not surprisingly, many such studies have confirmed a common intuitive association of wood material with healthfulness and general desirability. Spaces are consistently perceived as warm, inviting, and pleasantly relaxing when outfitted with wooden paneling, timber, or furniture; lobbies and reception areas with wooden finishes are uniformly seen as more prestigious, energetic, innovative, and comfortable, and are frequently associated with organizations that would be more desirable to work for.

If one has spent close to a lifetime working wood with one's own hands, fashioning everything from furniture to sculpture to whole houses from wood, none of the foregoing recitation of the beneficial effects of wood is really cause for amazement. Yes, the psychophysiometric and statistical studies and poetic and philosophical meditations have certainly brought much to light that is worth knowing about our innate responses to wood and timber materials. But what is genuinely amazing is just how obvious these conclusions sometimes appear to be. Of course we prefer interior environments that are furnished in wood; of course we find such spaces more relaxing and comfortable; of course a piney scent transports and calms us. This isn't meant to diminish the importance of environmental psychology studies, but merely to emphasize how commonsensical, how intuitively right its conclusions are, and how elemental our relationship with wood truly is.

And yet, in spite of what appears to be an almost genetically determined favorable predisposition toward wood and other natural materials, and in spite of the sheer obvious logic of our attraction to wood, there persists a number of common, vague prejudices and misconceptions about wood as a building material.

A Structurally Gifted Material

One such notion is that wood as a structural material (as opposed to a decorative material) is somehow the poor stepchild of construction. This idea has an interesting and convoluted provenance in enlightenment and industrial revolution notions of absolute progress. When the Eiffel Tower was built, people marveled at a structure the likes of which human eyes had never before seen. The tower's technological and psychological triumph was that it transcended the limitations of traditional building materials and methods. In the euphoria surrounding this landmark engineering achievement, traditional materials like wood came to be relegated to secondary status.

This notion obscures the fact that timber is, in a manner of speaking, structurally gifted. Its resilience and tensile strength have allowed ancient structures to survive earthquakes more successfully than masonry structures. In typical sizes, heavy timbers retain their structural integrity in a fire longer than unprotected steel. While wood as a primary structural material has been supplanted to a great extent by ferroconcrete and steel structures, it has made a significant comeback in the form of engineered timber products, and given rise to the highly innovative and exciting technology of cross-laminated timber (CLT). These structural components, used in engineered mass timber structures, are beginning to make inroads in the construction of middle and high rise buildings.

An Environmentally Positive Material

There are some who bemoan these developments. Another vague prejudice about wood as a construction material is that its use substantially contributes to the destruction of the environment. This idea is a natural outgrowth of efforts beginning in the 1960s, to raise awareness of environmental damage caused by a wide range of industrial and commercial practices. Nonetheless, it is quite reasonable to argue that the use of wood and timber in construction is actually environmentally positive. In fact, timber is the only renewable structural building material we have. According to the National Report on Sustainable Forests, for at least the last sixty years the total area of forests in the United States has been stable, and the volume of wood found on them has actually increased.

Timber is organic and during its life cycle it absorbs carbon dioxide and releases oxygen. As a finished product, it remains a carbon sink, and at the end of its service it can be recycled. Virtually all of a harvested tree finds its way into a useful product. Additionally, timber is hypoallergenic, moderates humidity, and is acoustically positive. Finally, its service life is measured not merely in years and decades, but in centuries and millennia.

An Economically Competitive Material

The concept of embodied energy has gained currency as a measure of relative environmental impact. Embodied energy is commonly defined as the sum of all the energy required to produce goods or services, and that energy is considered to be embodied in the product itself. Timber and wood products fare well from this perspective. The production of steel, concrete, and glass requires approximately twenty-four, sixteen, and fourteen times more energy, respectively, than timber production. This lower embodied energy also helps to make timber and wood economically competitive in construction. In addition, in many areas timber is an indigenous material, reducing transportation costs. These products also play a substantial role in the modern economy, continuing to provide significant employment and support of rural economies. As environmental initiatives in the wood industry take root, the markets provide financial incentives for landowners and governments to invest in their forests to keep them healthy for future generations.

A Historically Significant Material

It hardly needs to be added that wood and heavy timber structures are historically significant. Heavy timber structures employing mortise and tenon joinery have been found in archaeological sites dating to at least 5,000 BCE in areas of China. A recent archaeological discovery in Germany has established a comparable age for true mortise and tenon joinery.[3] Even today, in Europe, many dwellings and buildings still in use were built more than 500 years ago. The role wood and timber have played in the master narrative of our architectural evolution is plainly written in innumerable surviving structures across many regions.

A Stylistically Versatile Building Material

Heavy timber construction, whether specifically traditional timber framing with mortise and tenon joinery, or, more generally, post and beam construction with visible or concealed connections, is a method of building, not an architectural style. Heavy timber construction has been employed in widely divergent architectural styles, and across vast expanses of space and time. The skeletal structure can be designed to complement almost any look and feel. A sampling of this range is contained in the following project case studies.

What is not always equally apparent, however, is the historical relationship between our contemporary light wood framing methods and the heavy timber construction methods they supplanted. Before the advent of the industrial revolution in the United States, virtually all domestic and public buildings utilized either masonry or heavy timber construction methods, or a combination of both. With the westward expansion and burgeoning populations of early nineteenth-century America, an acute need for more economical and more rapidly built dwellings helped to drive the development of

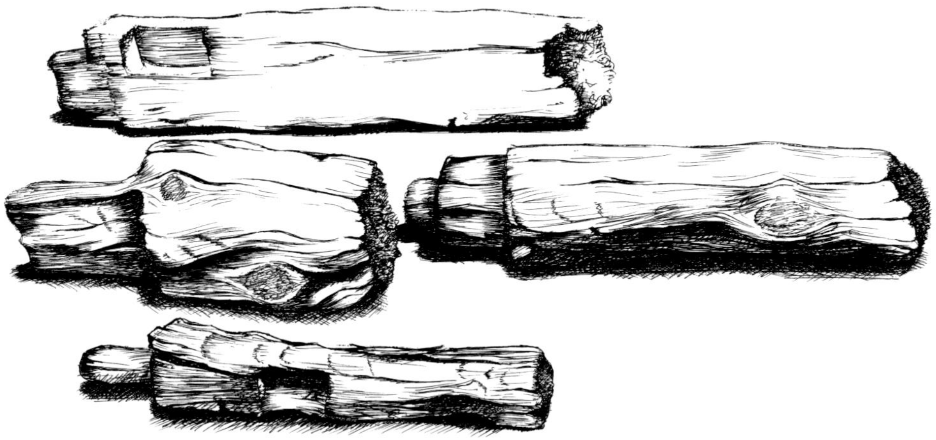

Samples of joinery dating to 5,000 BCE from the Hemudu culture, modern-day Zhejiang Province, China.

light stud framing methods. The technical advances of the industrial revolution—water-driven saw mills, machine-cut nails, railways to move timber material, coupled with abundant softwood forests—provided the conditions necessary for the proliferation of the stud framing methods we are familiar with today. In diametric opposition to construction utilizing heavy timbers as a primary structural element, stud framing is notable in that it is defined by the need to conceal its structure behind a veneer that evokes a material other than what it is; it is defined by a lack of material integrity, by the absence of authenticity.

Most of us live in stick-built houses, but we tell ourselves that if we'd had the good sense to be born with a silver spoon in our mouths, that would surely be otherwise. Indeed, much of our contemporary architectural and interior design ethic is focused on disguising and concealing the wood skeleton of the structures we inhabit. That's not too surprising, really, in view of the construction industry's aesthetically challenged light wood framing methods: who really wants to look at a stud wall skinned with oriented strand board, or any of the other materials married to it to give us comfort and access to conveniences? Our dwellings and public structures are often clad in materials that obscure the structural and mechanical systems that support them, and these materials embody our aspirations with respect to what we wish our buildings were really made of. The resurgence of heavy timber in residential and commercial applications should be viewed in light of these aspirations. With a heavy timber frame, both the structural system supporting the enveloping shell of a building and the primary aesthetic focus are equally on display.

In the middle of an address on the rebuilding of the British House of Commons Chamber, the rhetorically inimitable Winston Churchill famously quipped, "We shape our buildings, and afterwards they shape us." Generations of architects have been raised to revere this maxim as an article of faith, and rightly so. But there was a beguilingly concrete context in which it was uttered: Churchill's famous dictum was offered in support of the proposition that the Commons Chamber, demolished by incendiary bombs during the Blitz, be rebuilt as it had been. The original chamber contained only 427 seats for 646 members of parliament, and organized that insufficient seating in such a way as to intensify the intimacy of the debate and confrontation that occurred there daily. By reconstructing the Commons Chamber along the adversarial rectangular pattern, rather than the semi-circular or horseshoe pattern favored by many legislative assemblies, he sought to ensure that debate would remain lively and robust, but also intimate. A few minutes of watching a live debate on the BBC is all it takes to convince us that Churchill was right.

Another heavenly body in the firmament of architectural thinking, Frank Lloyd Wright wrote in a 1928 essay that "[Wood] is the most humanly intimate of all materials. Man loves his association with it, likes to feel it under his hand, sympathetic to his touch and to his eye. Wood is universally beautiful to Man" ("In the Cause of Architecture, IV. The Meaning of Materials—Wood," *Architectural Record*). Much of the rest of Wright's essay is an impassioned plea—a tirade, some might say—to respect the nature of wood as material, to eschew the violence done upon it by Western traditions of carpentry, which to him was all but a term of opprobrium. But while Wright's opinionated vitriol might tickle, his aim is as honorable as Churchill's. Wright knew that the environments into which the craft of the woodworker is poured will ever affect those who inhabit those places. He knew, too, that in the triumvirate of dominant structural building materials—wood, metals, and masonry—each has its own strengths and advantages, but none are as intertwined with the human mind, spirit, and heart as wood.

Houses of Worship

Wood has long occupied pride of place in ecclesiastical architecture. No structure exemplifies this standing better than the first project in the following series of case studies: the St. Joseph Adoration Chapel of Belmont Abbey College. The meditative interior space of the chapel, through its abstract re-imagination of the surrounding trees, communes directly with the natural environment right outside its almost fully glazed walls. The St. Thomas the Apostle Orthodox Church and the atrium at the St. Peter the Apostle Church both use their intricate timber frame structures to reference centuries-old building methods in their respective traditions, strengthening the confessional identity and continuity. So too the St. John Neumann Center attached to the St. Peter the Apostle Church and shrine. In contrast, the porte cochère of the St. Matthew Evangelical Lutheran Church calls attention to both the robust stylistic traditions of church architecture and its own departure from those conventions. All strive to welcome and calm, to instill awe, to draw the eyes and the mind upwards.

St. Joseph Adoration Chapel at Belmont Abbey College

Charlotte, North Carolina, 2008

Owner
Belmont Abbey College,
Belmont, North Carolina

Architect
WGM Design,
Charlotte, North Carolina

Engineer
D. Remy & Company,
Hayesville, North Carolina

General contractor
Spectrum Building Company,
Mooresville, North Carolina

Belmont Abbey College is a highly rated Catholic liberal arts college near Charlotte, North Carolina. The Benedictine monks wanted a haven in the woods near the college residence halls so that students and visitors could have a quiet place in which to pray and reflect. This haven was to be named the St. Joseph Adoration Chapel.

The monks tasked the architect, William Monroe of WGM Design, with designing a structure that, both from the interior and exterior, looked and felt like it belonged in the forest. They also requested that its impact on the forest environment be close to zero. The latter was accomplished in large part by securing the building to piers. The former was realized by bifurcating the slender timber columns into an orderly tangle of diagonal timber members that mimicked the surrounding trees.

Typically, glass panes in a timber structure are set in the exterior wall envelope. Not so here. The architect wanted the glass recessed between the timbers, and since virtually every exterior plane is either glass or timber, the tolerance for racking was extremely tight. A series of intersecting turn-buckled stainless steel tie rods, as well as concealed engineered steel connectors at all timber intersections, allowed the structure to resist lateral forces. The timbers are all 6×6 in section and are kiln-dried Douglas fir, select structural grade, and free of heart center.

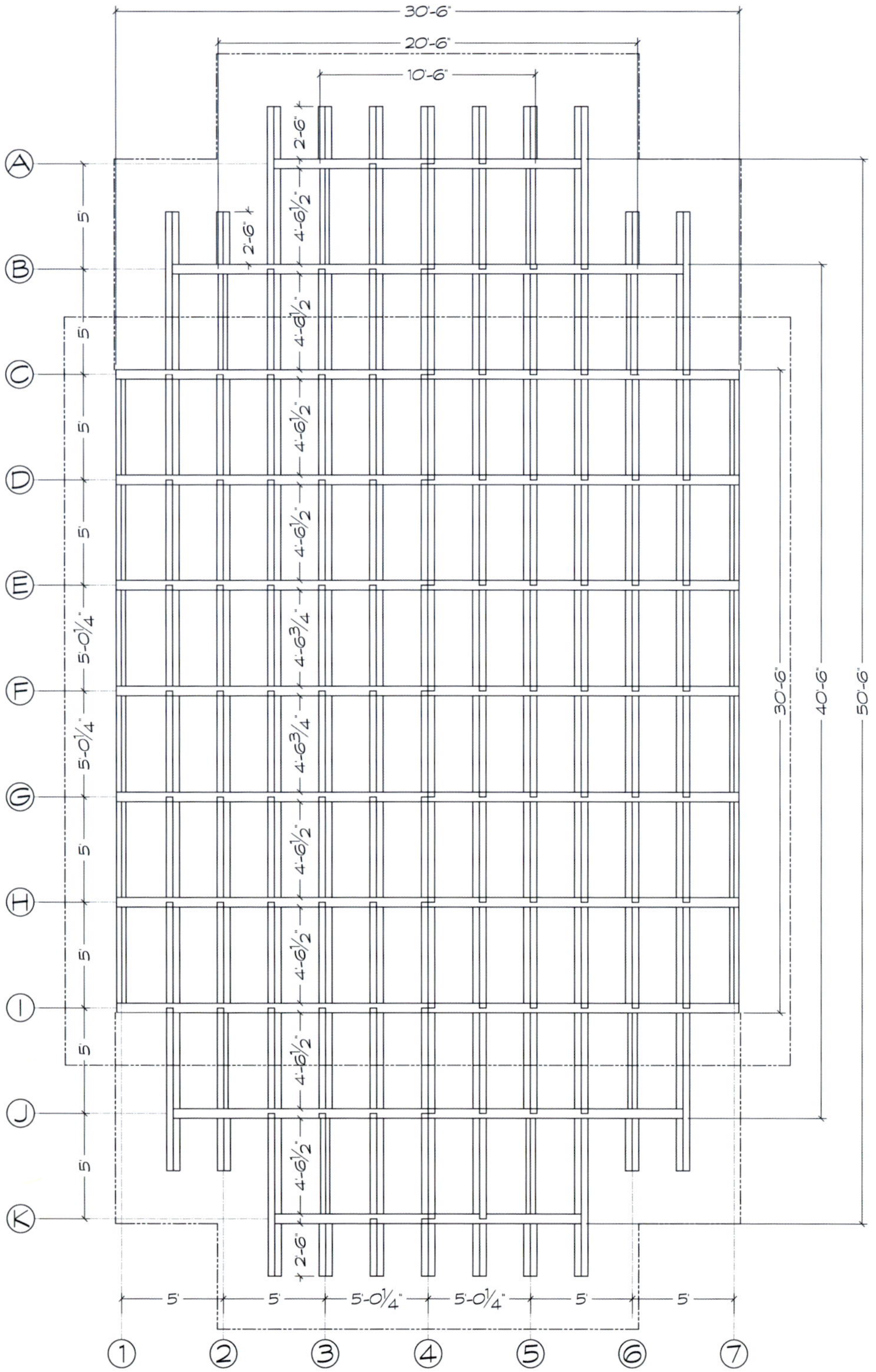
30'-6"
20'-6"
10'-6"
2'-6"
4'-6½"
4'-6¾"
5'
5'-0¼"
30'-6"
40'-6"
50'-6"
A
B
C
D
E
F
G
H
I
J
K
1
2
3
4
5
6
7

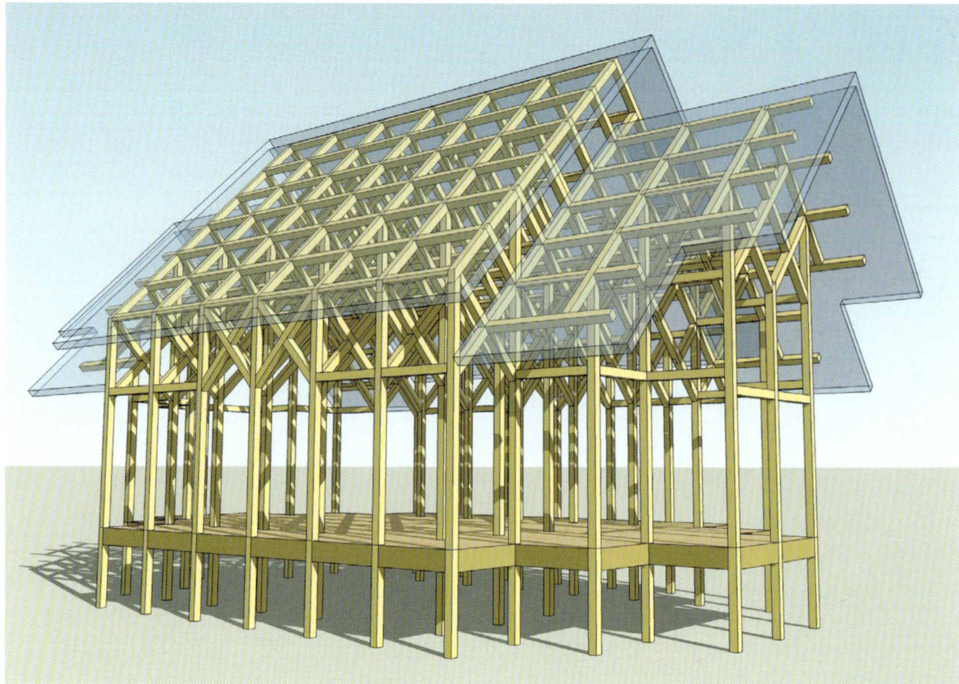

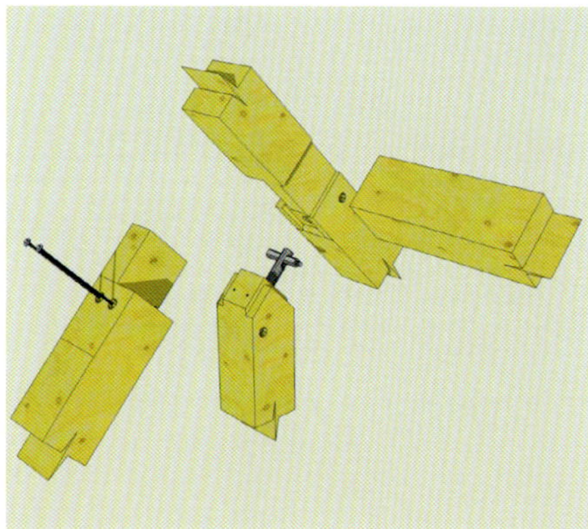

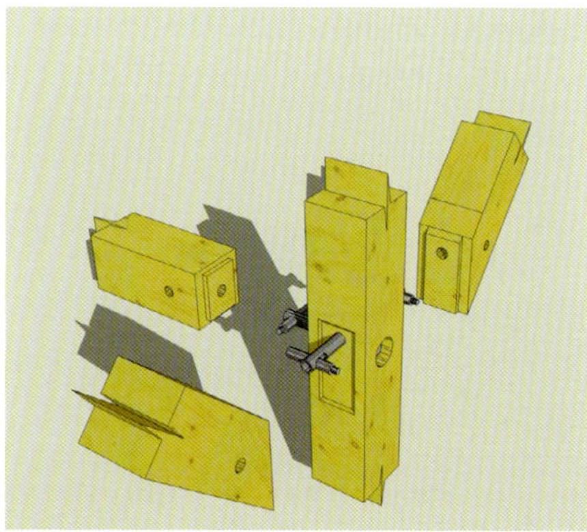

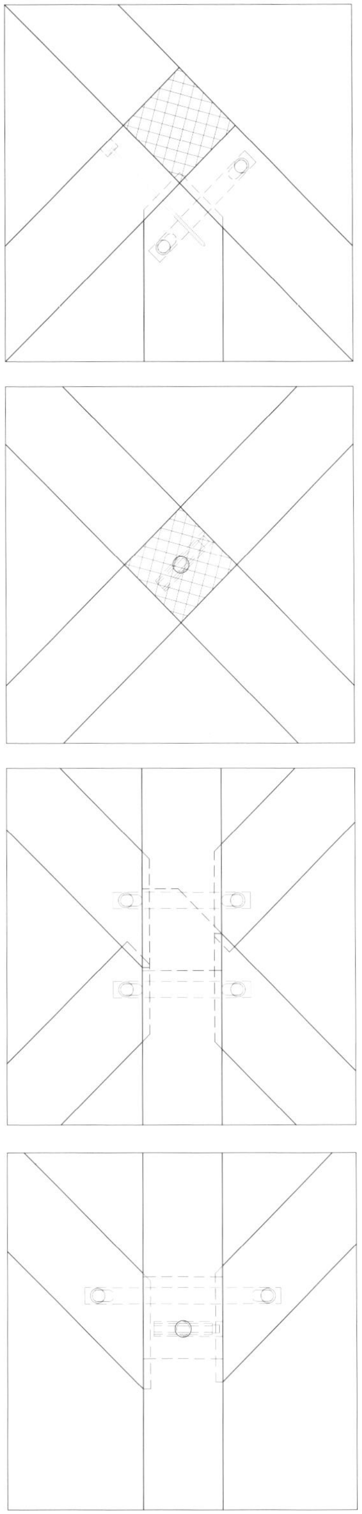

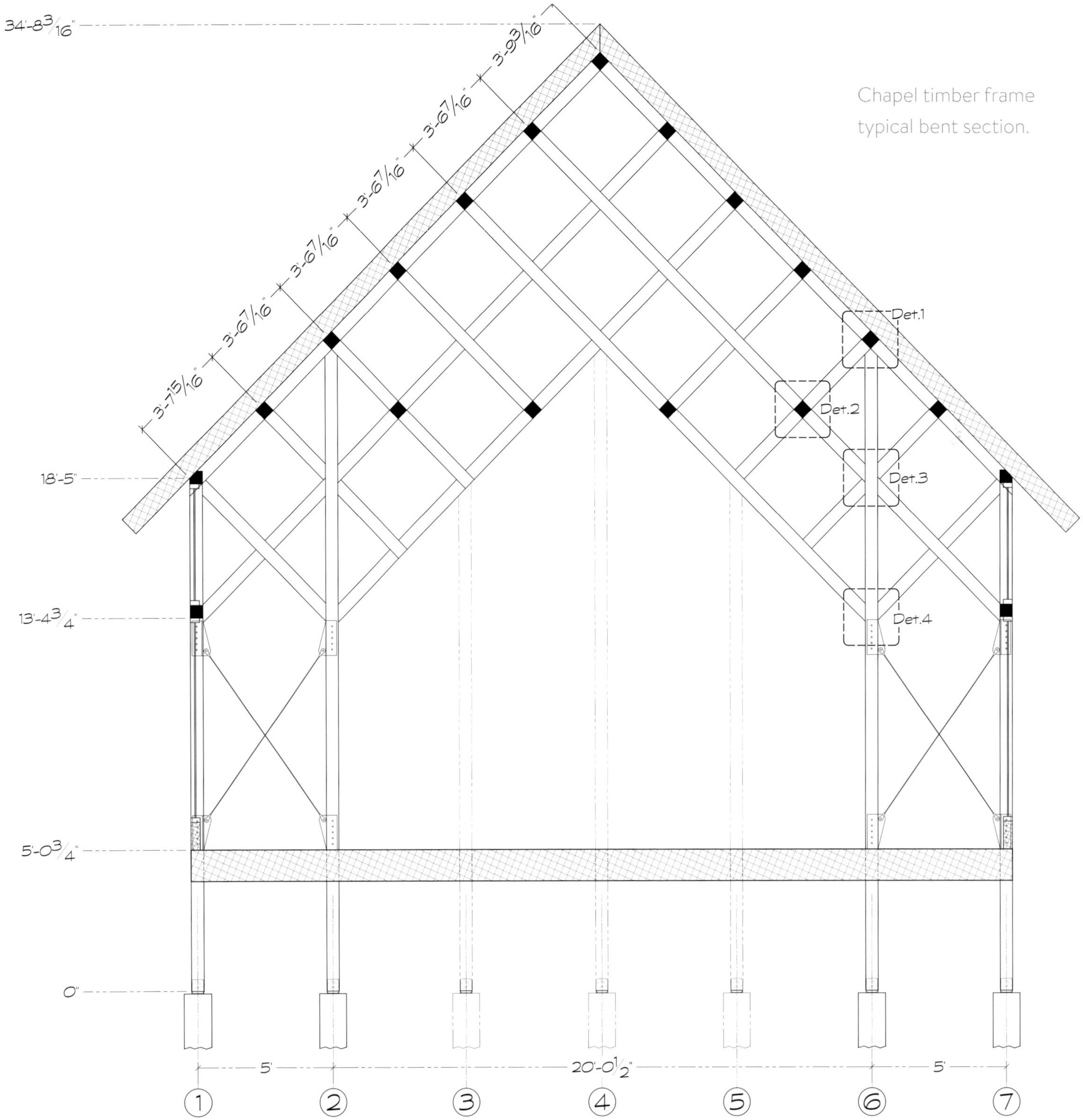

Chapel timber frame typical bent section.

St. Thomas the Apostle Orthodox Church

Waldorf, Maryland, 2011

Owner
St. Thomas the Apostle Parish,
Waldorf, Maryland

Architect
PAS Architecture,

Engineer
D. Remy & Company,
Hayesville, North Carolina

General contractor
St. Thomas the Apostle Parish

When we first met to discuss this project with Father Joseph Edgington, the architect, and the church building committee, it was in a rather modest rancher whose modified garage was being used for Sunday services. In our minds, their proposal for a new church required a huge leap of faith to bring to reality. Apparently in this parish, faith was not in short supply.

The design stays as close as reasonably possible to the traditional architecture of the Orthodox churches of the Carpathian region of Eastern Europe, with concessions to modern engineering, materials, and building codes. The timbers are Douglas fir, select structural grade, and free of heart center. Most of the timber connections are traditional mortise and tenon configurations. Where tension loads were high, steel, in the form of bed bolts, was employed. The rafter plates had to act as tension rings to contain the downward and outward thrust of the rafters, so the steel bed bolts were put into service at those corners. The three turrets or towers were built on the ground and then craned into position.

EXIT

Our first "pinwheel" convergence, at the peak of the church cupola roofs.

A "bed bolt" joint at the cupola corner post tops.

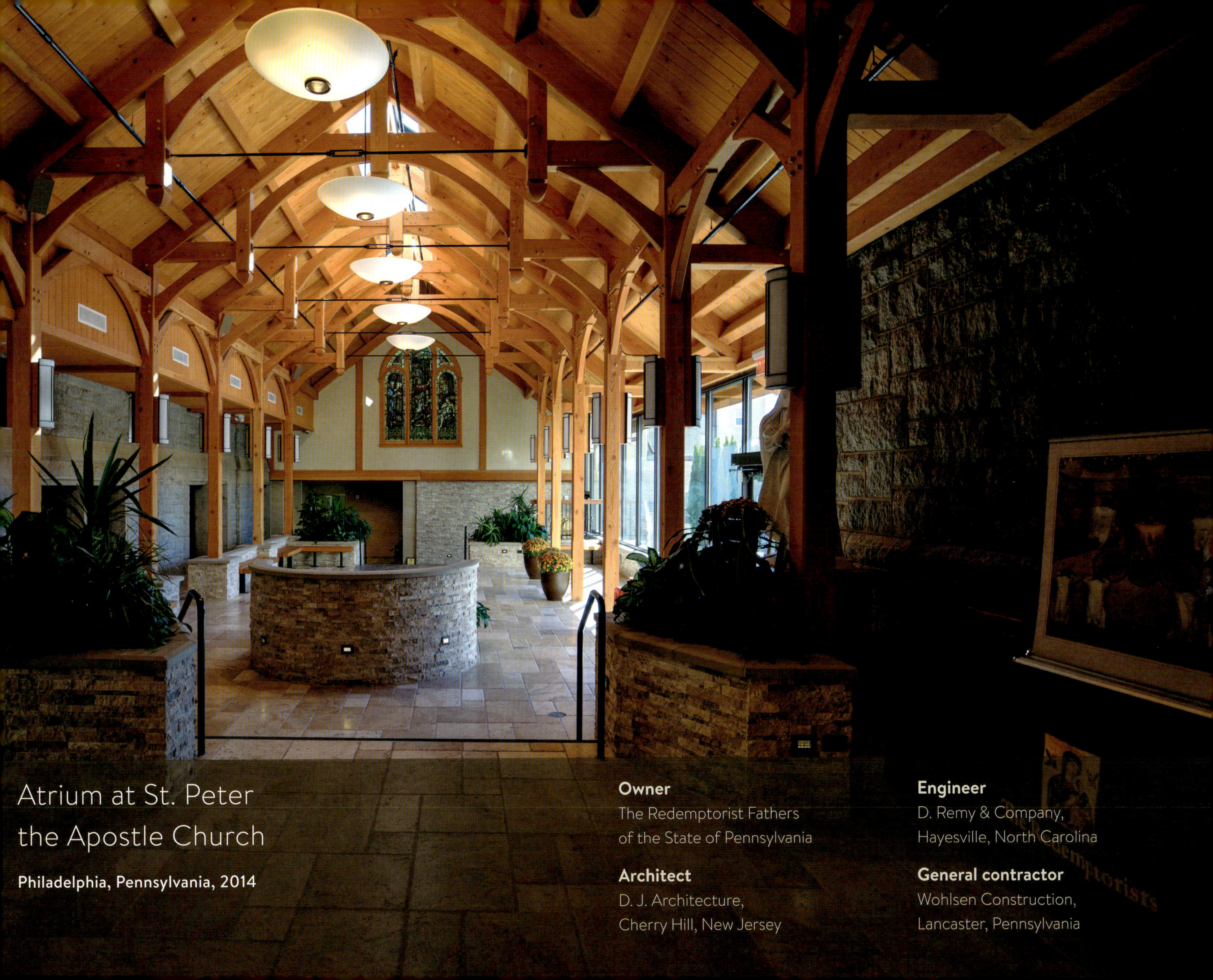

Atrium at St. Peter the Apostle Church

Philadelphia, Pennsylvania, 2014

Owner
The Redemptorist Fathers of the State of Pennsylvania

Architect
D. J. Architecture, Cherry Hill, New Jersey

Engineer
D. Remy & Company, Hayesville, North Carolina

General contractor
Wohlsen Construction, Lancaster, Pennsylvania

The Redemptorist Fathers of the State of Pennsylvania selected Lancaster County Timber Frames (LCTF) to design, engineer, carve, and erect a six-bent hammer beam atrium adjoining St. Peter the Apostle Church and the National Shrine of St. John Neumann at 5th Street and Girard Avenue in Philadelphia. St. Peter's is one of Philadelphia's oldest and most historic churches. It is also one of the city's most ethnically diverse parishes.

LCTF was the only non-union subcontractor on the project, and as a large number of St. Peter's parishioners are union members, we weren't surprised when a union shop asked to work with us. We set up a meeting and quickly reached a harmonious agreement. LCTF would hire one of their men for each of ours, excluding our site manager, plus one apprentice, creating a "blended crew." Apparently, this practice is the norm for union jobs involving specialty trades for which there are no available union members. The union guys on this job were top notch.

Two construction issues caused some trepidation. The target date for completion was quite aggressive

and totally inflexible. The atrium had to be finished and furbished before Pope Francis's visit to the city and the concurrent World Meeting of Families. As LCTF's range of responsibilities expanded beyond the initial scope of timber frame and tongue and groove ceiling boards and into trim work, in the last few weeks we shared working space with plumbers, mechanical contractors, electricians, tile setters, painters, fixture installers, and inspectors. No one took breaks for fear of relinquishing the precious few square inches under their feet.

The other issue dealt with an underground tunnel. The tunnel's existence was known and a month-long survey mapped the course of the tunnel on which the foundation design and engineering were then based. When the frame was almost fully designed and engineered, some significant inaccuracies were discovered in the tunnel survey. Until a foundation engineering resolution could be devised and the timber frame design modified and analyzed, work had to cease, thus compounding the effects of an already aggressive schedule. In spite of these setbacks and issues, the project finished on schedule.

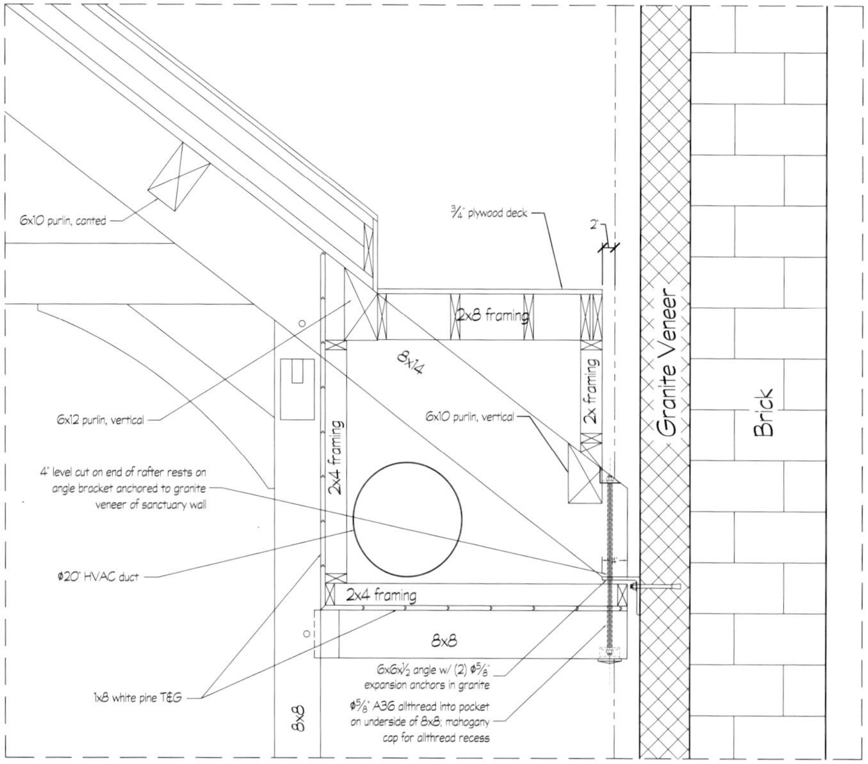
6x10 purlin, canted
3/4" plywood deck
2"
2x8 framing
8x14
Granite Veneer
Brick
2x framing
6x12 purlin, vertical
6x10 purlin, vertical
2x4 framing
4" level cut on end of rafter rests on angle bracket anchored to granite veneer of sanctuary wall
ϕ20" HVAC duct
2x4 framing
8x8
6x6x1/2 angle w/ (2) ϕ5/8" expansion anchors in granite
1x8 white pine T&G
ϕ5/8" A36 allthread into pocket on underside of 8x8; mahogany cap for allthread recess
8x8

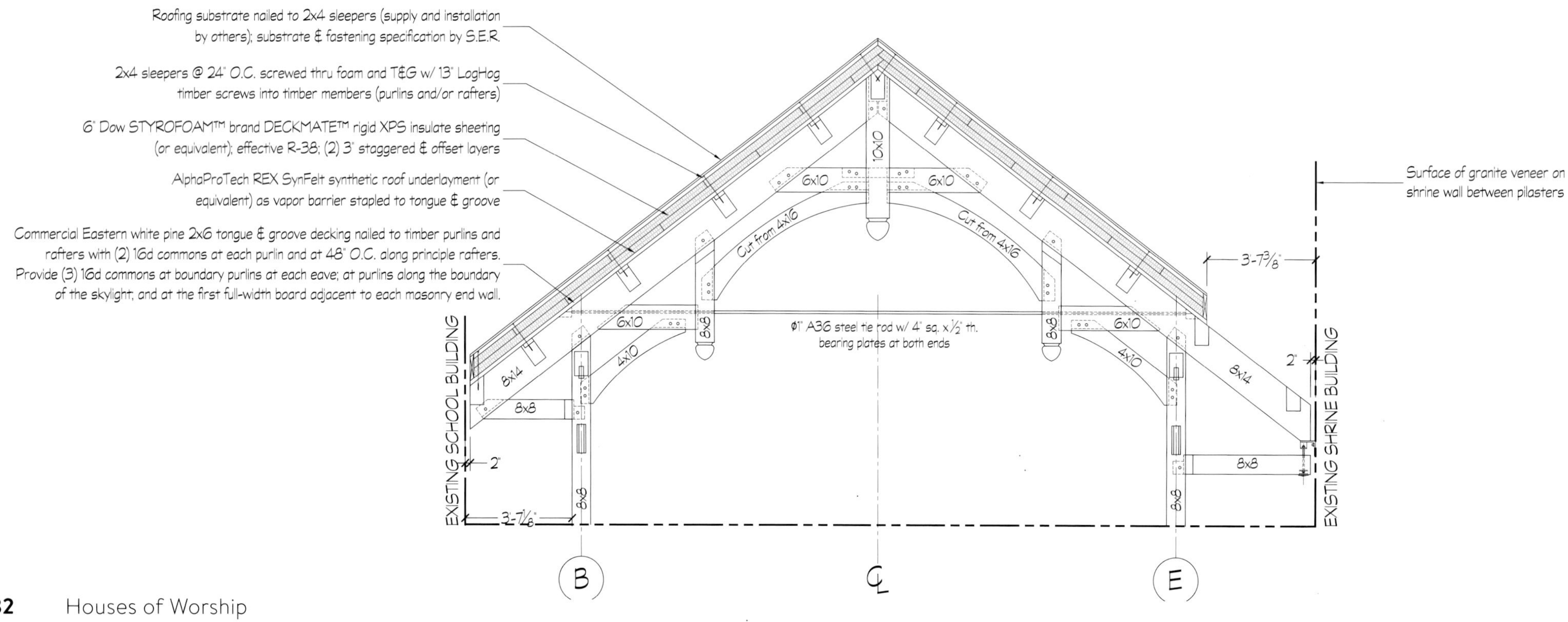
Roofing substrate nailed to 2x4 sleepers (supply and installation by others); substrate & fastening specification by S.E.R.
2x4 sleepers @ 24" O.C. screwed thru foam and T&G w/ 13" LogHog timber screws into timber members (purlins and/or rafters)
6" Dow STYROFOAM™ brand DECKMATE™ rigid XPS insulate sheeting (or equivalent); effective R-38; (2) 3" staggered & offset layers
AlphaProTech REX SynFelt synthetic roof underlayment (or equivalent) as vapor barrier stapled to tongue & groove
Commercial Eastern white pine 2x6 tongue & groove decking nailed to timber purlins and rafters with (2) 16d commons at each purlin and at 48" O.C. along principle rafters. Provide (3) 16d commons at boundary purlins at each eave; at purlins along the boundary of the skylight, and at the first full-width board adjacent to each masonry end wall.
Surface of granite veneer on shrine wall between pilasters
10x10
6x10
6x10
Cut from 4x16
Cut from 4x16
3'-7 3/8"
6x10
6x10
8x8
8x8
ϕ1" A36 steel tie rod w/ 4" sq. x 1/2" th. bearing plates at both ends
4x10
4x10
8x14
8x14
8x8
8x8
2"
2"
EXISTING SCHOOL BUILDING
EXISTING SHRINE BUILDING
3'-7 1/8"
8x8
8x8
B
CL
E

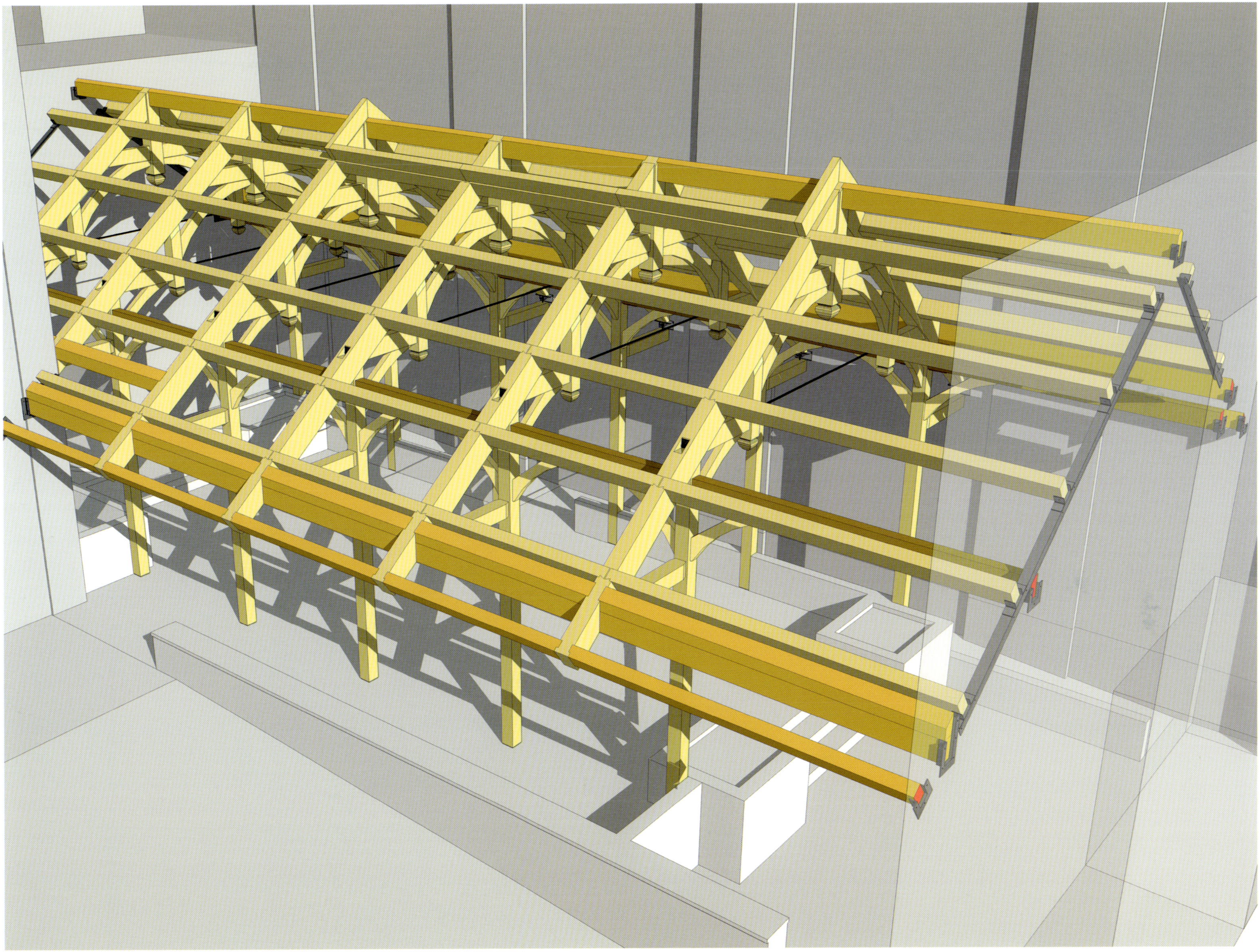

Pre-fitting the hammer beam trusses on the Lancaster County Timber Frames shop floor.

Hammer post bottom pendant.

Students and teachers from the adjacent Catholic school signed the top side of the roof boards.

The entire student body at the adjacent Catholic school observed the start of the erection work.

The finished timber posts were wrapped with lauan plywood to protect them during construction.

A panoramic view of Philadelphia from the church bell tower.

The timber frame atrium is wedged between the existing sanctuary, a rectory, and a Catholic elementary and middle school.

St. John Neumann Center

Philadelphia, Pennsylvania, 2015

Owner
The Redemptorist Fathers
of the State of Pennsylvania

Engineer
D. Remy & Company,
Hayesville, North Carolina

To the rear of St. Peter the Apostle Church and the Shrine of St. John Neumann, and across a narrow city street, sat a long and narrow flat-roofed brick building that the parish had been using for storage. When the design work for the atrium was winding down, the parish proceeded with plans to convert the warehouse into a community center and library for the St. John archives. Lancaster County Timber Frames's work consisted of a timber-framed truss system for the lobby and a 100-foot-long bracketed-brace roof for the exterior.

Every project presents surprises and challenges. Prior to giving the Fathers of this parish an estimate for the work, we asked the union crane company that we had used for the atrium to map out a staging and lift plan for the timber-framed lobby. Of particular concern to us were the phone and power lines that ran the length of the street (more like an alley) behind the church and in front of the brick storage building. The crane company representative advised that they could set the crane on the church parking lot and lift the trusses over the power lines to set them in place. On the day of the raising, the crane operator, after seeing the situation for himself and hearing what his company rep had told us, said "absolutely not!" He soon eased a little and informed us that "maybe if we were willing to spend a week or two dealing with government agencies, we might get lucky." We didn't have one or two

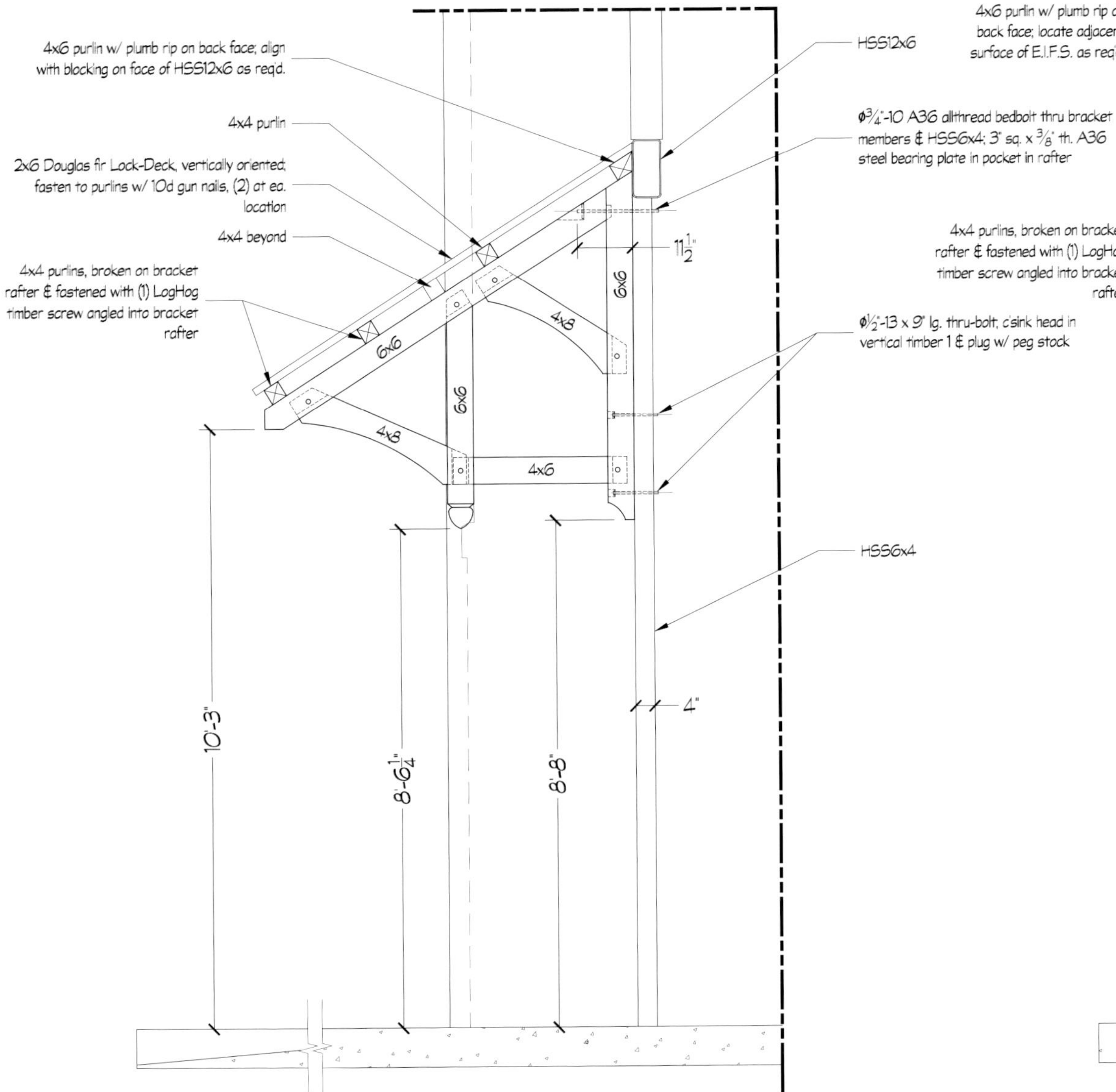

1 TYPICAL LARGE BRACKET SECTION AT ENTRY - (3) THUS REQD.
TF4 1" = 1'-0"

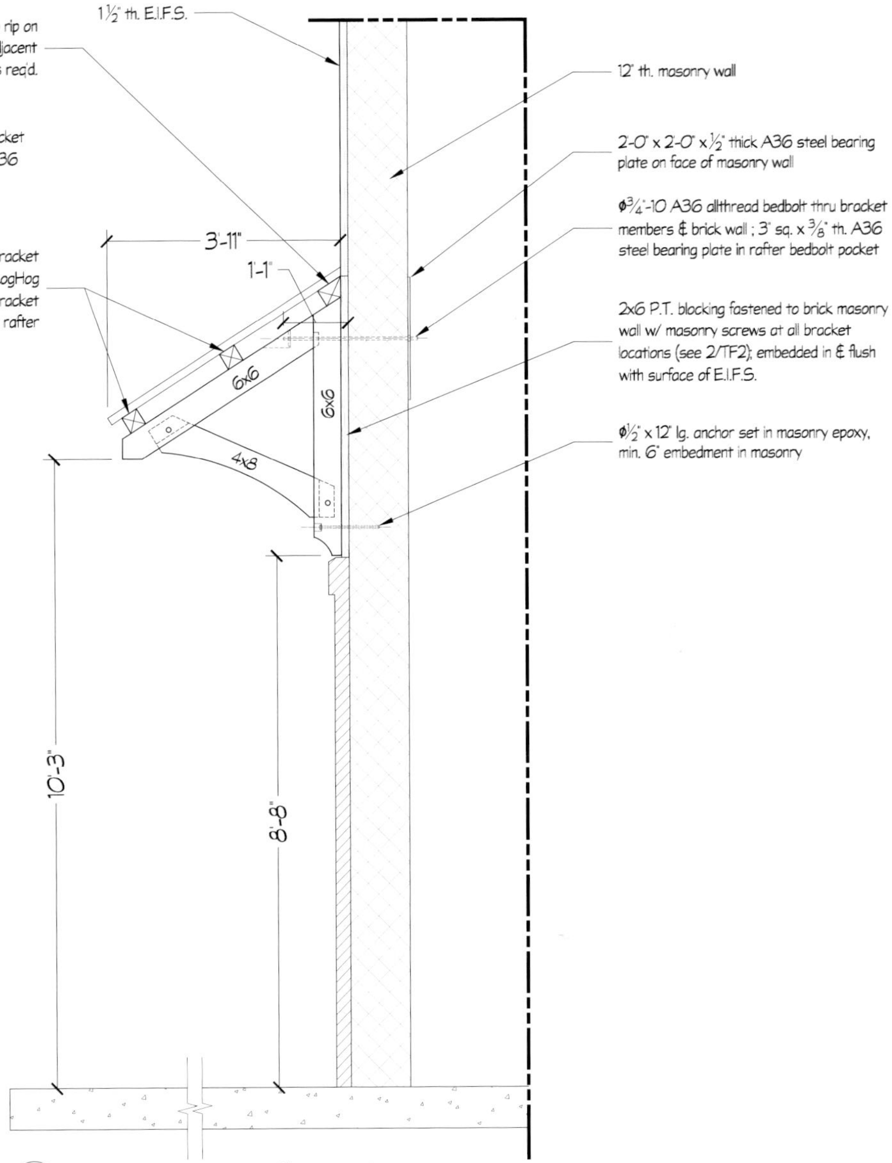

1 SMALL BRACKET SECTION - (11) THUS REQD.
TF4 1" = 1'-0"

weeks; the crane was already there as was the truck delivering the timbers.

Unfortunately, a line of tightly parked cars would need to be moved to afford us the space needed for the crane and staging. The crane company's president secured police permission to close the street, and our men went door-to-door, asking owners of the townhouses to please move their cars. We had to attach a jib extension to lift the trusses from the rear of the building, over the building, and to the front. This was no easy task to perform in the tight back alleys of Philadelphia. Luckily, there were only four trusses involved and we were able to complete the job that day.

St. Matthew Evangelical Lutheran Church

York, Pennsylvania, 2011

Owner
St. Matthew Evangelical Lutheran Church, York, Pennsylvania

Architect
Murphy & Dittenhafer Architects, York, Pennsylvania

Engineer
C. S. Davidson, York, Pennsylvania

General contractor
eciConstruction, Dillsburg, Pennsylvania

This projecting canopy serves as a porte cochère for the community service areas of a large Lutheran church in York, Pennsylvania. More than one hundred years old, the church architecture conforms to the norms of its time—rectilinear, formal, and classical in its inspiration. As such, the gentle arc of the glulam canopy is certainly unexpected, and yet it seems to enhance rather than detract from the church's traditional architectural aesthetic.

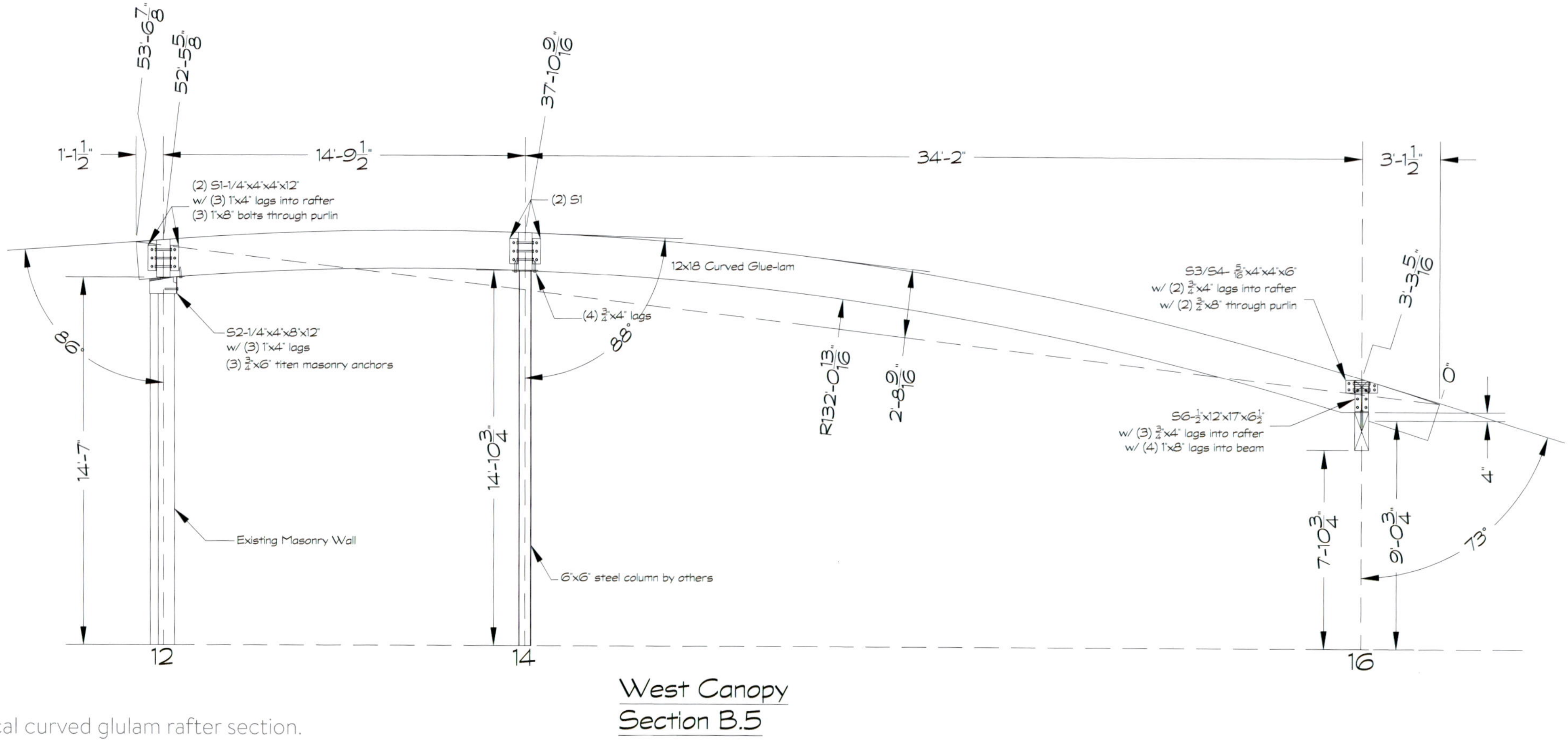

Typical curved glulam rafter section.

ST. MATTHEW LUTHERAN CHURCH

2

Hospitality

Hospitality spaces such as restaurants, winery tasting rooms, hotels, and brew pubs become more engaging when they offer a multi-level sensory experience, inviting visitors to pause and appreciate their surroundings. And when the restaurant or pub is timber framed, this engagement isn't so much an invitation as a demand. It is hardly possible to remain indifferent to the timbers overhead, to ignore the celebration of an open structure.

The following projects illustrate this demand. All are places where people come together to share food and drink, to listen to music, to celebrate life's events.

The River Company Restaurant & Brewery

Radford, Virginia, 2007

Owner
Hall & Sons Developers, Radford, Virginia

Designer
Josh Coleman/Lancaster County Timber Frames, York, Pennsylvania

Engineer
D. Remy & Company, Hayesville, North Carolina

General contractor
Hall & Sons Developers

For this restaurant and brewery building, we were asked to provide not only the frame design and engineering, but also design development and construction documents. The 17,500-square-foot, 350-seat, fully timber-framed restaurant and micro-brewery is situated on 21½ acres on a bluff overlooking the New River, one of the five oldest rivers in the world. The main dining room occupies the main level and overlooks the brewery on the lower level. Also on the lower level is a large banquet hall and restaurant facilities, including a refrigerated drying room for the Angus beef, which is organically raised on the surrounding farmland.

The main body of the structure is defined and supported by twelve major king post bents, which on the interior are tied one to another by minor purlins. The exterior bents, supporting the entrance porch and the rear dining porch, are tied back to the main structure by plates and major purlins that hold minor rafters. The drop to the New River, hundreds of feet below, looked to be nearly vertical, and as the deck system for the rear porch was to be supported by our posts, the positioning of the crane and the setting of the bents supporting that area presented a significant challenge.

STOUT
The River Room
The
RIVER
COMPANY
Restaurant & Brewery, Inc
Thank You for dining with us!

View from the restaurant main level down into the brewery.

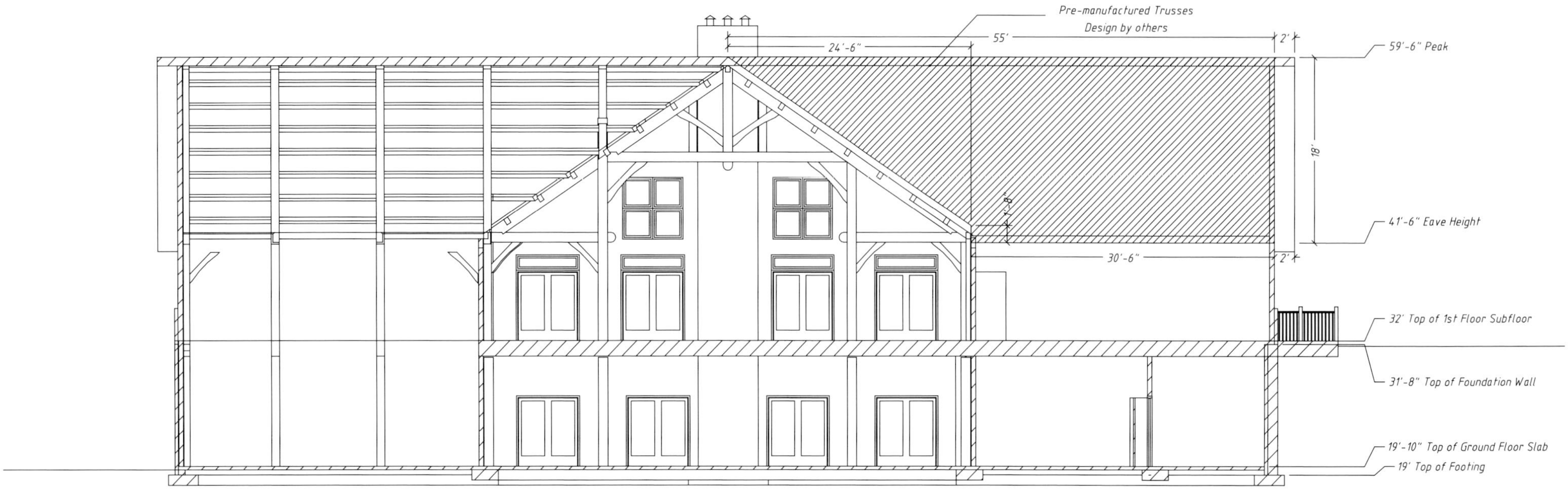

Section A

Scale 1/8"=1'-0"

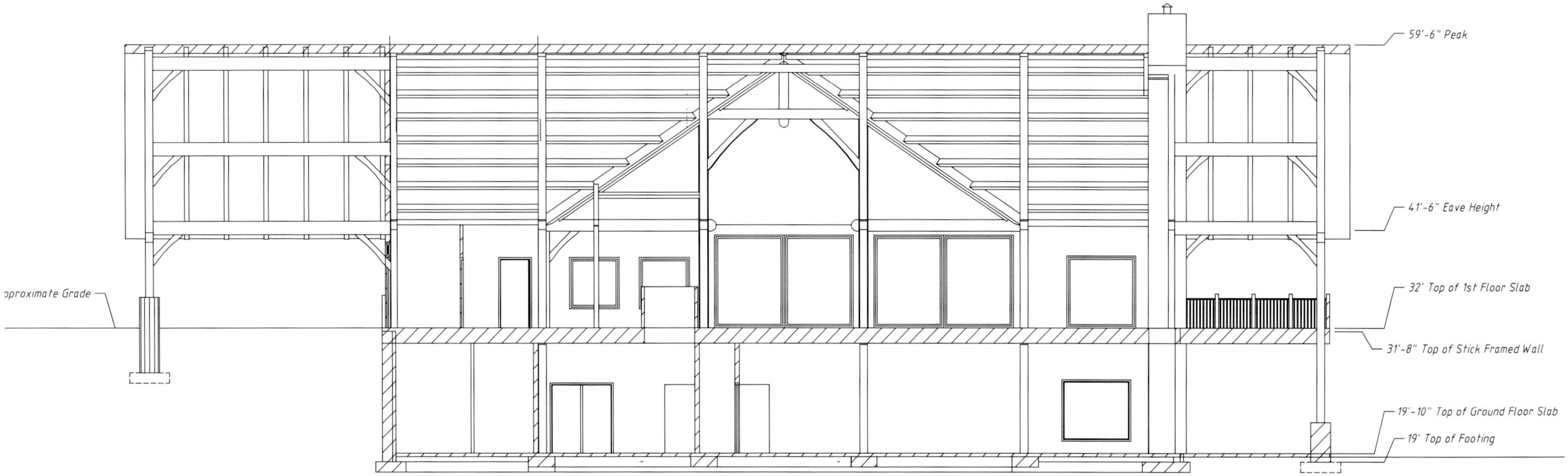

Section B

Sacle 1/8"=1'-0"

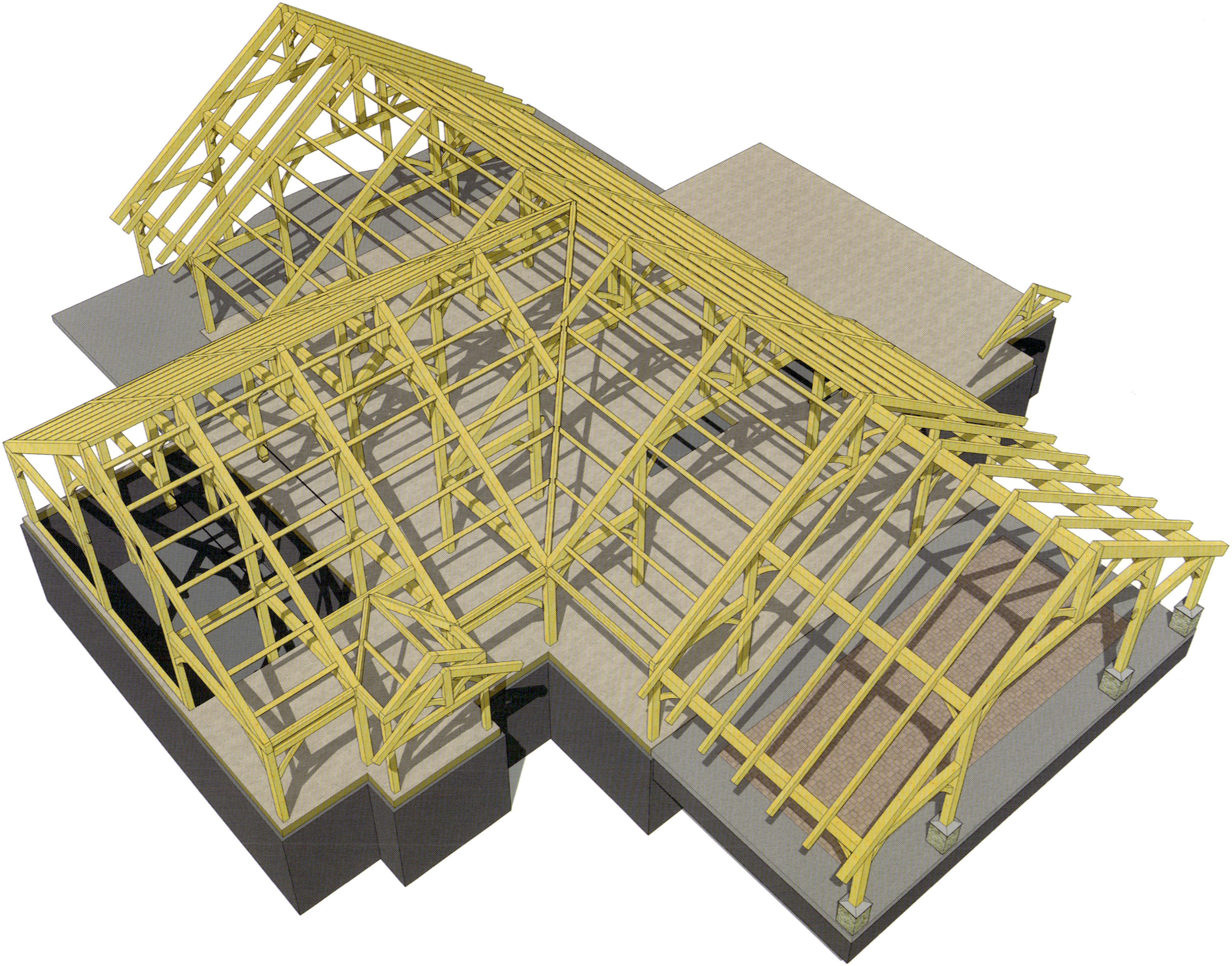

Eight timbers converging in one complex joint, at the root of the roof valleys.

John Wright Restaurant

Wrightsville, Pennsylvania, 2009

Owner
Donsco/John Wright Store & Restaurant;
Wrightsville, Pennsylvania

Designer
Tim Diener/Lancaster County
Timber Frames, York, Pennsylvania

Engineer
Ruff Engineering,
Douglassville, Pennsylvania

General contractor
Donsco

When Donsco, a family-owned business since 1906 and North America's leading single-source provider of machined iron castings, decided to expand their restaurant seating, they requested that their patrons be able to fully enjoy the views and sounds of the Susquehanna River, just a stone's throw away. They also wanted glass doors enclosing all three sides of the addition. The expansion was so successful that a few years later, we were called back to enlarge the seating area again.

The existing restaurant was housed in a late nineteenth-century silk mill, repurposed over the years first to provide pattern storage for the foundry, then to house the company store and restaurant. The timber-framed addition was intended to create an "almost outdoors" dining experience.

The layout of the timber columns is based on the geometry of the old mill building to which it is attached, and is fully modular. The basic module is a 10-foot by 13-foot grid with some columns removed to allow for uninterrupted spans. The roof timbers were sized to allow for a future dining terrace above.

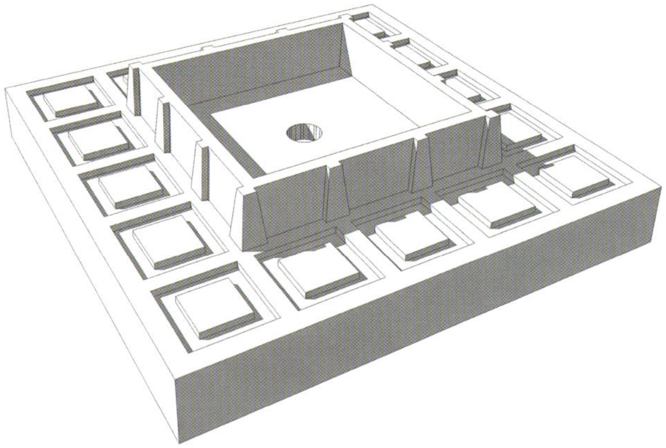

Since the client's primary business is metal casting, it seemed fitting to incorporate castings into the design. Shown left and right are the plinths for the 12×12 timber posts. The plinth castings extend 2-1/2 inches below the surface of the finish floor and about the same distance above. The timber posts are socketed into a recess as shown at left, with an anchor rod embedded in the post base above, and in the concrete foundation wall below. The design of the plinths was partly inspired by a vast online digital collection of cast iron manhole covers, something we all see and walk over but seldom pay much attention to.

Cast ductile metal brackets were also used in place of timber knee braces. The bracket design was inspired by the arches of the Wrightsville-Columbia bridge—shown at right—visible from inside the restaurant addition. The bridge is one of at least four bridges built at this site; at just a few feet short of a mile long, it is the longest multi-arched concrete bridge in the world.

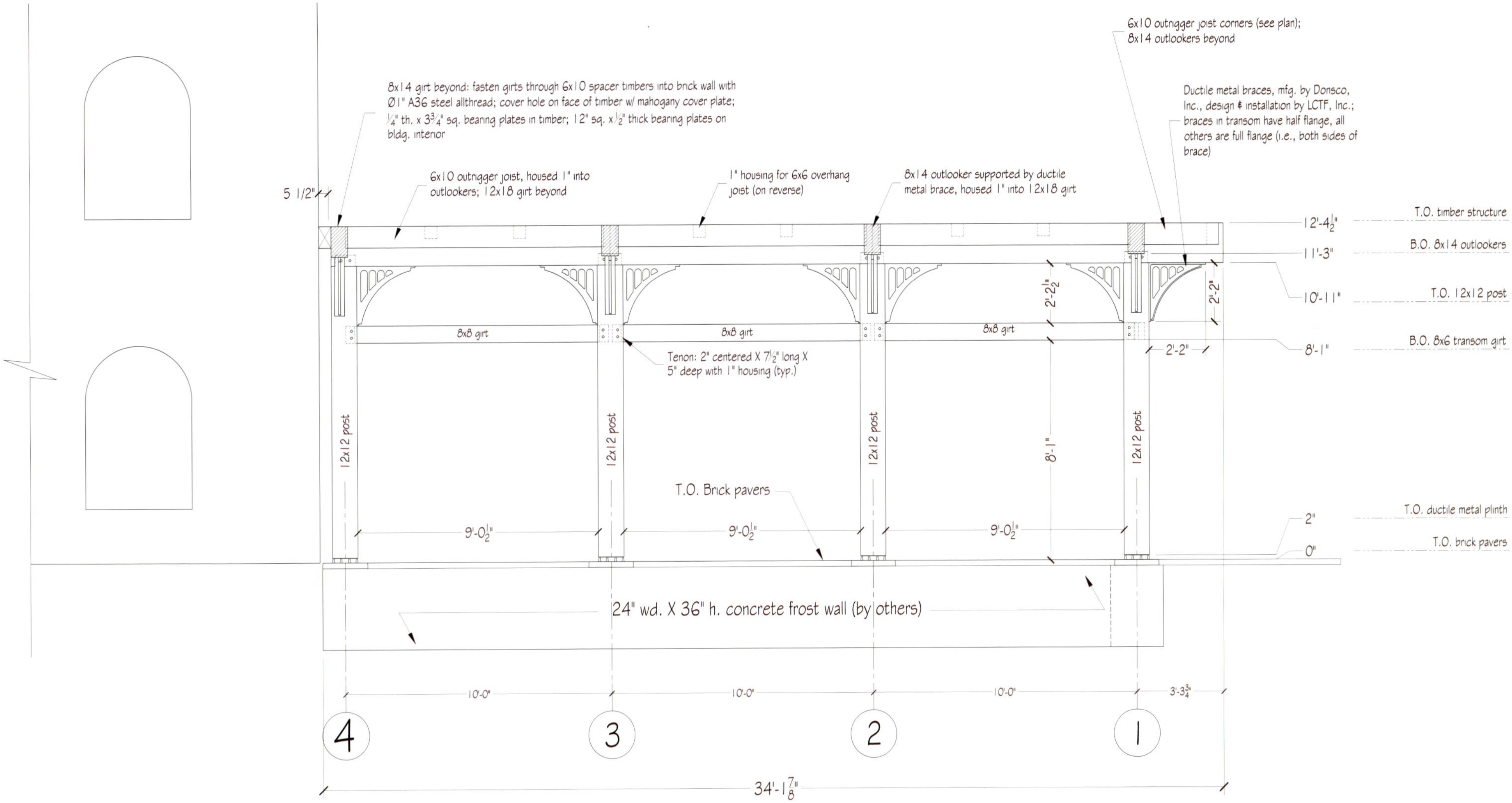

Iron Rooster Restaurant

Baltimore, Maryland, 2013

Owner
BCP Investors,
Baltimore, Maryland

Architect
Brown Craig Turner Architects,
Baltimore, Maryland

Engineer
D. Remy & Company,
Hayesville, North Carolina

General contractor
Chesapeake Contracting Group,
Reisterstown, Maryland

The Iron Rooster, formerly the Farmstead Grill, is part of Canton Crossing, a commercial development occupying sixty-five acres of a former industrial zone in southeast Baltimore. The original Iron Rooster is in Annapolis and is known for serving "breakfast all day." Canton Crossing is much like the King of Prussia Town Center project shown in the retail projects section of this book, with restaurants, small boutique-style shops, and large anchor department stores commingling with green spaces, creating a comfortable town-like feeling in a walkable area close to a major metropolitan center.

The restaurant, which opened in 2014, seats 200 people. Its frame is composed of six tall Douglas fir king-post bents joined with visible through-bolted steel plates at most interfaces and with embedded hardwood pegged splines at others. The solid timbers are finished with a semi-transparent white stain often referred to as pickling or whitewashing. The steel hardware is powder coated a light metallic gray.

FARMSTEAD

FARMSTEAD GRILL

Landing a truss on the post tops.

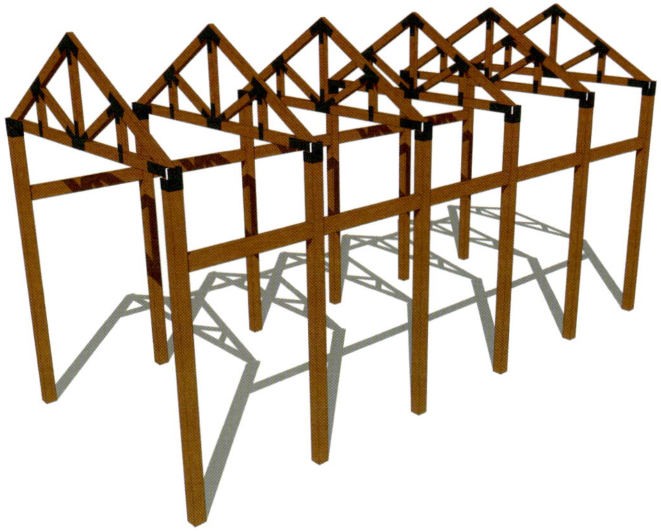

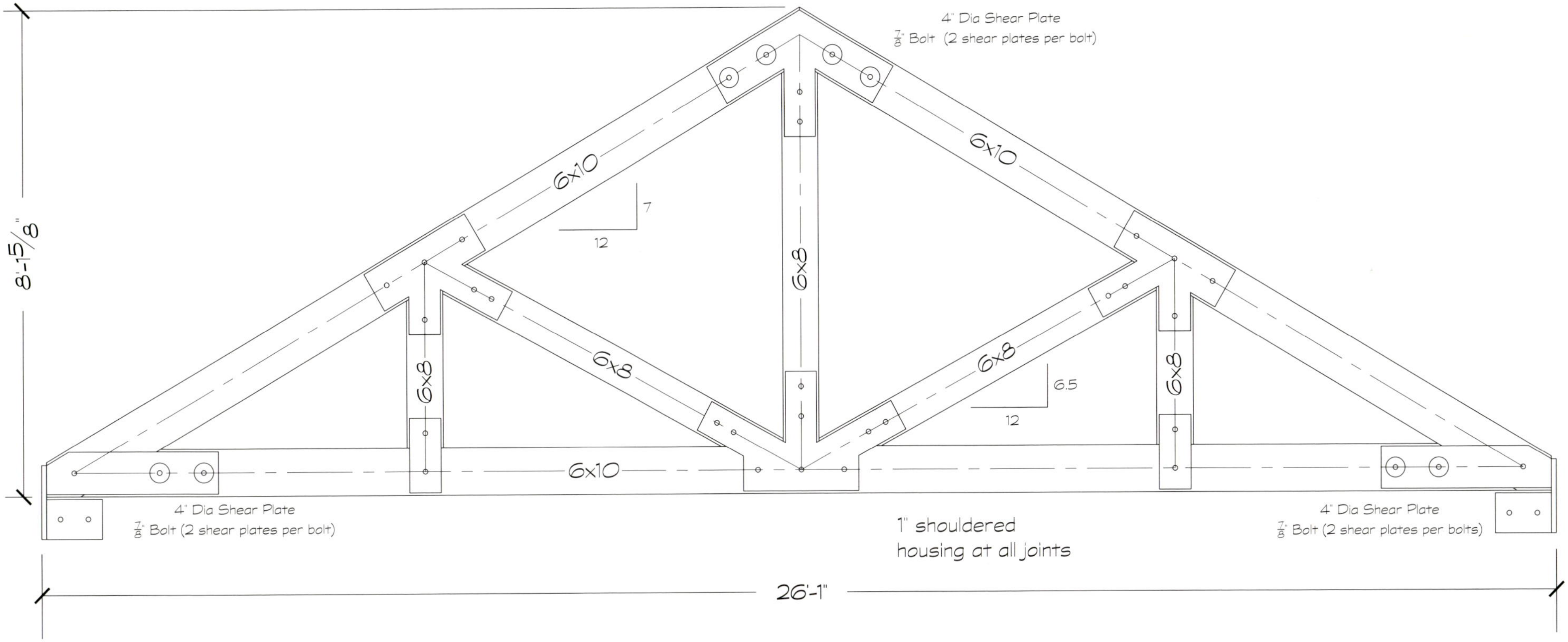

Typical Truss (qty 6)

Scale: 3/4"=1'-0"

The Lodge at Liberty Forge Golf Course

Mechanicsburg, Pennsylvania, 2002

Owner
John Williams/Altland House Hospitality Group, Mechanicsburg, Pennsylvania

Designer
Joe Barnard/Lancaster County Timber Frames, York, Pennsylvania

Engineer
Centerpoint Engineering, Mechanicsburg, Pennsylvania

General contractor
Liberty Forge Golf Course, Mechanicsburg, Pennsylvania

This 5,700-square-foot restaurant and bar lounge was Lancaster County Timber Frames's first commercial design commission and included everything from conceptual drawings to construction documents. The project required 31,000 board feet of red pine tongue and groove ceiling boards atop its frame of 350 Douglas fir timbers.

The frame was raised in the middle of winter during a mean cold spell. Because we were anxious to install the tongue and groove ceiling boards and water shield before the next snowfall, our site manager hired an Amish carpenter who offered to bring several other carpenters who could get the project roofed in short order. The man showed up on schedule with three family members who were between twelve and fourteen years of age. This seemed like a really bad idea, and we politely turned away his "crew."

Bridge trusses connect the king post bents along the building's length, and lower-pitched wings expand the space outward on both sides. The frame design has some interesting details, such as the "quirks" (plowed grooves) running to the top of the king posts, and lower chords whose arcs terminate short of the timber columns to which they connect.

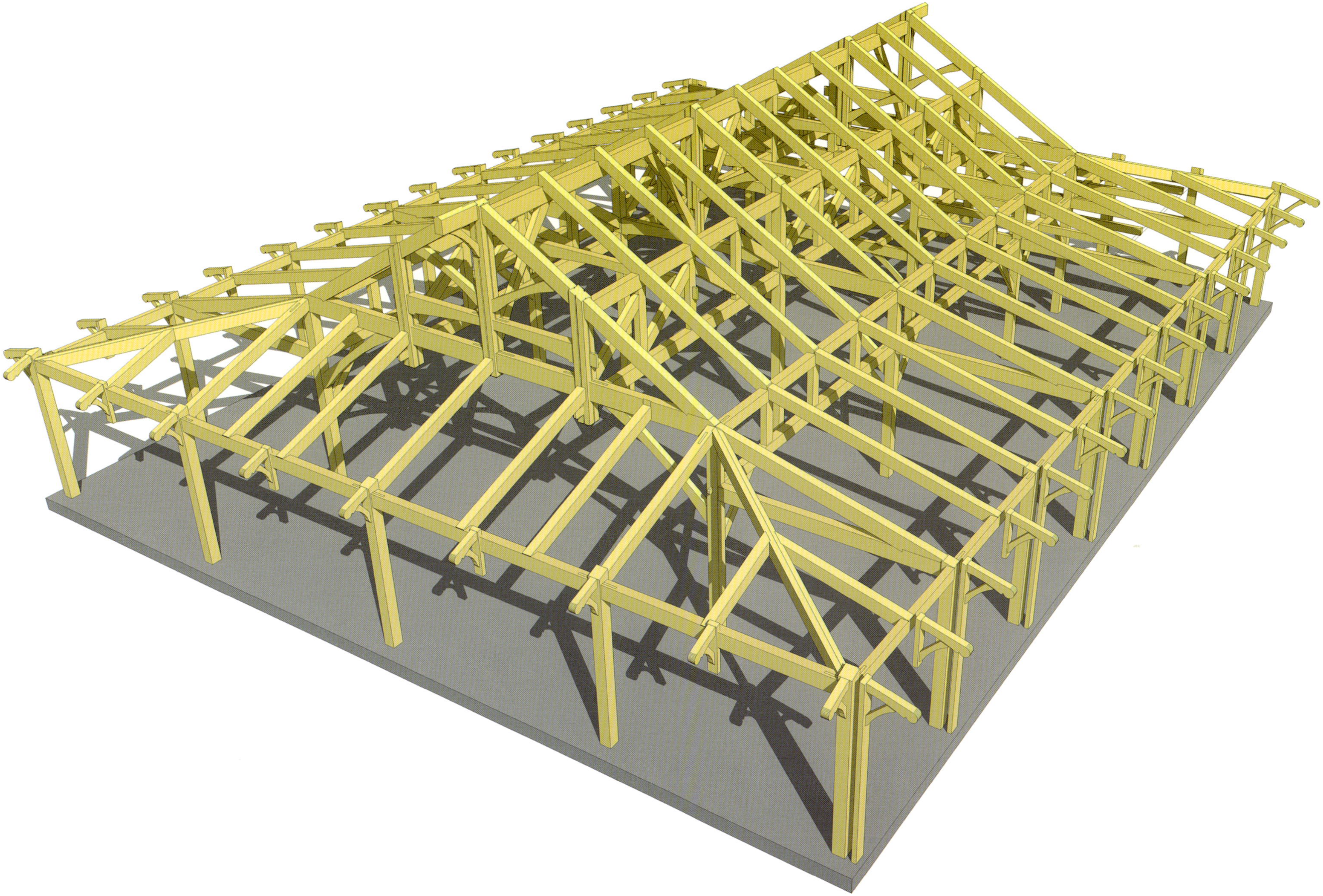

A pegged spline joint. Hardwood spline caps conceal the engineered lumber spline material

A wedged through-tenon.

The king posts were given a "quirk"—a groove or reveal plowed from top to bottom.

Jambo Grill at the Pittsburgh Zoo & PPG Aquarium

Pittsburgh, Pennsylvania, 2015

Owner
Pittsburgh Zoological Society,
Pittsburgh, Pennsylvania

Architect
Indovina Associates Architects,
Pittsburgh, Pennsylvania

Engineer
Sellers Treybal Structural Engineers,
Williston, Vermont

General contractor
Bradley Smith, AIA,
Pittsburgh, Pennsylvania

This 7,000-square-foot building contains nine scissor truss bents; it seats 160 patrons under roof and 140 outside. Douglas fir timbers are stained with Sikkens Cetol SRD in mahogany. Most of the joinery is traditional mortise and tenon with the balance being exposed through-bolted steel gusset plates.

Two issues made this project difficult. A week before we were to arrive on-site for the raising, we called the general contractor to verify that the concrete floor would be cured enough to bring in a material handling machine. We were assured that it would be. Of course, what we found upon arrival was a mud bog, but as the photo illustrates, the show had to go on.

The second issue was access and staging. With meandering walkways leading from one exhibit to another, we knew there would be challenges. Initially, we believed that the raising site would be off-limits to pedestrian and cart traffic. Late in the game we were informed that a four-foot pedestrian path would have to be maintained at all times. That meant we needed to have multiple staging areas, some of them 100 yards from the raising area. Due to the narrow paths (in some places barely 8 feet) trucks and equipment had to be backed in over considerable distances. The outriggers for the 40-ton crane required that the cheetahs be temporarily relocated to a different enclosure—there was no other way.

This 77-acre zoo is known for its naturalistic exhibits. There are 475 animal species represented, twenty of which are threatened or endangered.

The Jambo Grill is named after a silverback gorilla that rose to fame in 1986, when a five-year-old

boy fell into the gorilla enclosure at the Jersey Zoo on the island of Jersey in the English Channel. As the boy lay unconscious, Jambo placed himself between the child and the other gorillas and stroked the boy to comfort him. Jambo then led his troop away, allowing the zoo staff to reach the boy.

Jambo Grill at the Pittsburgh Zoo & PPG Aquarium

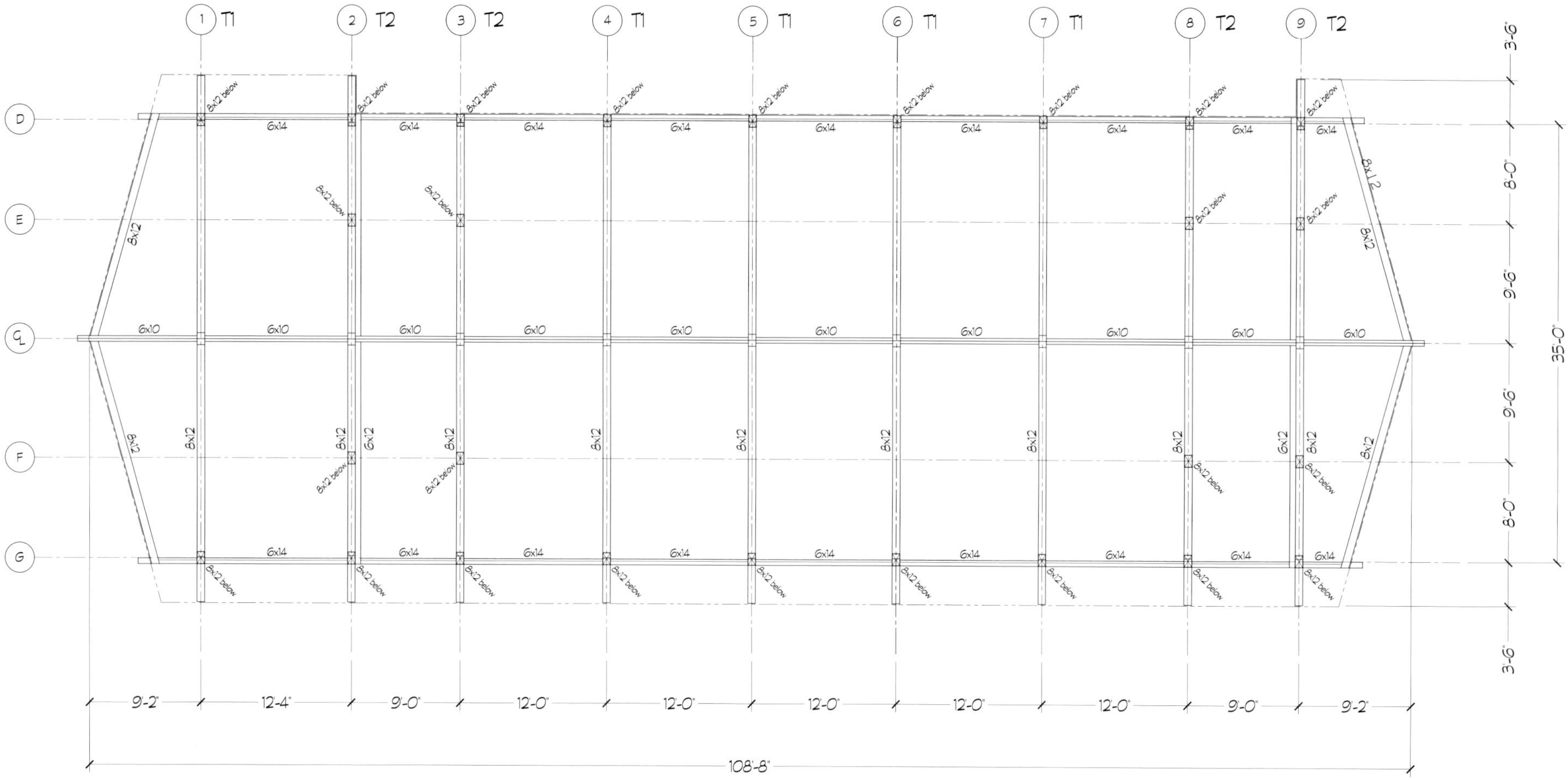

ROOF PLAN

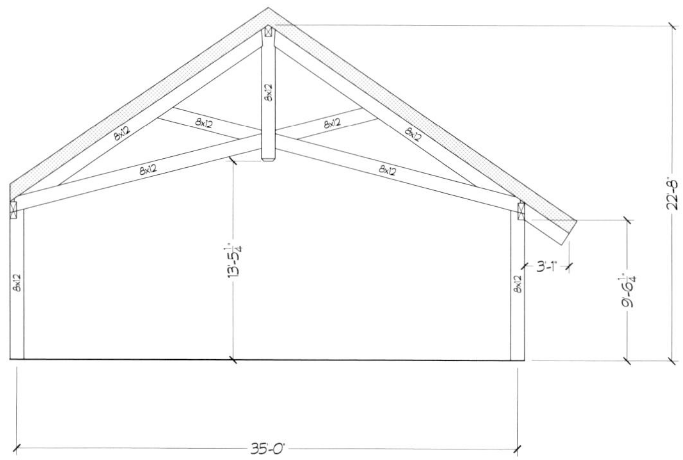

Truss 1

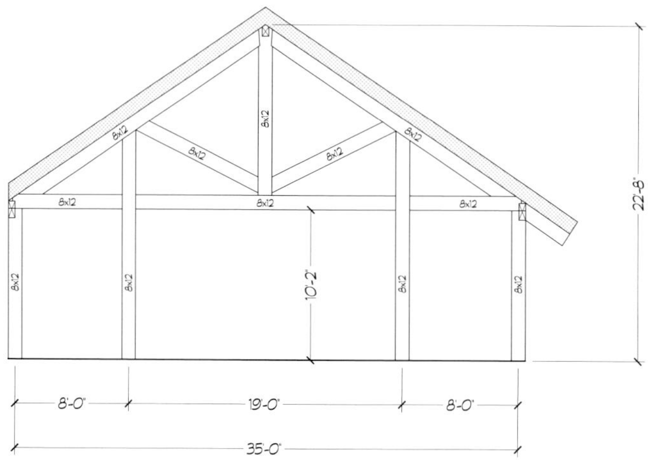

Truss 2

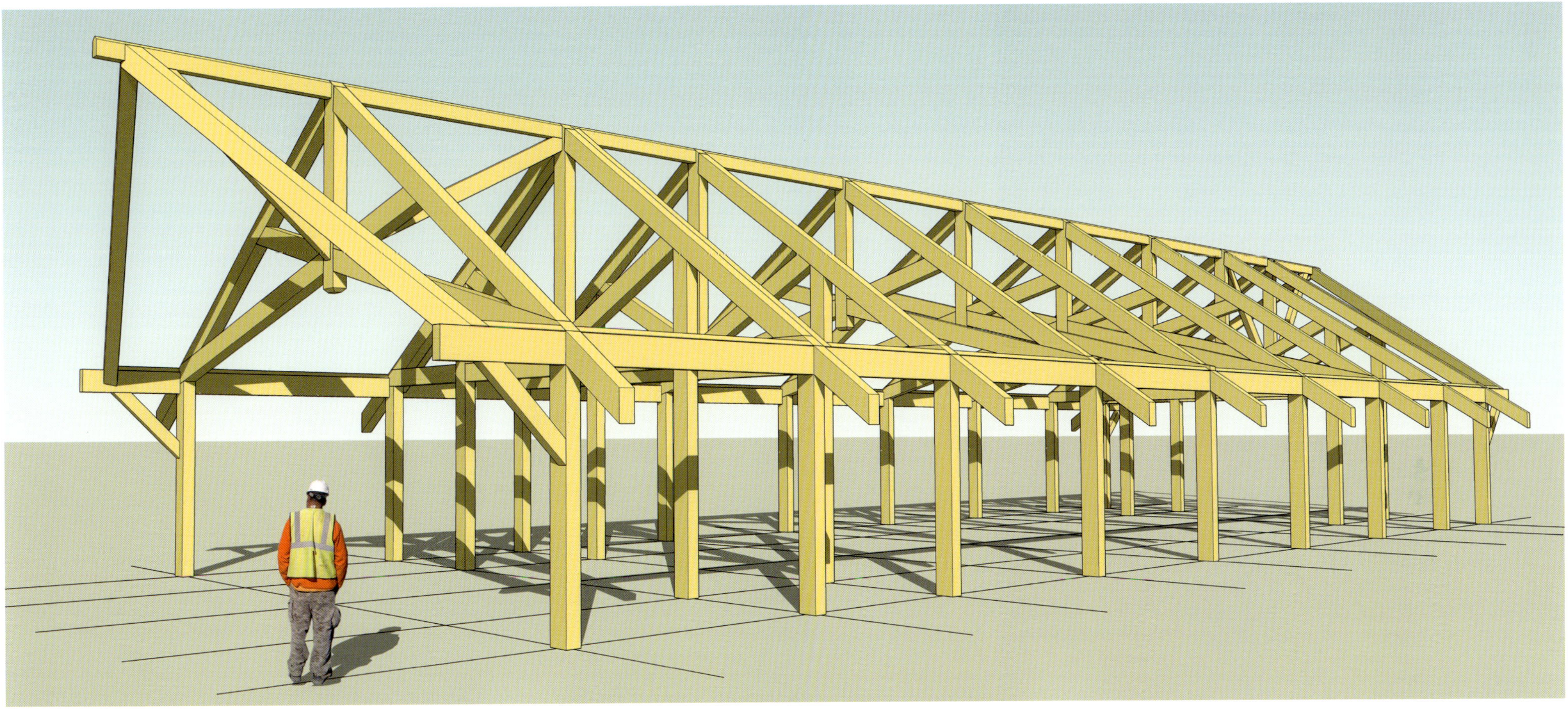

The frame was erected in late winter, just after the ground had thawed.

An interior view of the restaurant, taken from roughly the same vantage point as the photo at left.

While the timber was being erected, the cheetahs were brought out from their winter pen to their summer enclosure across from the job site.

Willow Creek Winery

Cape May, New Jersey, 2010

Owner
Barbara Bray Wilde,
Cape May, New Jersey

Architect
Philip Giambri Architect, PC,
Cape May, New Jersey

Engineer
Ruff Engineering,
Douglassville, Pennsylvania

General contractor
James Regan Construction,
Cape May, New Jersey

This hand-carved post-and-beam winery building sits on a 50-acre vineyard on New Jersey's Outer Coastal Plain. The main section of the timber frame consists of nine bents. With the exception of the end bents, the trusses span 50 feet. The frame and building were designed to withstand coastal wind speeds of up to 120 mph. The lower chord is segmented and connected at the king post by an embedded and concealed steel plate spline with hardened steel pins. Steel spline plates and other connectors are used throughout, all concealed inside the timber members. The timbers are Douglas fir, select structural, and free of heart center.

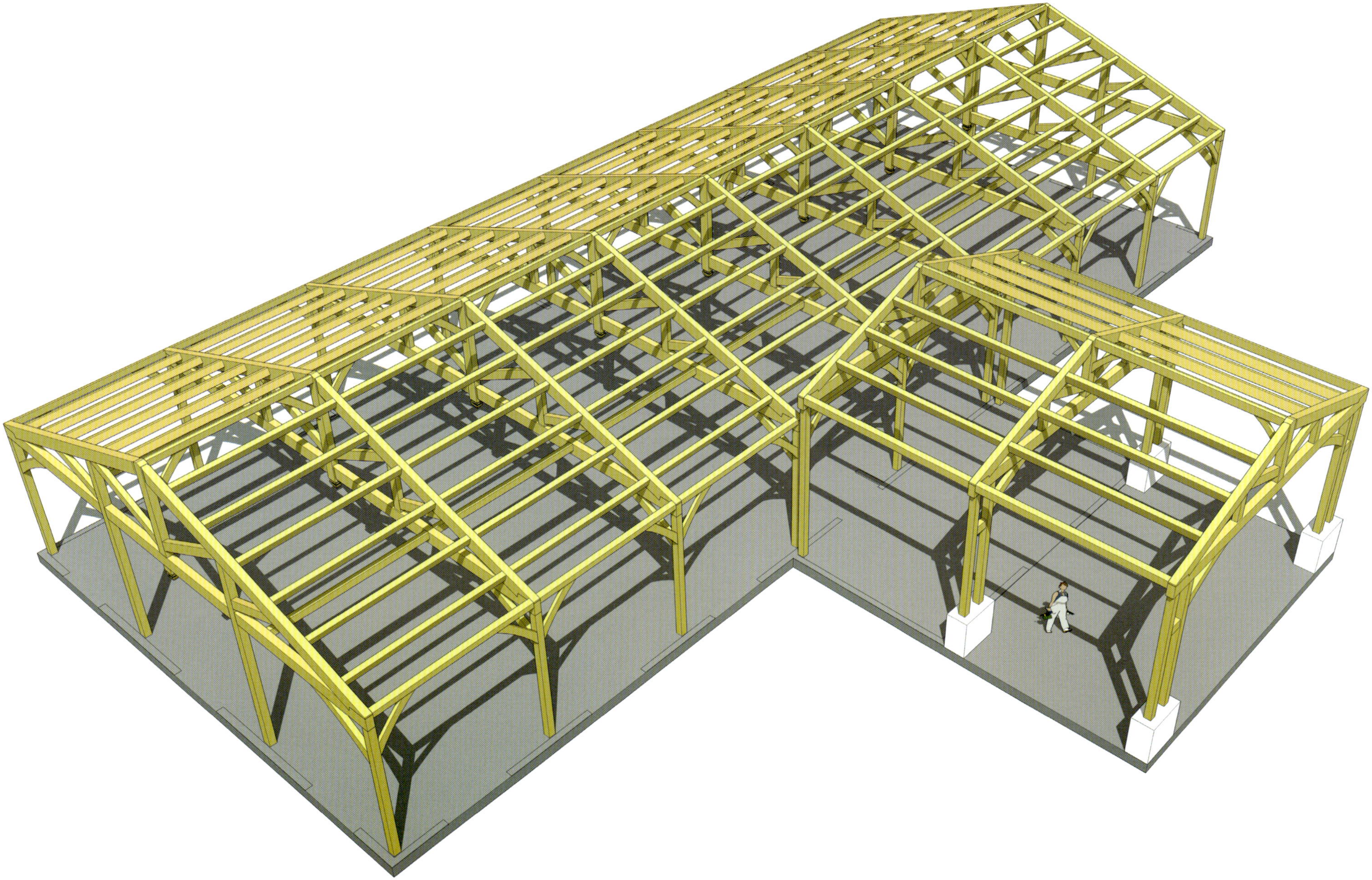

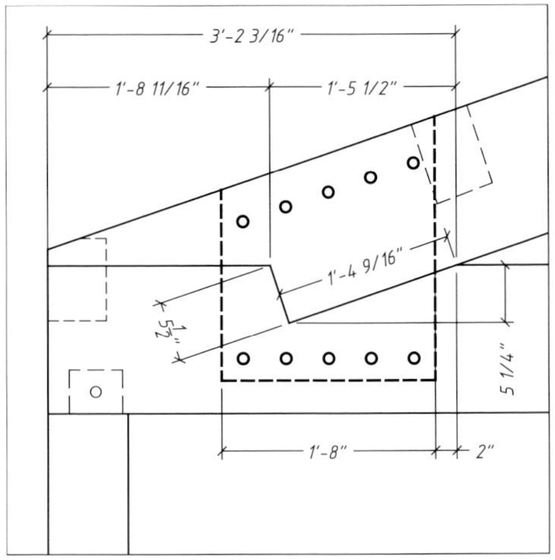

BIRD'S MOUTH DETAIL

NOTES:
1) ALL STRUTS & BRACES FLUSH TO OBVERSE THIS BENT
2) REF. SHEETS TF15-17 FOR ALL STEEL SPLINE
& TIMBERLINX CONNECTOR DETAILS

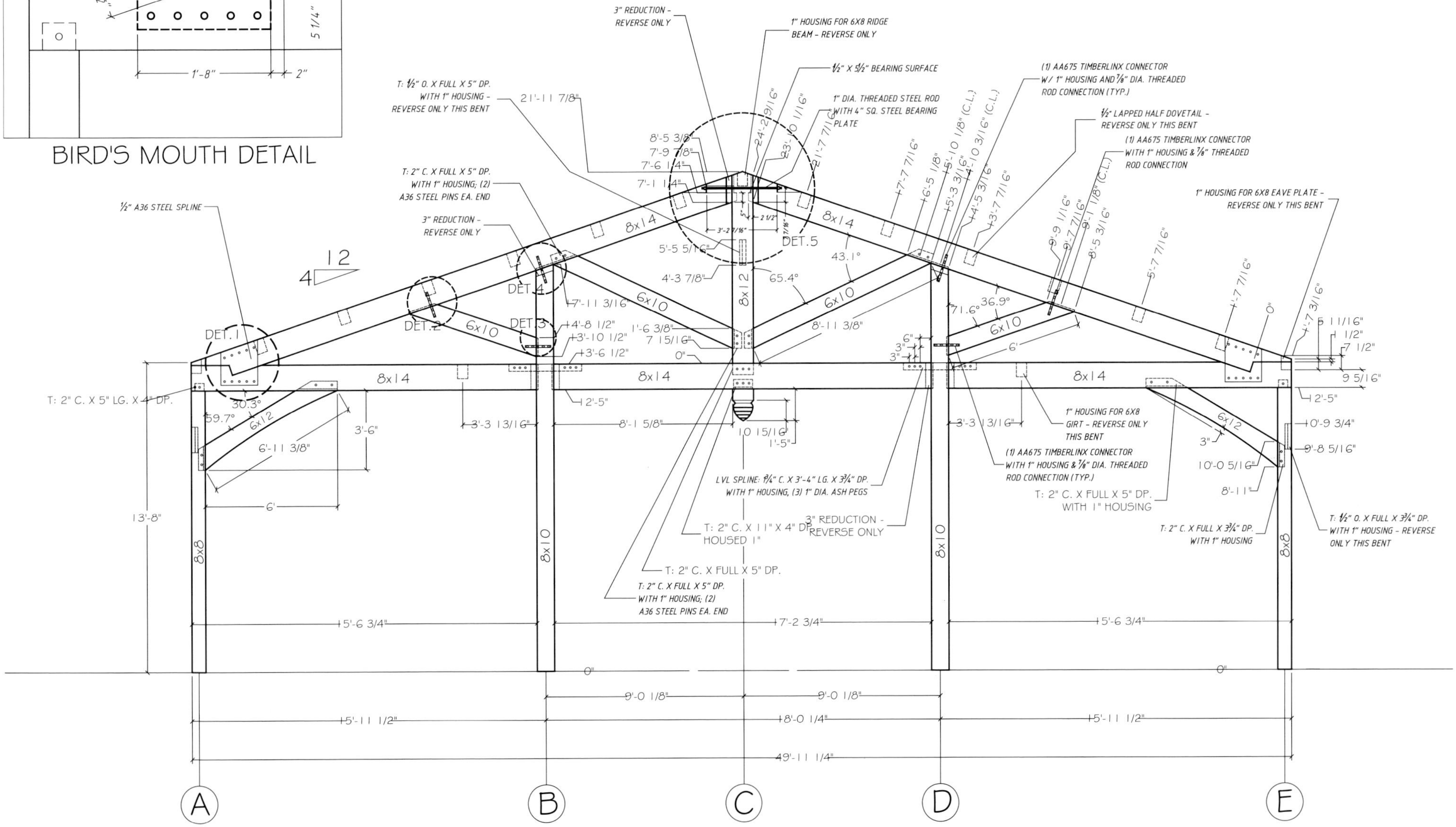

THE VINEYARD - BENT 1

NOT TO SCALE

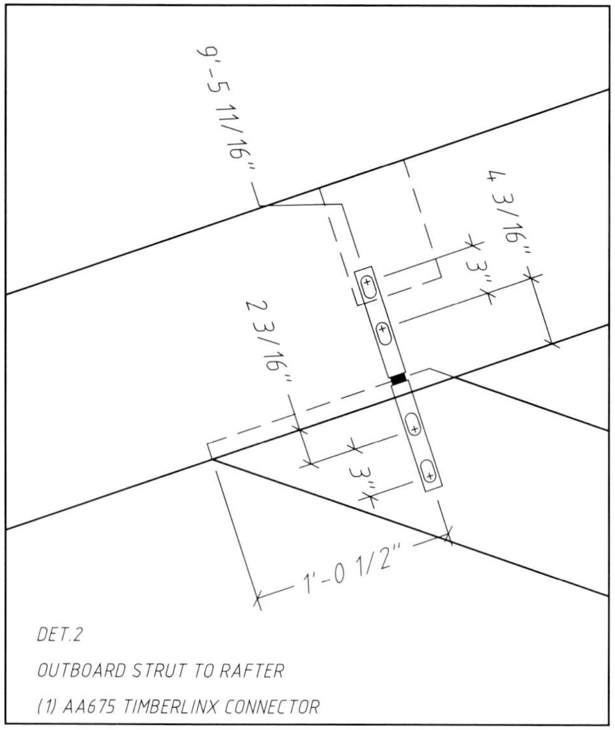

DET.2

OUTBOARD STRUT TO RAFTER

(1) AA675 TIMBERLINX CONNECTOR

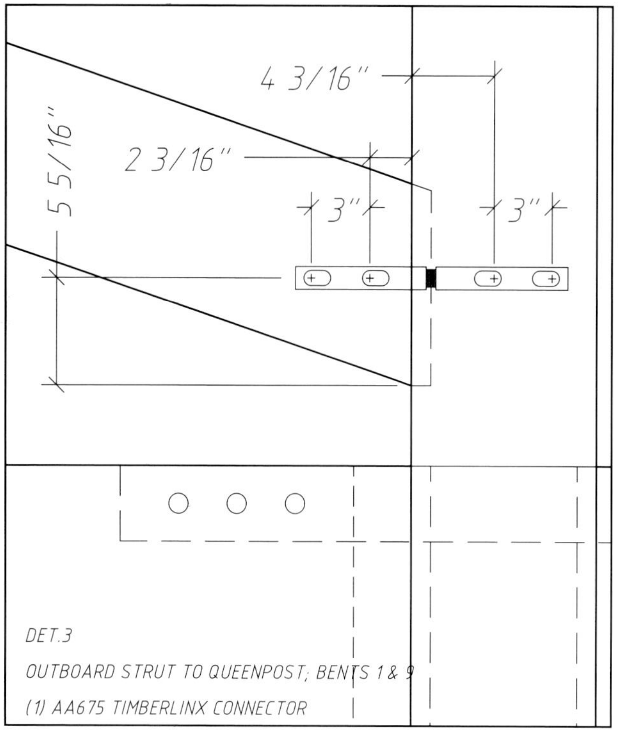

DET.3

OUTBOARD STRUT TO QUEENPOST; BENTS 1 & 9

(1) AA675 TIMBERLINX CONNECTOR

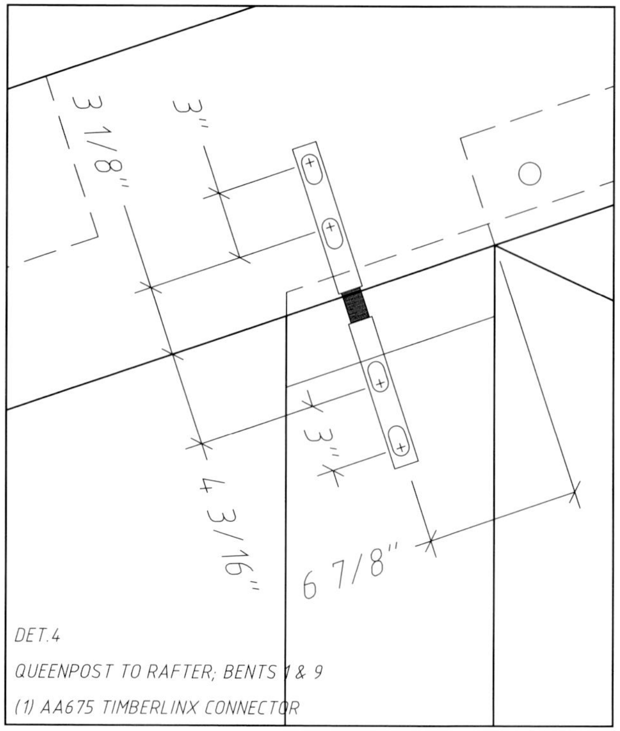

DET.4

QUEENPOST TO RAFTER; BENTS 1 & 9

(1) AA675 TIMBERLINX CONNECTOR

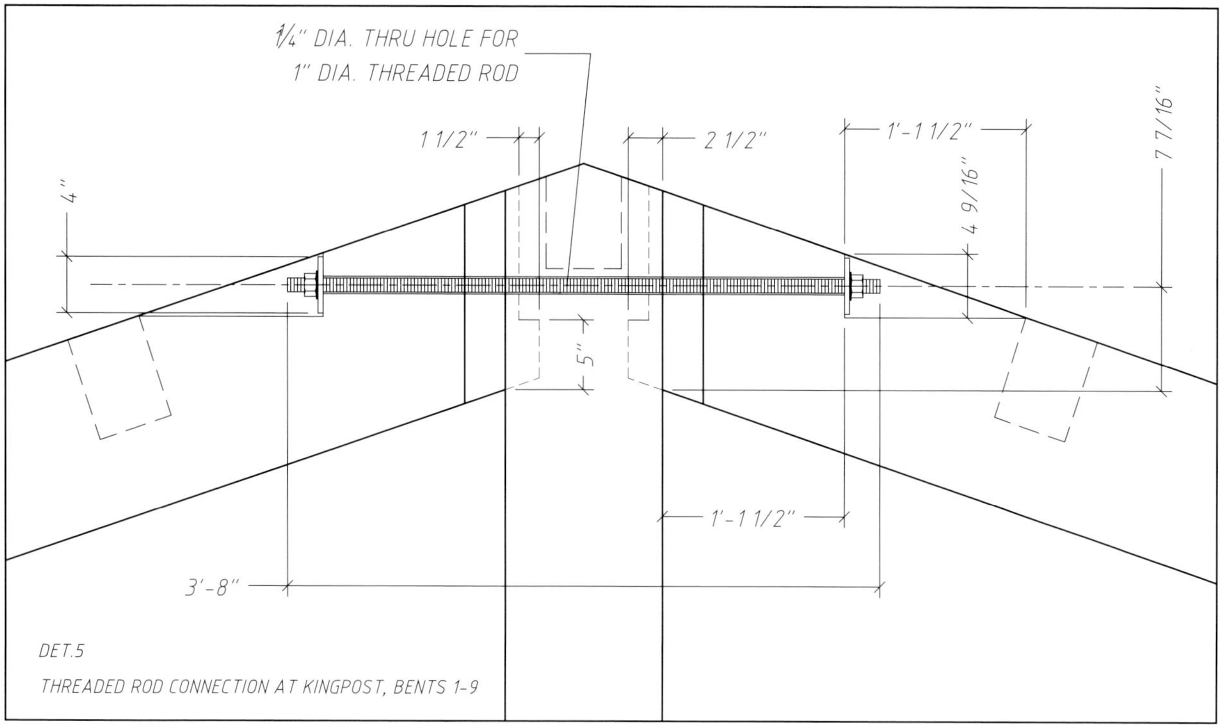

DET.5

THREADED ROD CONNECTION AT KINGPOST, BENTS 1-9

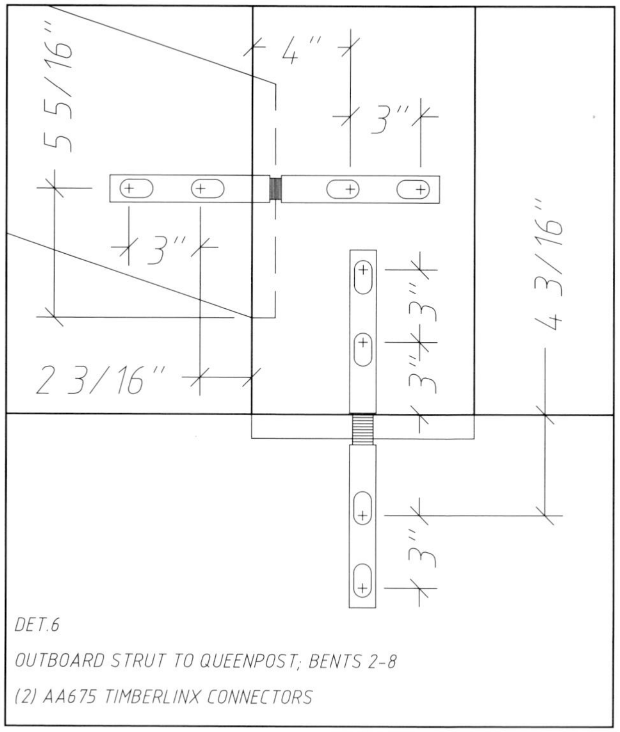

DET.6

OUTBOARD STRUT TO QUEENPOST; BENTS 2-8

(2) AA675 TIMBERLINX CONNECTORS

Notaviva Vineyards

Purcellville, Virginia, 2006

Owner
Stephen and Shannon Mackey,
Purcellville, Virginia

Designer
Stephen Mackey

Engineer
D. Remy & Company,
Hayesville, North Carolina

General contractor
Ronald M. Hawes,
Lovettsville, Virginia

The clients, Stephen and Shannon Mackey, were a young couple who had recently become parents. Both worked in music promotion, and they had the high energy, enthusiasm, and irrepressible personalities that often go with that kind of work. They had just purchased land in northern Virginia and were ready to pursue their dream of leaving their careers to start a vineyard.

The lower level of this 4,300-square-foot structure serves as their home. Wine tasting and music/event/dining areas are on the main level. Above is a mezzanine with guest seating, and a second mezzanine provides a stage for musical performances.

As design development got underway, the couple successfully pitched the project to HGTV. This was no small feat, as that year HGTV received more than 6,000 pitches from all over the country. The project was filmed from April 2006 to July 2007 for the HGTV series *Dream House*. It aired in 2008 and has been shown in re-runs several times since.

The film crew was a constant presence at the job site during the nearly two weeks of frame-raising and panel installation. We frequently had to delay our work until their crew was ready to shoot. And, of course, the crew was always on the alert for any drama, real or imagined. This was, after all, reality TV.

For several days, rain was another constant presence. It started when we were ready to build the eight stress-skin panel gable dormers. We covered the rear of the structure with a makeshift plastic sheet and spent the rain days building those dormers on the ground under the plastic cover. When the skies cleared, we craned them into place.

All Because Two
People Fell In Love

Lancaster County Timber Frames craftsmen carved grape bunches for the Notaviva timber frame.

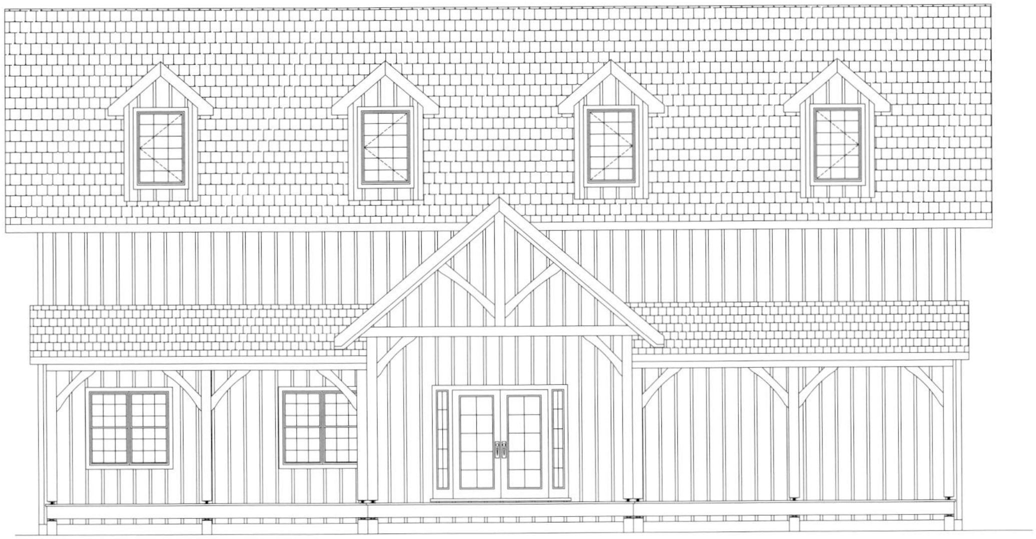

FRONT SIDE ELEVATION

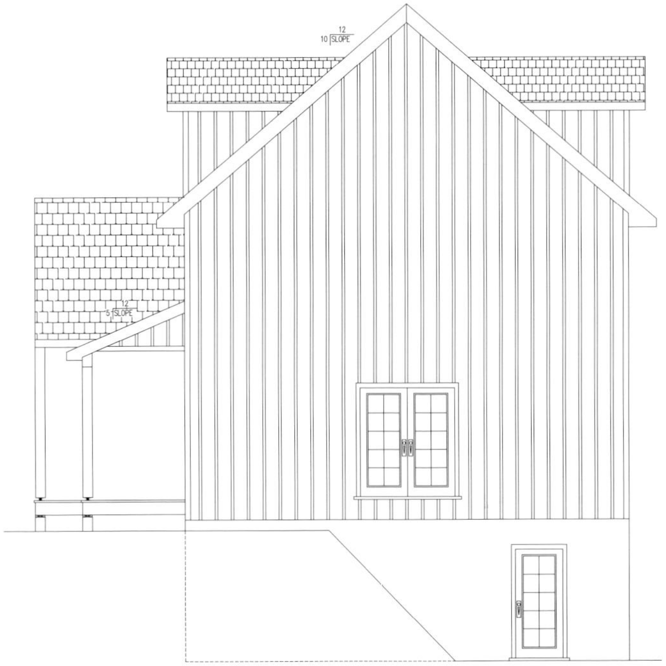

RIGHT SIDE ELEVATION

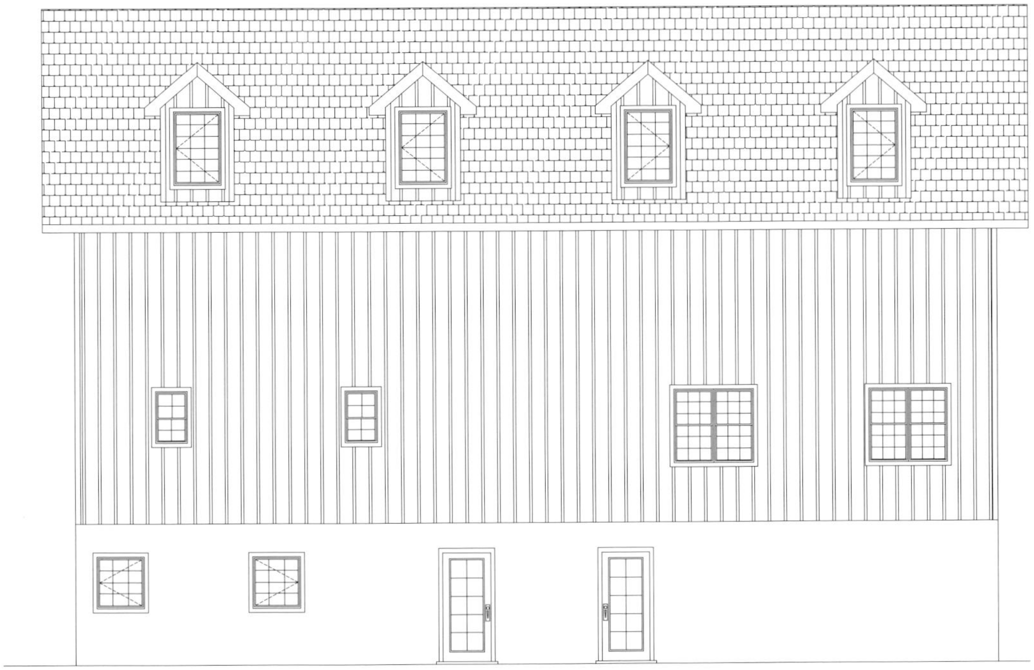

REAR SIDE ELEVATION

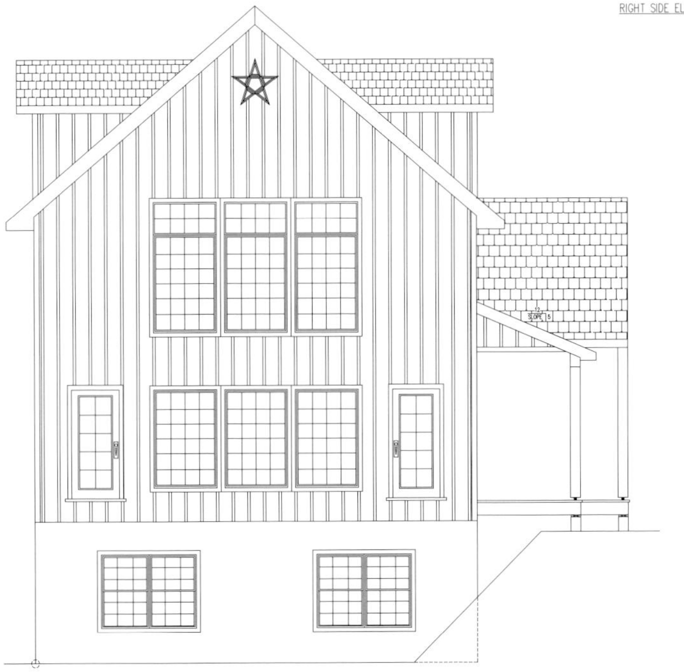

LEFT SIDE ELEVATION

Health Care

Until relatively recently, when we thought of health care facilities, we thought of hospitals. They conjured images of florescent-lit halls, vast expanses of antiseptic linoleum floors, and drab, monochromatic, "tasteful" paint schemes.

Today, however, the specialization of health care functions has led to a proliferation of facility types: nursing homes that cater to specific needs groups; senior living complexes that offer all levels of assistance, from independence to "total immersion;" rehab clinics for substance abuse; diagnostic centers; behavioral health centers; birthing centers, and so on. Many of the facilities, and even traditional hospitals, now strive to create a warmer, more welcoming, and less stress-inducing environment.

With the emergence of environmental psychology studies and the resulting heightened interest in biophilic design, architects and their clients are increasingly seeking to include natural materials in their health-care facility projects. The following four projects illustrate some of the possibilities, from the simple and straightforward porte cochère that welcomes visitors and residents to the Solana at Marlboro, an assisted living facility for Alzheimer's patients; to the unconventional lobby of the Lebanon VA behavioral health center.

Lebanon, Pennsylvania, 2015

Architect
Array Architects,
Conshohocken, Pennsylvania

General contractor
Arthur Funk and Sons,
Lebanon, Pennsylvania

The US Department of Veterans Affairs maintains a major health-care complex in Lebanon, Pennsylvania. This facility was added to expand the range and quality of behavioral health services for veterans. From the start, priority was given to the incorporation of wood into the main reception and waiting area to capitalize on its warmth and calming influence.

The timber frame occupies a space approximately 45 feet wide by 60 feet long and 45 feet high. Atypically, the main posts land well inboard of the perimeter walls. Every timber member measures a nominal 10×10. Although the timber frame is designed to handle gravity loads only, under normal loading conditions, significant tension loads arise in several of the timber-to-timber connections.

These loads could easily have been handled with through-bolted, surface-applied steel gusset plates. The driving aesthetic consideration, however, was to preserve the clean, uninterrupted, and consistently weighted lines of the timber members. Applying hardware to the timbers' exterior faces would have been visually distracting and would have evoked a more utilitarian design idiom. Instead, concealed fasteners to handle the design loads were custom-designed.

The timber is select structural Douglas fir, free of heart center, surfaced on four sides to a half-inch under nominal dimensions. The timbers were sanded dead smooth and finished with clear polymerized tung oil.

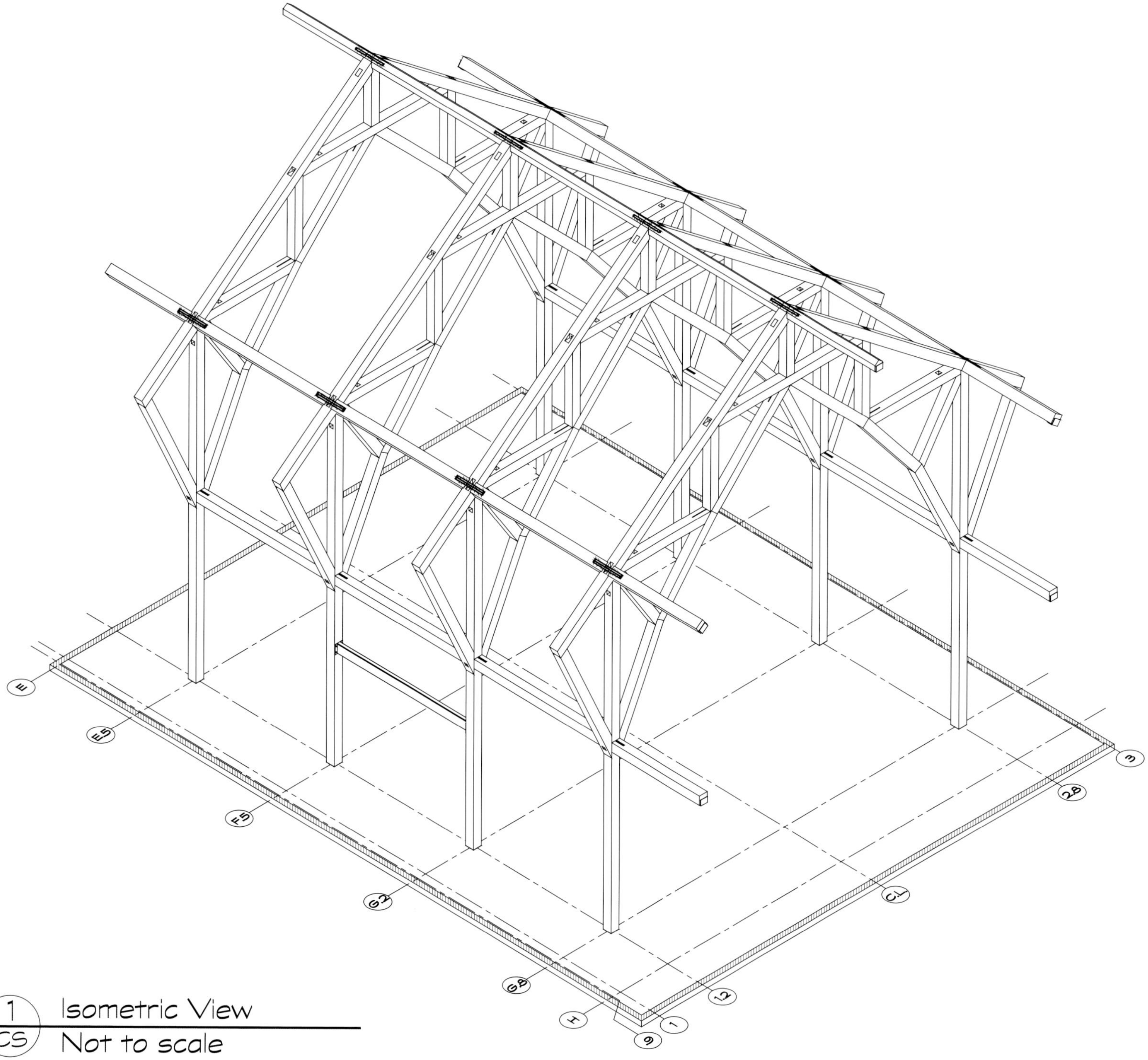

1 / CS Isometric View
Not to scale

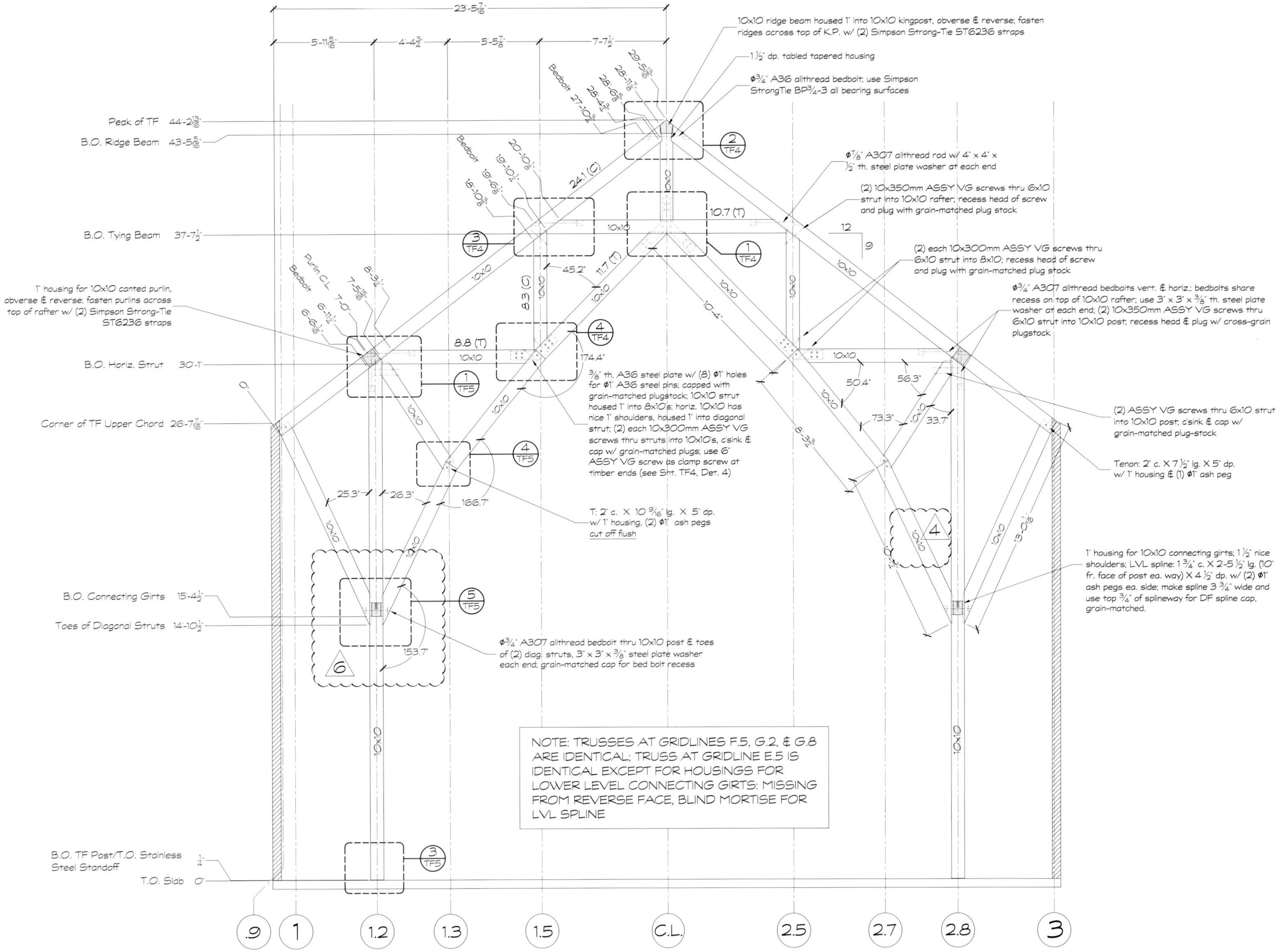

1/TF2 Typical truss section

3/8" = 1'-0"

Pre-fitting a bent on the floor at the Lancaster County Timber Frames shop.

The first bent being lifted into position.

The finished frame stands approximately 45 feet tall at the peak.

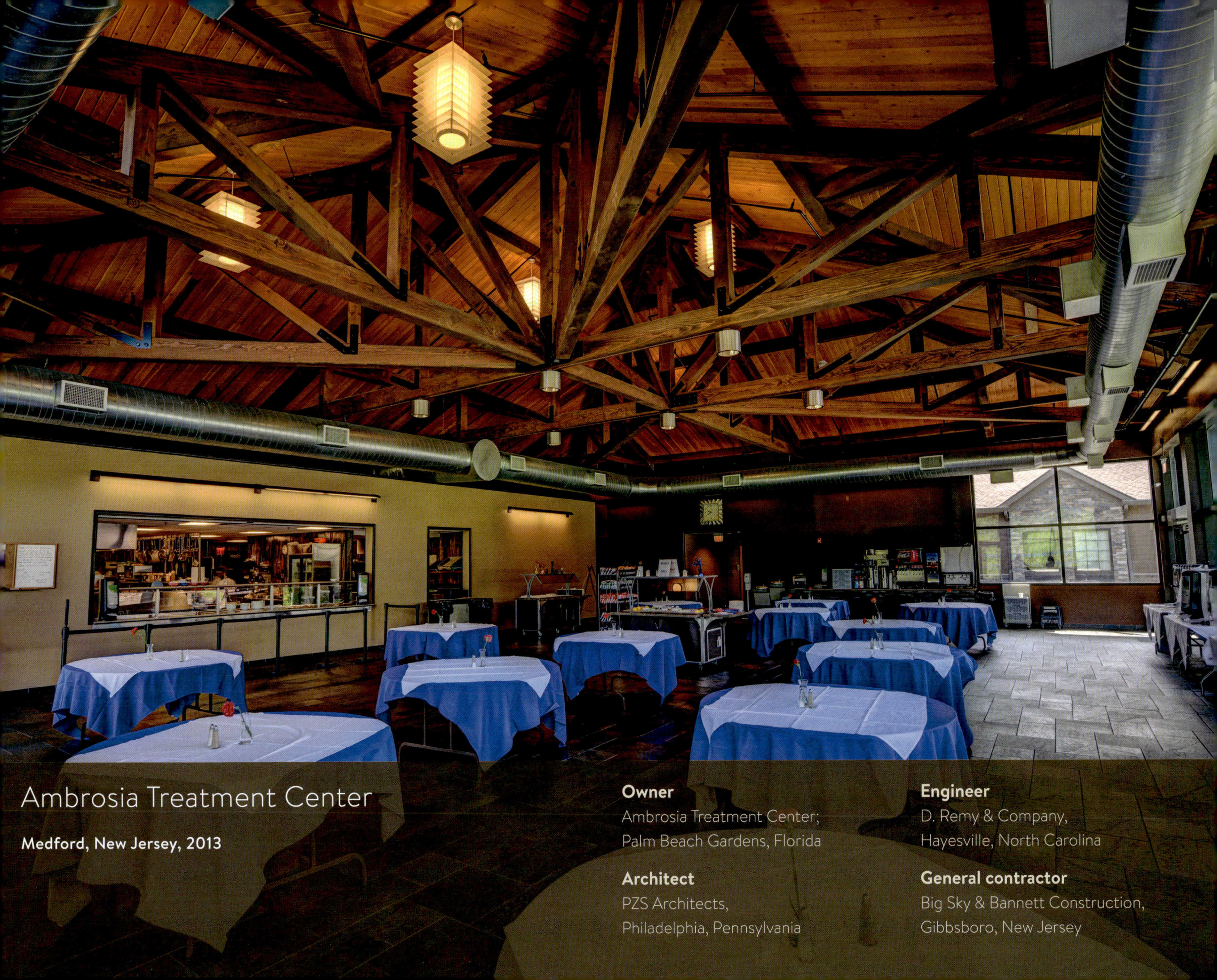

Ambrosia Treatment Center

Medford, New Jersey, 2013

Owner
Ambrosia Treatment Center;
Palm Beach Gardens, Florida

Architect
PZS Architects,
Philadelphia, Pennsylvania

Engineer
D. Remy & Company,
Hayesville, North Carolina

General contractor
Big Sky & Bannett Construction,
Gibbsboro, New Jersey

Lancaster County Timber Framers's work at this treatment center consisted of two heavy timber roof systems supported by steel columns embedded in conventionally framed walls. The smaller structure, the lobby, measures 35 feet by 43 feet and has a simple gabled roof. The larger dining hall measures 53 feet by 63 feet and is a hip roof. The timbers, 230 of them, were solid Douglas fir and the total timber material for both areas was 21,000 board feet.

Other than the need to be mindful of the bolting sequence through the multi-flanged steel connectors at the top and bottom of the king posts, particularly at levels where the angles are acute, and contending with a very muddy site, this project was completely devoid of challenges and drama.

Custom-fabricated steel hub at one of two points of convergence of the roof framing members.

The structural timber purlins penetrated the front wall and were reduced at the ends so as not to project too far below the fascia board.

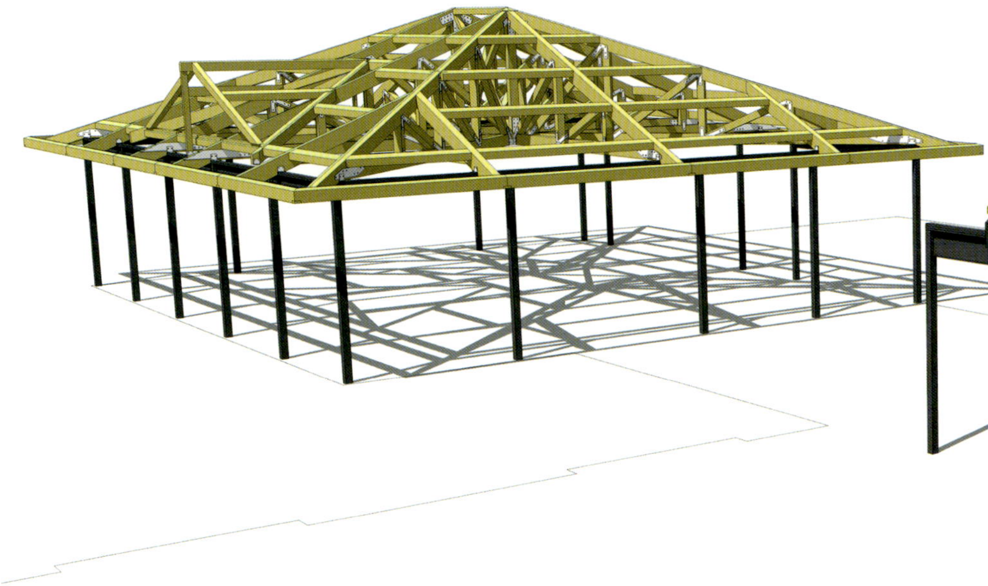

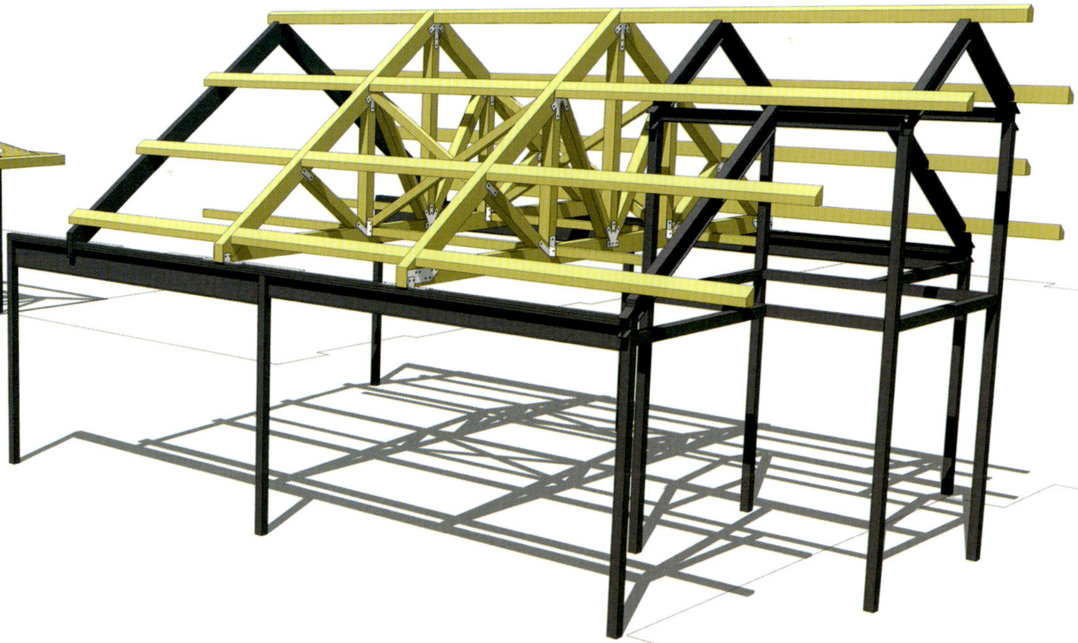

Solana Marlboro

Marlboro Township, New Jersey, 2014

Owner
Formation-Shelbourne Senior Living Services,
Radnor, Pennsylvania

Architect
PRDG,
Dallas, Texas

Engineer
Sellers Treybal Structural Engineers,
Williston, Vermont

General contractor
Wohlsen Construction,
Lancaster, Pennsylvania

The roof of the Solana Marlboro porte cochère was decked in laminated Douglas fir tongue and groove, which has a warm glow even when not lit.

This free-standing heavy timber porte cochère at a New Jersey assisted living facility consists of a series of four king post trusses attached to two longitudinal eave plates supported at the corners by four posts. The corner posts land on stone-veneered piers. All connections are through-bolted, face-mounted steel plates, which are powder coated for corrosion protection. Such face-mounted steel plates are generally custom fabricated for a project, allowing these components to become an expressive element of the design, going well beyond the prosaic minimum requirements of engineering. Often, however, the industrial look is all the design statement that is sought.

Other than the two eave plates, which are glulams, all of the timbers are solid Douglas fir. Solid timbers could have been used in place of the glulam eave plates, but because of their relatively long span, they would have had to have been significantly more massive than the glulams. The solid timbers and the glulams are the same species and are coated with the same finish, so their combination in this project doesn't appear incongruous.

Country Meadows Retirement Community

York, Pennsylvania, 2011

Owner
Country Meadows Retirement Communities
Hershey, Pennsylvania

Architect
Alexander Design Studio,
Ellicott City, Maryland

Engineer
Ruff Engineering,
Douglassville, Pennsylvania

General contractor
eciConstruction,
Dillsburg, Pennsylvania

One of the more intriguing design challenges we deal with from time to time is the octagonal timber frame. This one—a dining and lounge facility in a high-end retirement community—was one of two octagonal timber frames we completed in 2011. The interior space is divided into an inner octagon and an outer octagon. The building filled in the space between two existing residential wings.

The whole building —measuring about 80 feet across—houses dining rooms, a bar, and several lounge areas. The inner octagon isn't timber framed, but the lofty clerestory windows look through to the timber-framed outer ring. The outer ring is outfitted with several 8-foot-diameter Big Ass ceiling fans (yes, that's the brand name).

The sixteen Douglas fir trusses are common trusses with vertical and diagonal struts. They're tied together with top plates, eave plates, and purlins, over which a structural deck of four-inch-thick Douglas fir Lock-Deck (tongue and groove boards) is installed.

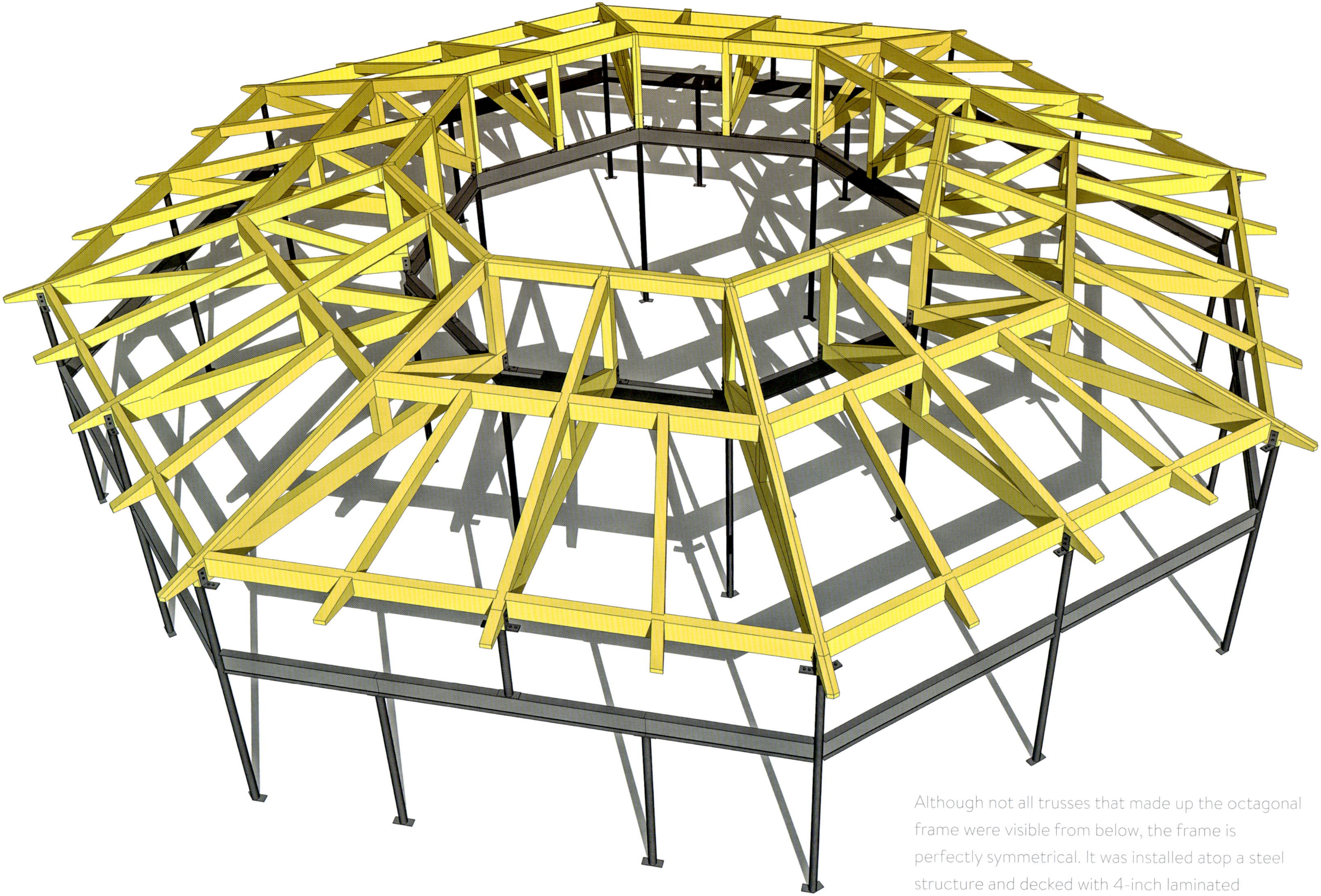

Although not all trusses that made up the octagonal frame were visible from below, the frame is perfectly symmetrical. It was installed atop a steel structure and decked with 4-inch laminated structural tongue and groove boards.

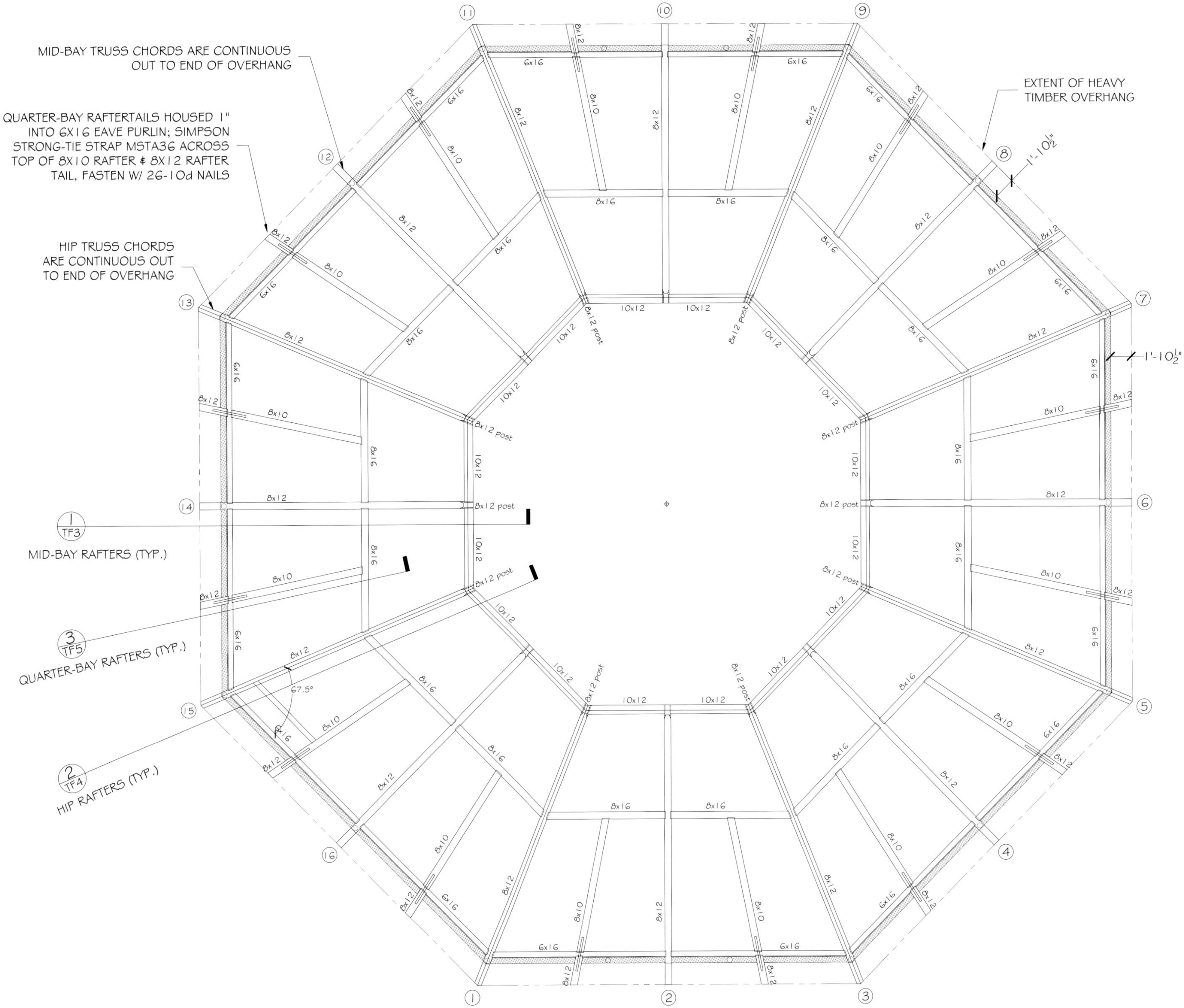
MID-BAY TRUSS CHORDS ARE CONTINUOUS OUT TO END OF OVERHANG
QUARTER-BAY RAFTERTAILS HOUSED 1" INTO 6X16 EAVE PURLIN; SIMPSON STRONG-TIE STRAP MSTA36 ACROSS TOP OF 8X10 RAFTER & 8X12 RAFTER TAIL, FASTEN W/ 26-10d NAILS
HIP TRUSS CHORDS ARE CONTINUOUS OUT TO END OF OVERHANG
EXTENT OF HEAVY TIMBER OVERHANG
1'-10½"
1 TF3 MID-BAY RAFTERS (TYP.)
3 TF5 QUARTER-BAY RAFTERS (TYP.)
2 TF4 HIP RAFTERS (TYP.)
67.5°

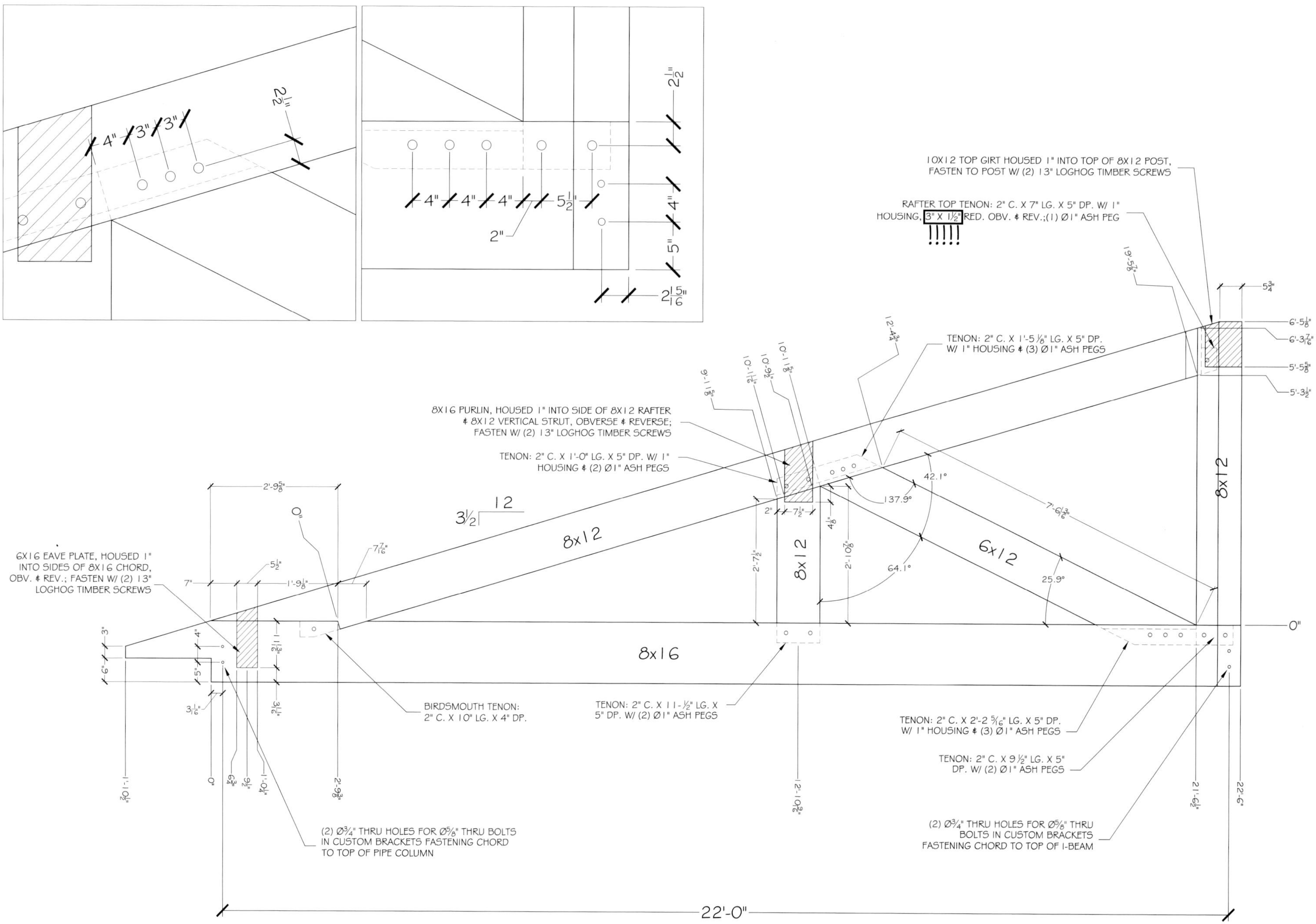

1 SECTION AT TRUSS T1 (MID-BAY RAFTERS; (8) THUS REQ'D.)

Scale: 1" = 1'-0"

4

Government Buildings

Heavy timber government projects— those financed and controlled, in whole or in part, by a federal, state, or local government agency—are typically larger than private projects. In this section, we see an exception to that pattern in the Zimmerman Center Pavilion in Wrightsville, Pennsylvania. Usually these projects are intended for common use, to maintain a cultural sense of identity, to commemorate a significant historic event (such as the Gettysburg National Military Park and Visitor Center), or to provide information and a public service (like the Maryland I-70 Welcome Centers and the Wildlife Center at Sinnemahoning State Park in Cameron County, Pennsylvania). Sometimes such structures do all these things well. We believe the projects in this section belong to that group.

The Wildlife Center at Sinnemahoning State Park

Austin, Pennsylvania, 2011

Owner
Department of Conservation & Natural Resources, Commonwealth of Pennsylvania

Architect
LSC Design,
York, Pennsylvania

Engineer
C. S. Davidson, York, Pennsylvania;
Carney Engineering, York, Pennsylvania

General contractor
Lobar,
Dillsburg, Pennsylvania

The Sinnemahoning State Park is in the heart of the Pennsylvania Wilds region in the north-central part of the state. The LEED-certified Wildlife Center, which houses state-of-the-art interpretive exhibits and park offices, covers approximately 10,000 square feet and cost $3.8 million to build. The center core of the building is a timber-framed atrium 30 feet wide by 70 feet long. The frame consists of eight groupings of four posts each, on which sit two longitudinal plates, on which sit eleven post-tensioned timber and stainless steel trusses. The timbers are FSC-certified Pennsylvania white oak; the steel is domestically manufactured 18/8 stainless steel with a bead-blasted satin finish. The two sets of exterior posts sit on 2.375-inch-thick stainless plates.

The project marked the first time that LCTF added snake bite kits to its on-site safety packages, as the site was in the heart of rattlesnake country. The crew members were continually admonished not to put a hand anywhere they couldn't see.

A typical post tensioning connection. All hardware was domestically manufactured, glass bead–blasted stainless steel.

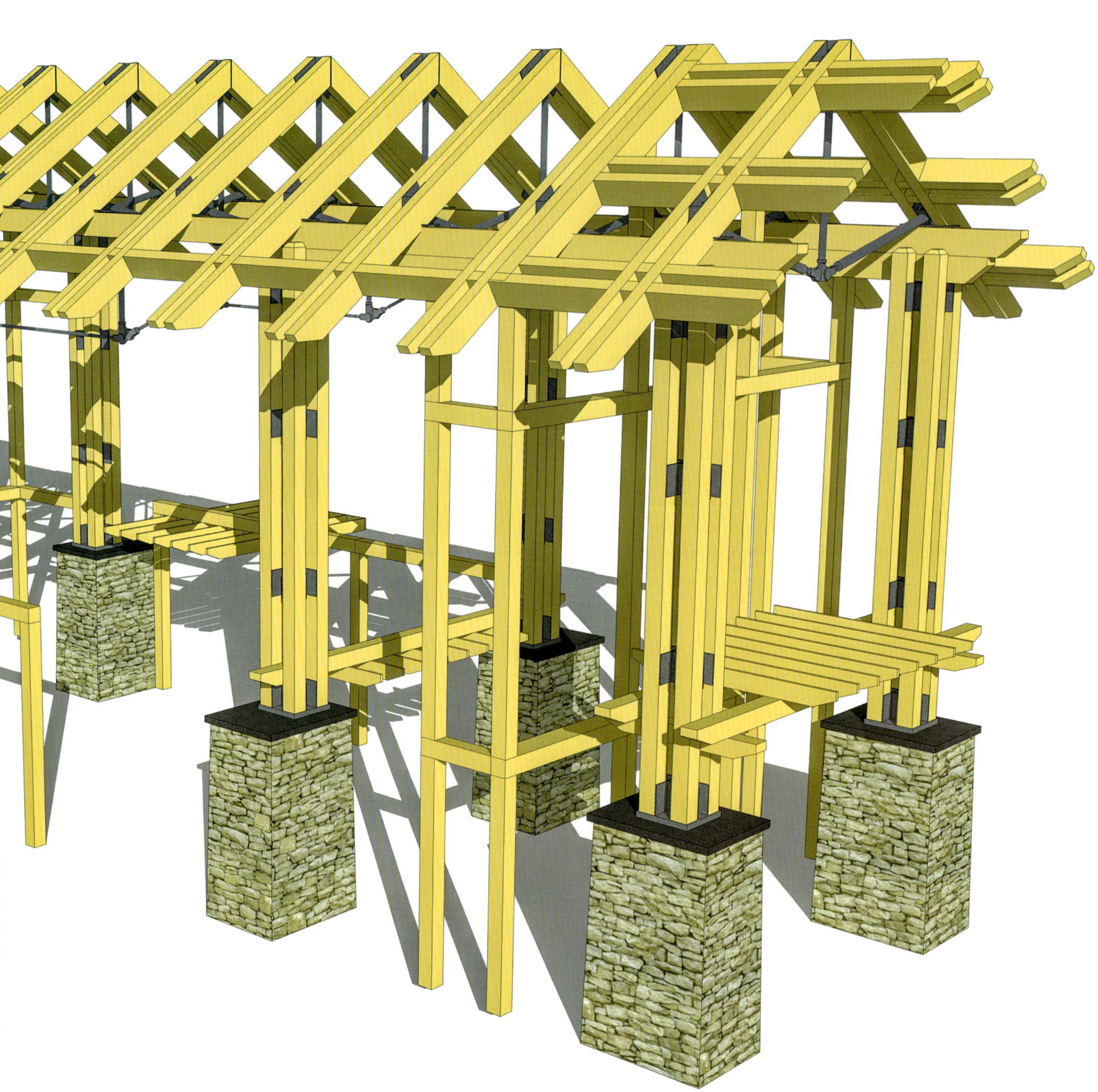

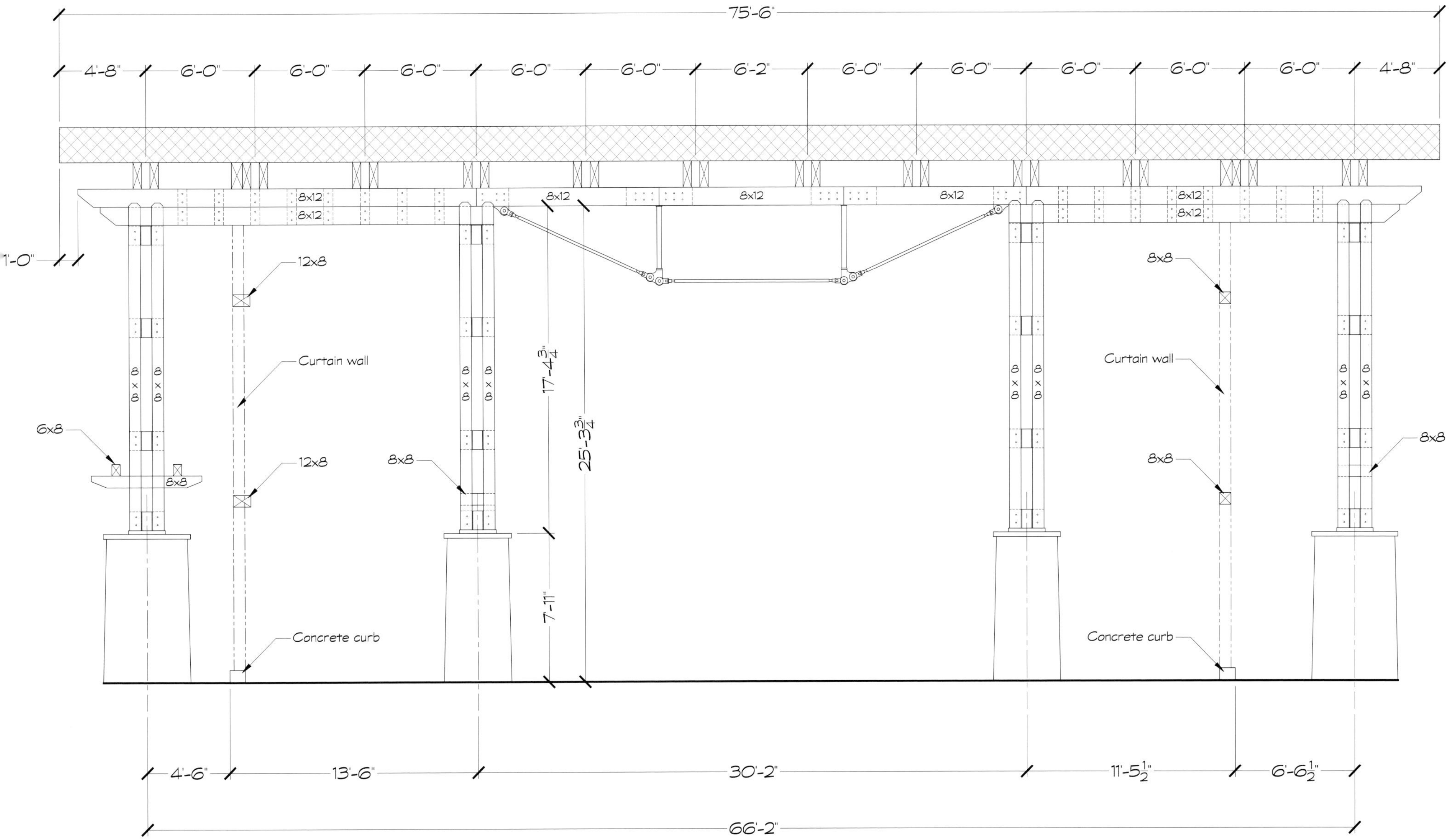
75'-6"
4'-8"
6'-0"
6'-0"
6'-0"
6'-0"
6'-0"
6'-2"
6'-0"
6'-0"
6'-0"
6'-0"
6'-0"
4'-8"
8x12
8x12
8x12
8x12
8x12
8x12
8x12
1'-0"
12x8
Curtain wall
12x8
6x8
8x8
8x8
8x8
Curtain wall
8x8
8x8
17'-4 3/4"
25'-3 3/4"
7'-11"
Concrete curb
Concrete curb
4'-6"
13'-6"
30'-2"
11'-5 1/2"
6'-6 1/2"
66'-2"

The Zimmerman Center for Heritage Pavilion

Wrightsville, Pennsylvania, 2014

Owner
Susquehanna Gateway Heritage Center,
Wrightsville, Pennsylvania

Architect
Murphy & Dittenhafer Architects,
York, Pennsylvania

Engineer
Baker, Ingram, & Associates,
Lancaster, Pennsylvania

General contractor
Kinsley Construction,
York, Pennsylvania

This modestly sized, roughly 600-square-foot pavilion sits on the west bank of the Susquehanna River in Wrightsville, York County, Pennsylvania. The architects maintained that "It's all about the river and the waterfront." They envisioned an elegant pavilion that would be structurally unobtrusive, and yet that could withstand seasonal flooding and severe winter ice flows. Employing just five beams and three columns, the building met that goal. The timbers are Douglas fir glulams (24F-V8), the roof decking is 4×6 Lock-Deck, and the steel is type 304 stainless with a D-3 glass bead-blasted satin finish.

As simple as this structure appears at first glance, consider that out of all the timber-to-timber connections not one is 90 degrees or even 45 degrees. The 4×6 tongue-and-grove Lock-Deck ceiling boards were laid out, cut, and then screwed together into three panels before being shipped to the site.

This pavilion was our first PennDot (Pennsylvania Department of Transportation)-monitored project. Every sub-zero day after sub-zero day for the week that we were on site, two PennDot employees sat in a heated pickup truck and watched the show.

The pavilion sits on the banks of the Susquehanna River a mile or so south of Wrightsville.

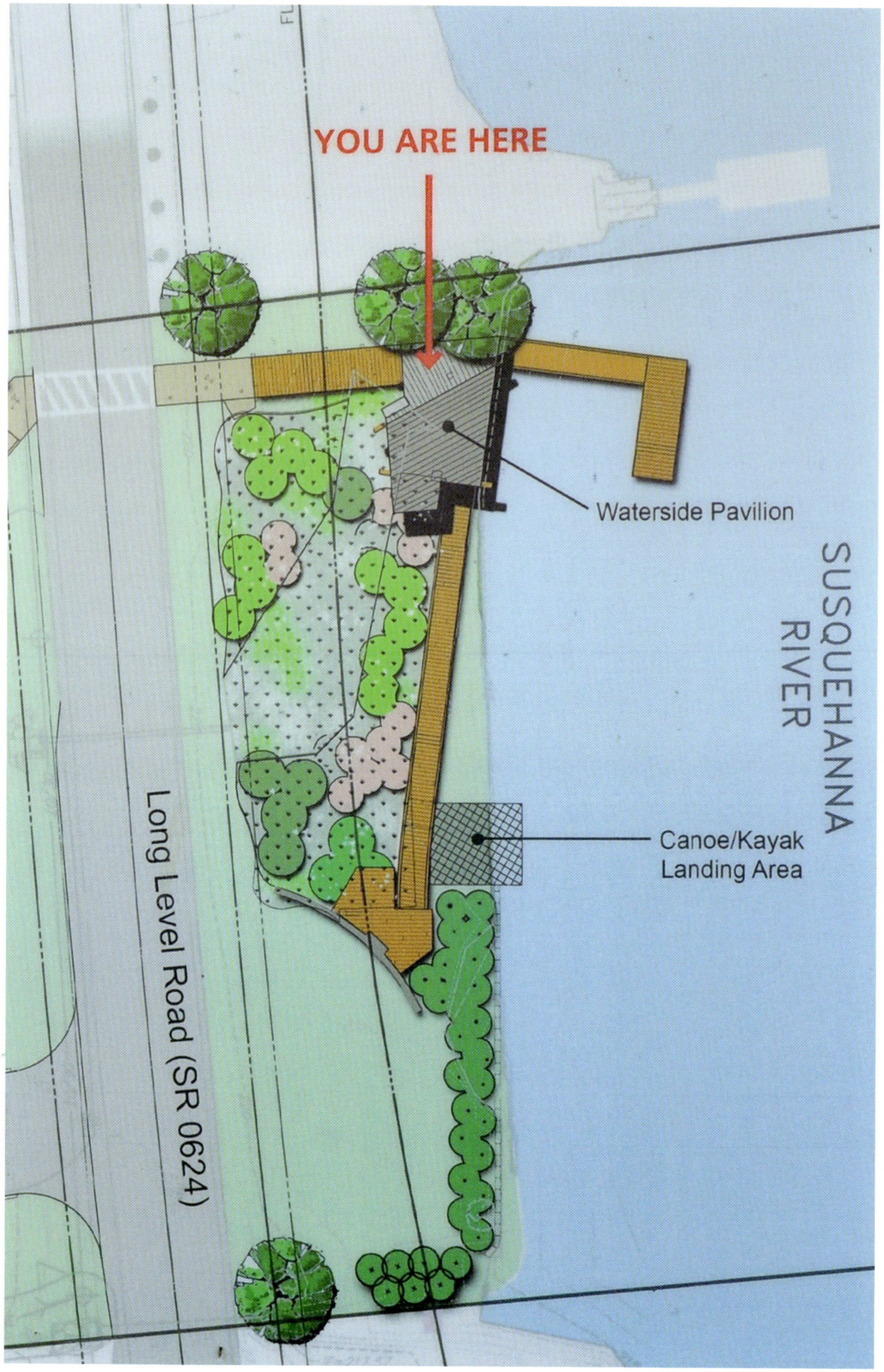
YOU ARE HERE
Waterside Pavilion
SUSQUEHANNA RIVER
Canoe/Kayak Landing Area
Long Level Road (SR 0624)

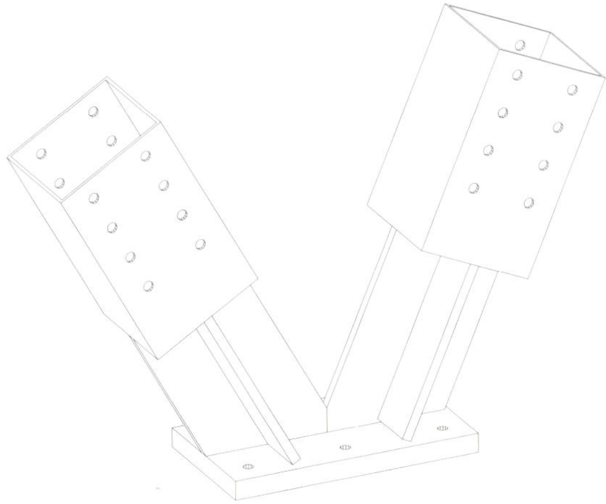

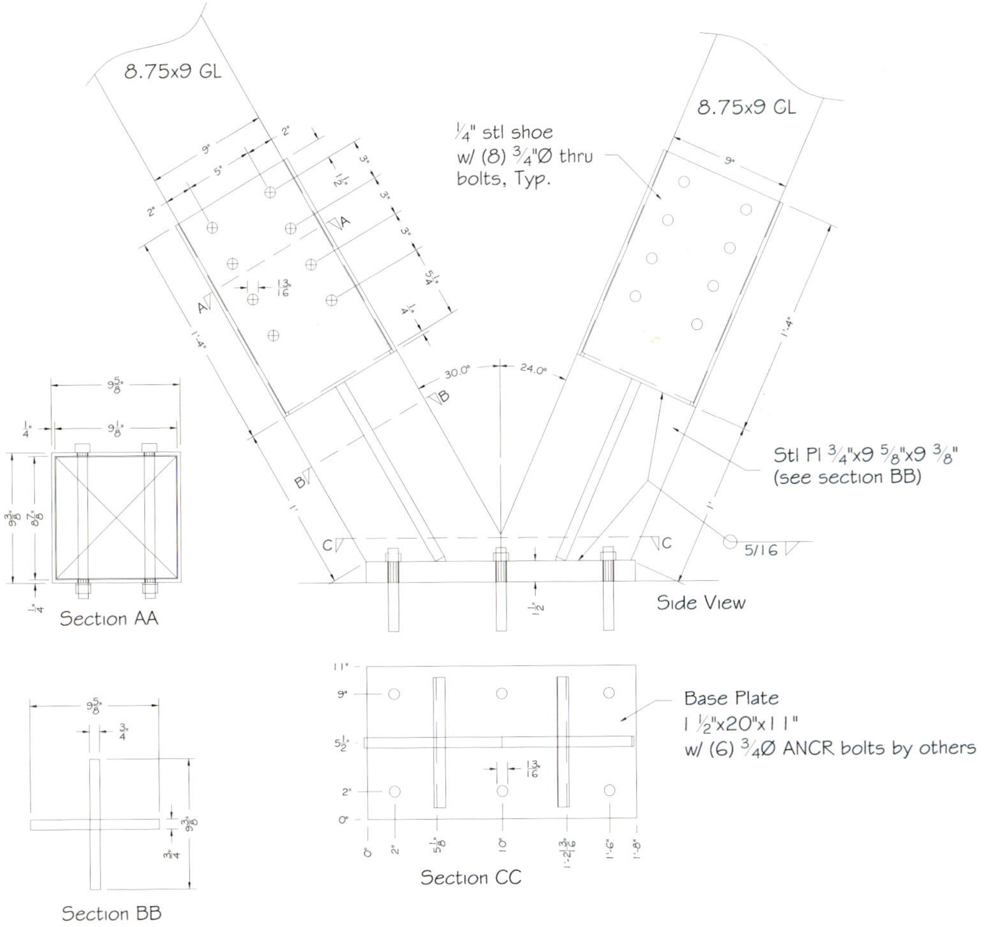

8.75x9 GL
8.75x9 GL
1/4" stl shoe
w/ (8) 3/4"Ø thru
bolts, Typ.
30.0°
24.0°
Stl Pl 3/4"x9 5/8"x9 3/8"
(see section BB)
5/16
Side View
Section AA
Section BB
Section CC
Base Plate
1 1/2"x20"x11"
w/ (6) 3/4Ø ANCR bolts by others

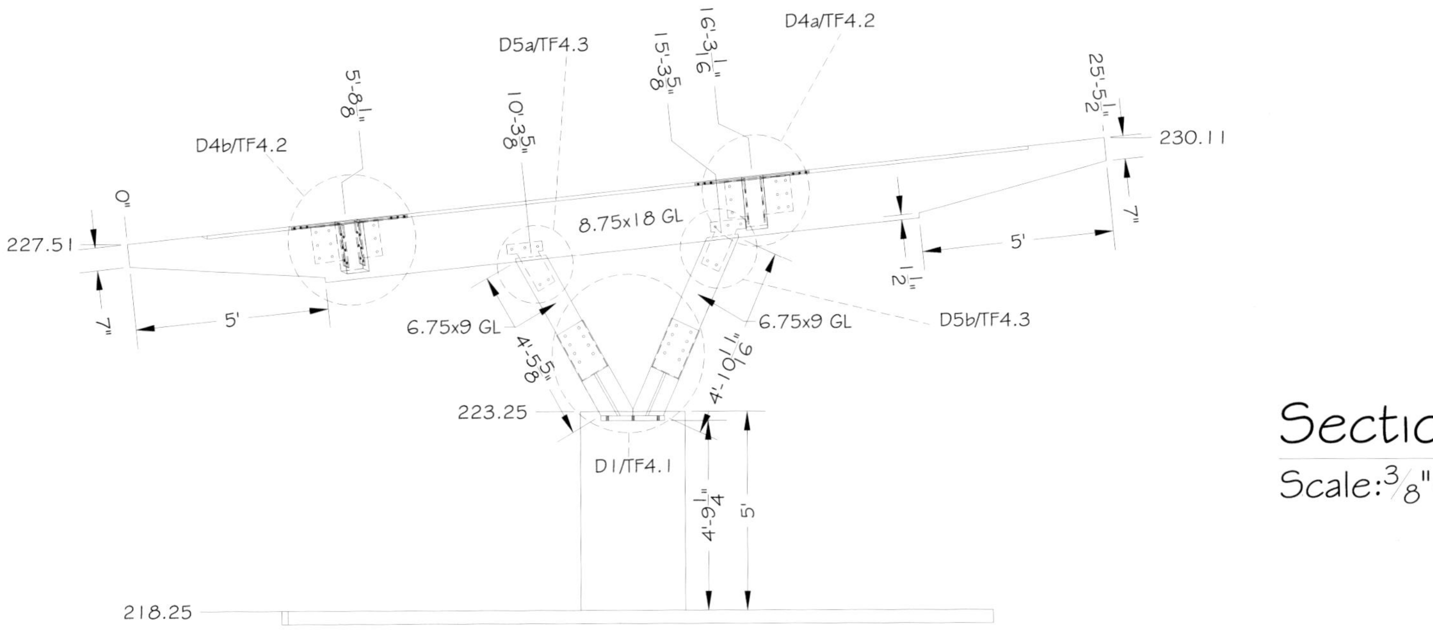

Section A'

Scale: 3/8" = 1'-0"

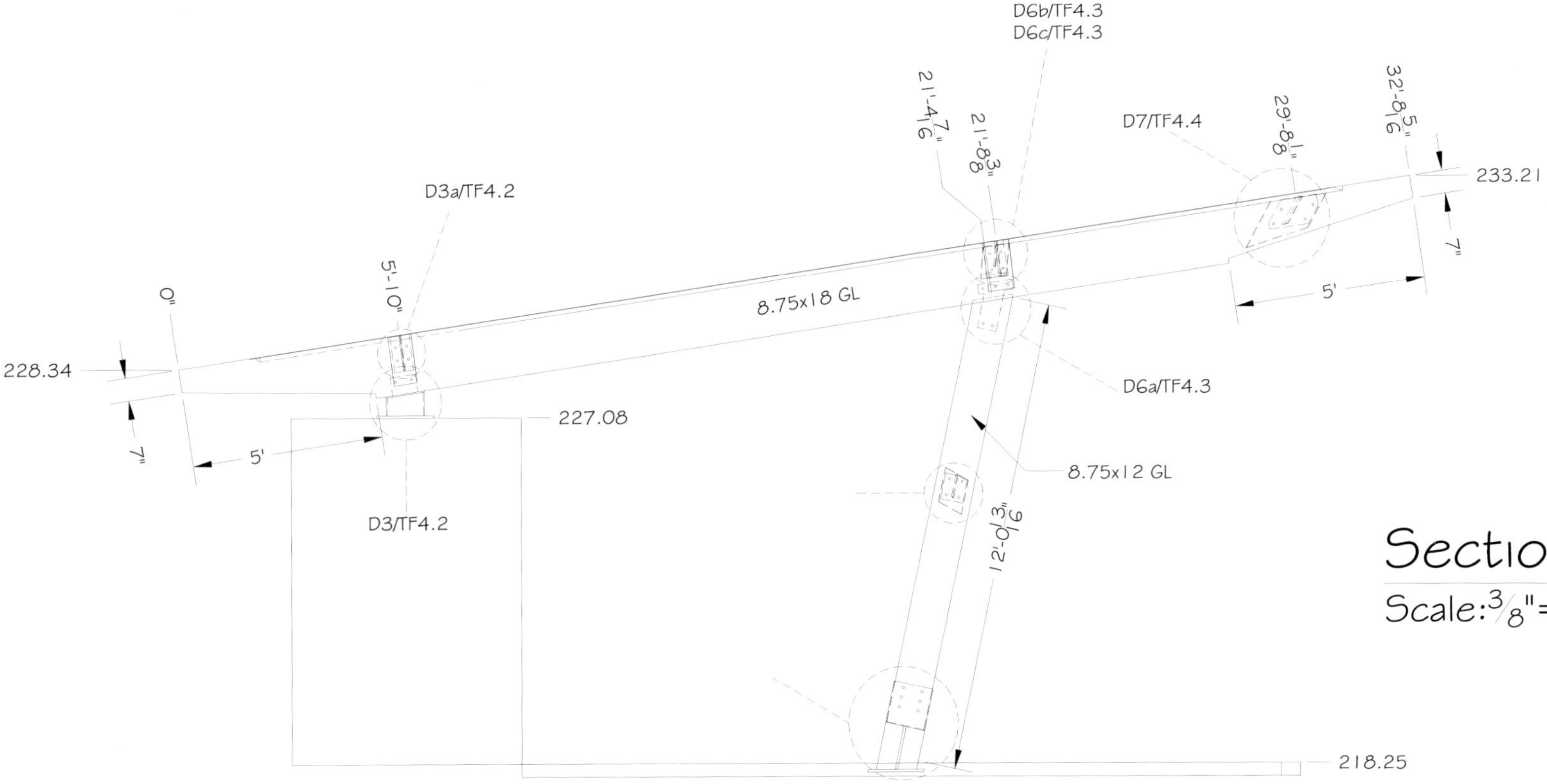

Section B'

Scale: 3/8" = 1'-0"

Gettysburg National Military Park Museum & Visitor Center

Gettysburg, Pennsylvania, 2008

Owner
US National Park Service

Architect
LSC Design,
York, Pennsylvania

Engineer
Ruff Engineering,
Douglassville, Pennsylvania

General contractor
Keystruct/Kinsley
Construction, York, Pennsylvania

This facility, more than 130,000 square feet, replaced the much smaller original structure that had served for 87 years. Three timber species were used: Port Orford cedar, fresh-sawn white oak, and reclaimed mixed oak. The latter two were the predominant species: the fresh-sawn oak was harvested in Pennsylvania, while the reclaimed mixed oak came from dismantled Pennsylvania barns. More than 400 timbers were worked and the total board footage was just shy of 10,000. The structure was the first US museum to achieve LEED Gold certification.

WELCOME TO THE GETTYSBURG
MILITARY PARK VISITOR CENTER
General Admission Tickets
PROGRAMS
ONE TICKET
s Come in all Sizes!

TRAYS
GRILL

A reclaimed timber post colonnade at the bus drop-off area for the museum.

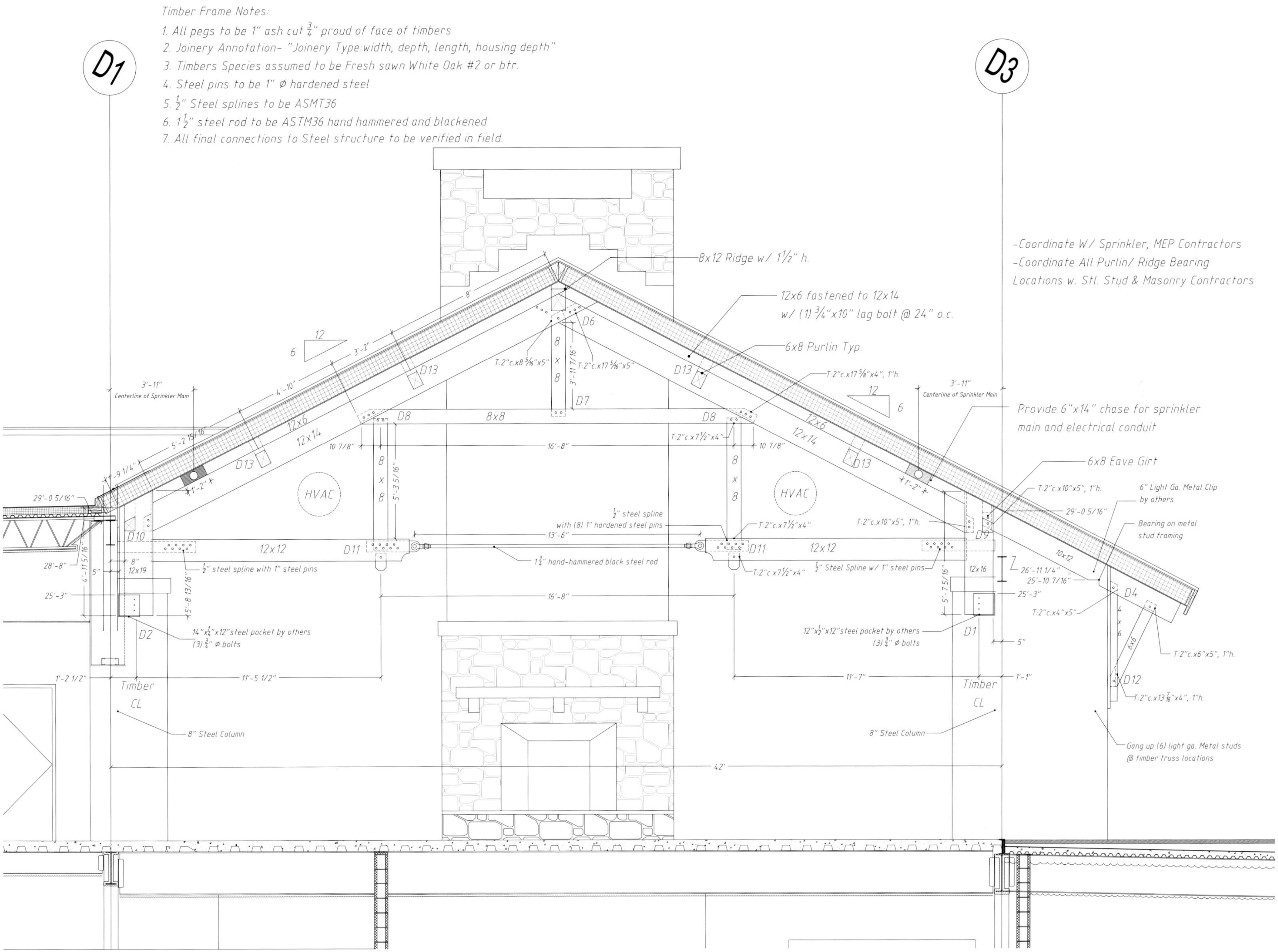
Timber Frame Notes:
1. All pegs to be 1" ash cut 3/4" proud of face of timbers
2. Joinery Annotation- "Joinery Type:width, depth, length, housing depth"
3. Timbers Species assumed to be Fresh sawn White Oak #2 or btr.
4. Steel pins to be 1" Ø hardened steel
5. 1/2" Steel splines to be ASMT36
6. 1 1/2" steel rod to be ASTM36 hand hammered and blackened
7. All final connections to Steel structure to be verified in field.
D1
D3
8x12 Ridge w/ 1 1/2" h.
12x6 fastened to 12x14
w/ (1) 3/4"x10" lag bolt @ 24" o.c.
6x8 Purlin Typ.
-Coordinate W/ Sprinkler, MEP Contractors
-Coordinate All Purlin/ Ridge Bearing
Locations w. Stl. Stud & Masonry Contractors
Provide 6"x14" chase for sprinkler
main and electrical conduit
6x8 Eave Girt
6" Light Ga. Metal Clip
by others
Bearing on metal
stud framing
Gang up (6) light ga. Metal studs
@ timber truss locations
HVAC
HVAC
1/2" steel spline
with (8) 1" hardened steel pins
1 3/4" hand-hammered black steel rod
1/2" steel spline with 1" steel pins
1/2" Steel Spline w/ 1" steel pins
14"x1/2"x12"steel pocket by others
(3) 3/4" Ø bolts
12"x1/2"x12"steel pocket by others
(3) 3/4" Ø bolts
Timber
CL
8" Steel Column
42'

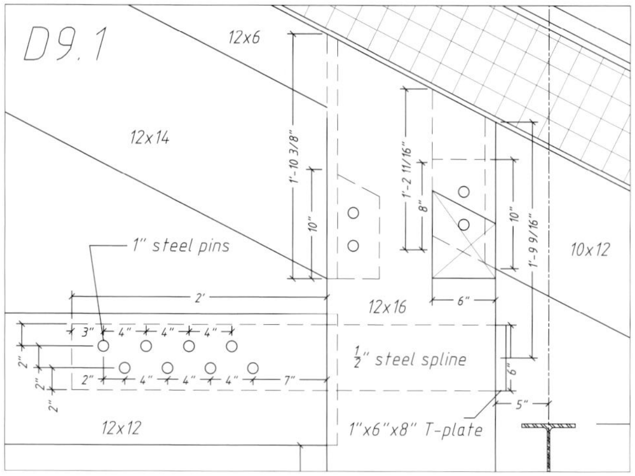

D9.1

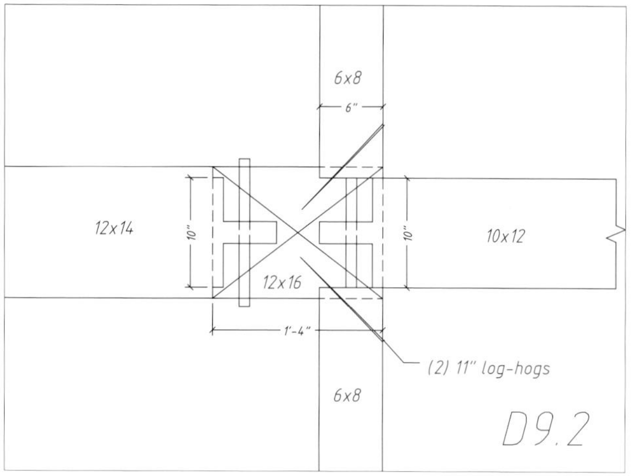

D9.2

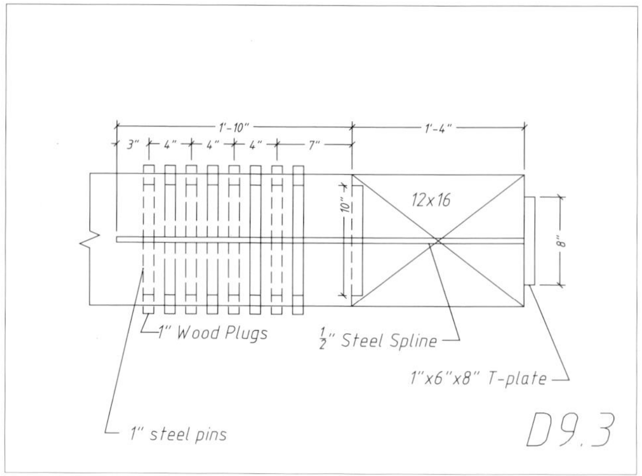

D9.3

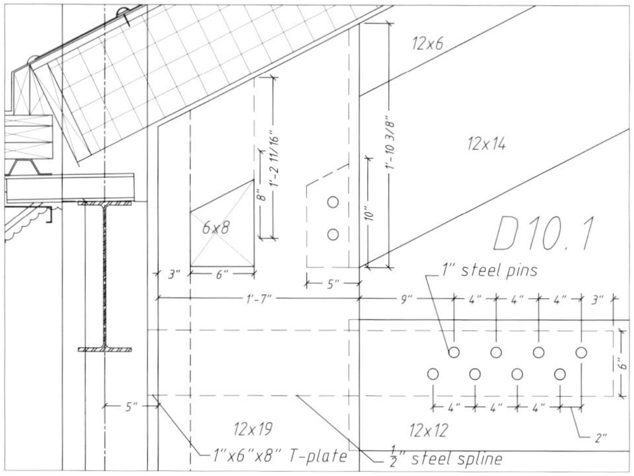

D10.1

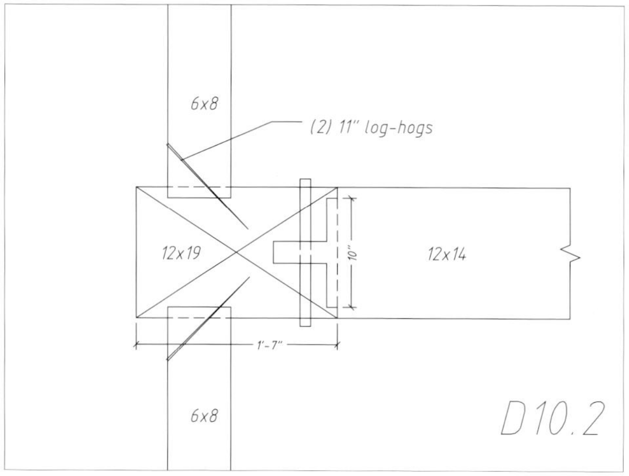

D10.2

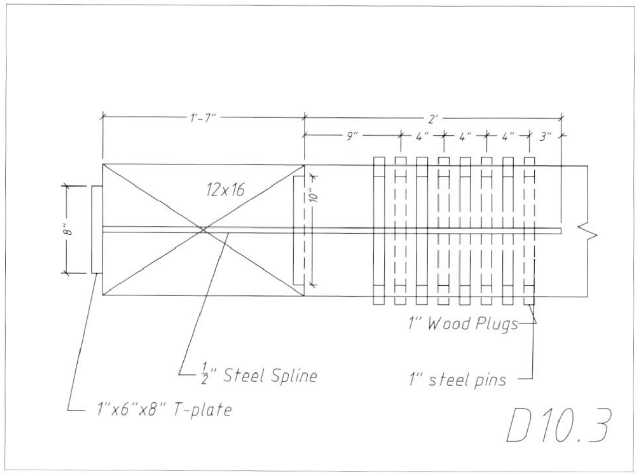

D10.3

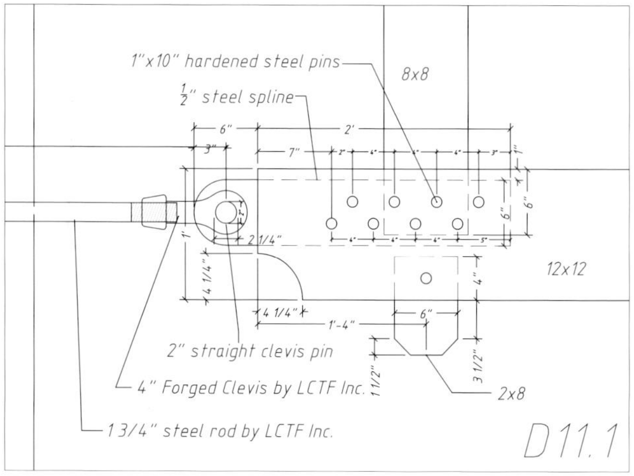

D11.1

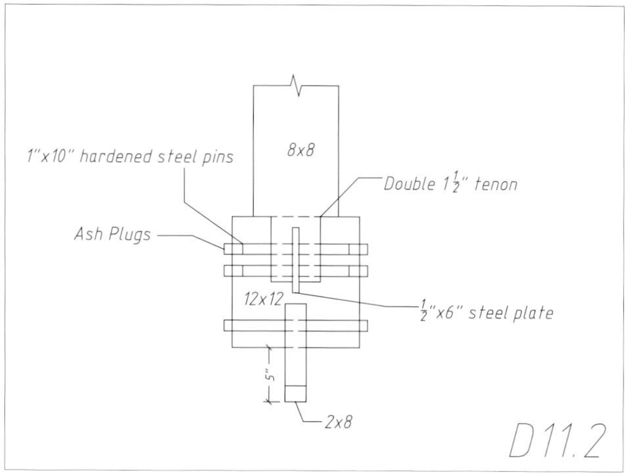

D11.2

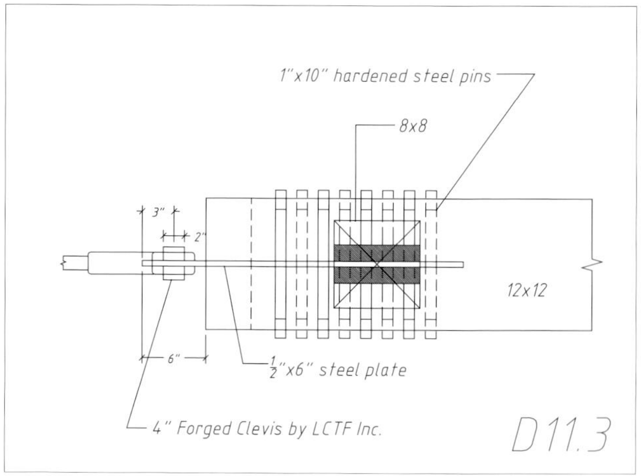

D11.3

Aerial view of the museum during construction. The fully erected saloon timber frame is visible at the top of the photograph.

Pre-fitting one of the saloon trusses on the floor of the Lancaster County Timber Frames shop.

An exterior timber-framed trellis with stainless steel fittings, during construction. The two parallel walls create a planter at the end of the terrace outside the dining saloon.

Maryland I-70 Welcome Centers at South Mountain

Myersville, Maryland, 2009

Owner
Maryland State Highway Administration

Architect
Waldon Studio Architects & Planners, Columbia, Maryland

Engineering
KCI Technologies, Sparks, Maryland

General contractor
Kinsley Construction, York, Pennsylvania

Two identical welcome centers, one on the eastbound side of Maryland's I-70 and the other on the westbound side, cover 10,200 square feet each and house a conference room, restrooms, breezeway, media room, and vending area. These two structures, the first operational facilities owned by the Maryland Highway Administration to be awarded LEED-Silver certification, replaced the two long-standing, much smaller centers. Each of the two structures is comprised of two enclosed buildings connected by a covered walkway.

The narrower building's primary interior roof supports are two parallel bridge trusses, while the larger building employs a pair of longitudinal glulams. The connecting covered walkway has a high shed roof that is also supported by a bridge truss, and its lower rear load is carried by solid wood girts, under which closely spaced wood posts disperse the load downward. This project used 1,000 timbers, and the board footage was just shy of 70,000. (A board foot is a standard volume of lumber and timber and is equal to 144 cubic inches, or a board measuring 1 foot square and 1 inch thick.) With the exception of a few glulam members, the entire project consisted of solid Douglas fir timbers. All have been stained a light gray.

In the early hours of October 24, 2002, police surrounded a blue 1990 Chevrolet Caprice in the parking lot on the eastbound side. They arrested the two men who had gained infamy as the Beltway/DC snipers.

MARYLAND
SO MUCH
SO CLOSE
SO MUCH
LOCAL FLAVOR
SO CLOSE
SO MUCH
HISTORY
SO CLOSE
SOUTH MOUNTAIN WELCOME CENTER
SOUTH MOUNTAIN RESTROOMS

TO ENJOY
SO CLOSE
MARYLAND
TRAIL

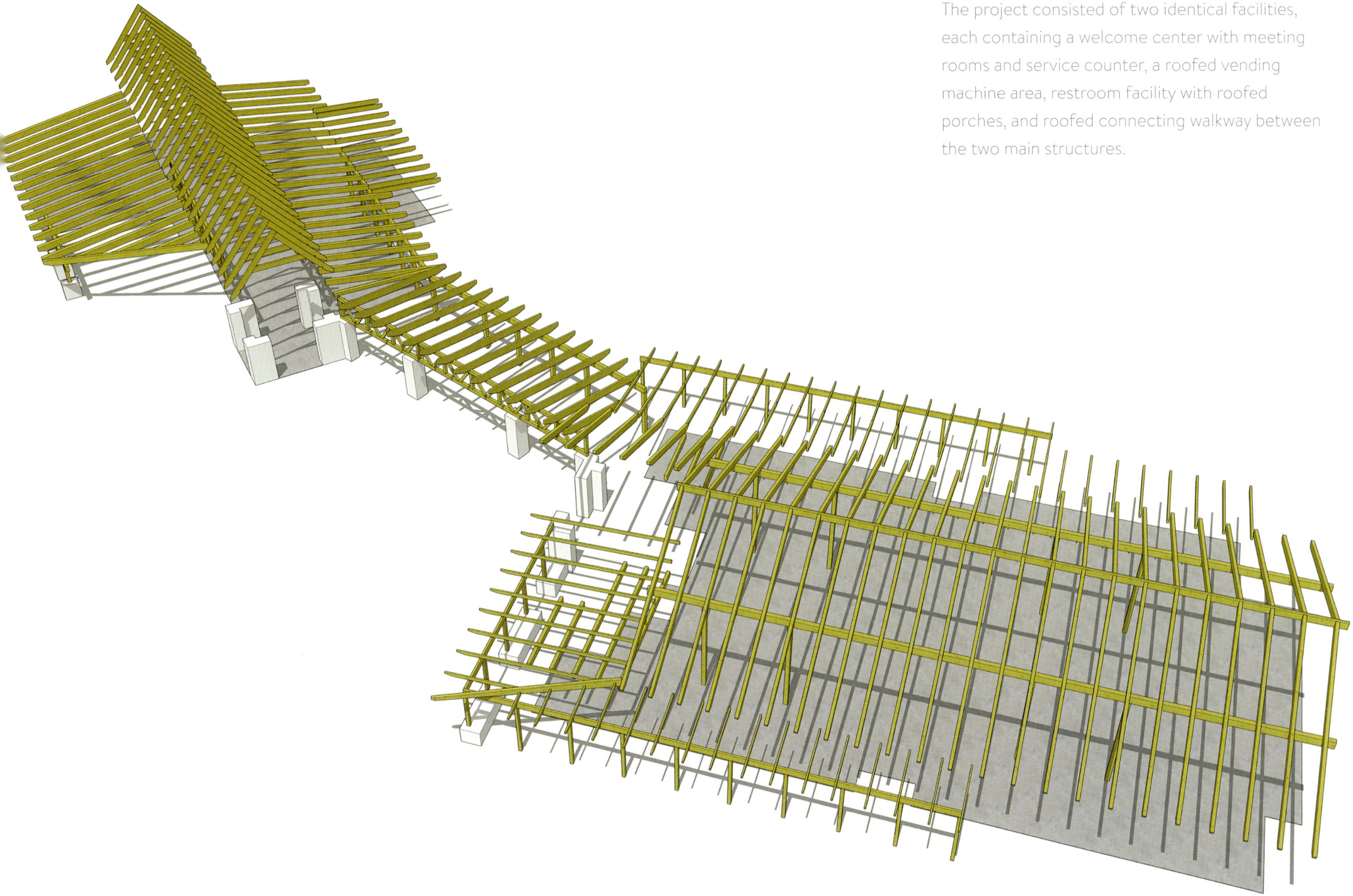

The project consisted of two identical facilities, each containing a welcome center with meeting rooms and service counter, a roofed vending machine area, restroom facility with roofed porches, and roofed connecting walkway between the two main structures.

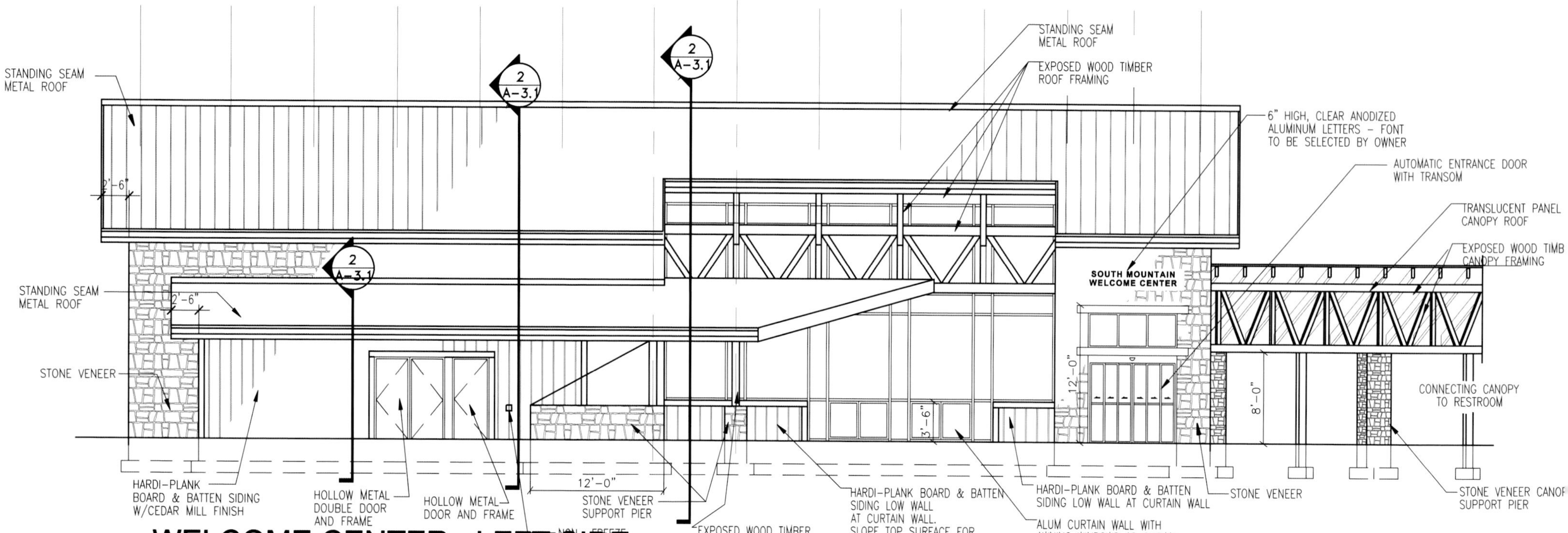

2 **WELCOME CENTER - LEFT SIDE**

SCALE: 1/8" = 1'-0"

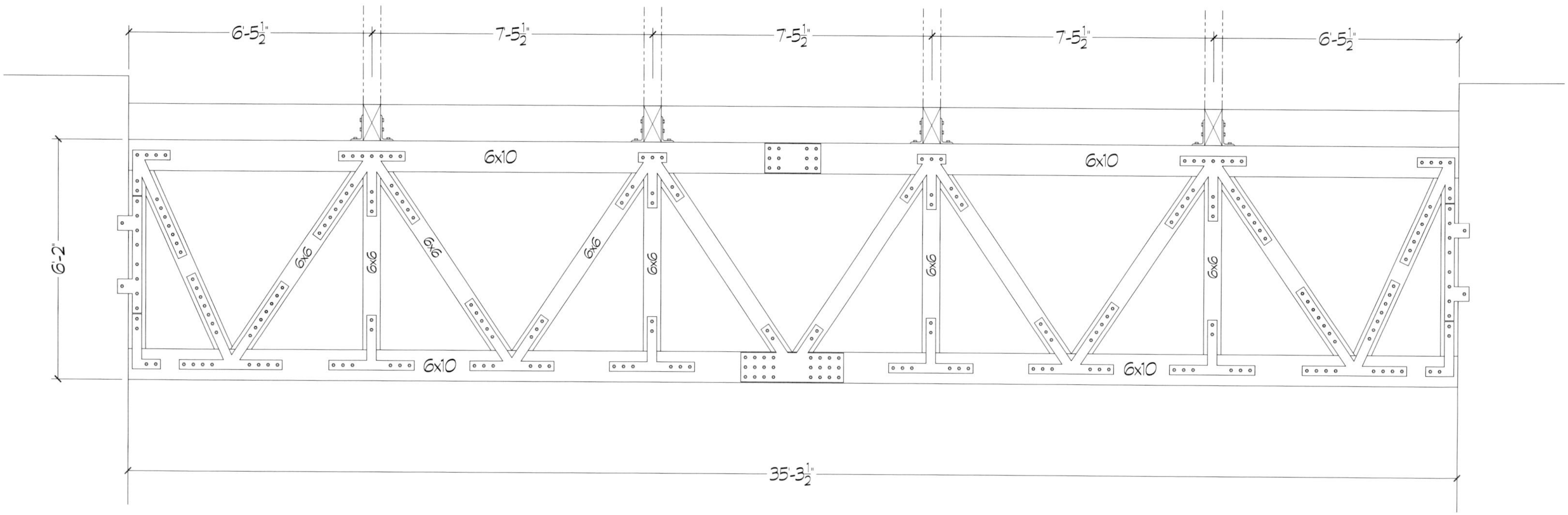

5

Clubhouses

For kids of past generations, the idea of a clubhouse had a strong appeal. Be it a backyard shed, a slapped together hut in the woods, a tree house with a rope ladder—a clubhouse was a place to trade baseball cards and comics, to tell scary stories, a place to be with your best friends, a place exclusive of parents.

Apparently even the passage of many decades doesn't diminish this appeal. This section looks at clubhouses (or, in the case of Hawk Pointe Golf Club in Washington, New Jersey, an entry to a clubhouse) that focus on golf, community, boats, and cars.

Three-Season Dining Room at Gulph Mills Golf Club

King of Prussia, Pennsylvania, 2006

Photo by John M. Lewis

Owner
Gulph Mills Golf Club,
King of Prussia, Pennsylvania

Architect
Moeckel Carbonell Associates,
Wilmington, Delaware

Engineer
Ruff Engineering,
Douglassville, Pennsylvania

General contractor
Ehret Construction,
Wilmington, Delaware

The membership of this private club wanted a covered outside dining area adjacent to the main clubhouse. This 2,500-square-foot, three-season room is open on three sides during the summer, but retractable walls hidden in the soffits allow it to be enjoyed in cool weather as well. Shed dormers with operable windows on both sides of the roof act as a thermal chimney by venting hot summer air out the top and drawing in cooler air from below. The timbers are Douglas fir, select structural grade, and free of heart center. The joinery is predominantly traditional mortise and tenon, but steel connectors are concealed in the timbers to handle high tension loads.

"Before" shot of the veranda where the three-season dining room was constructed.

"After" view from roughly the same vantage point as the previous photograph. *Photo by John M. Lewis*

Concealed curtain walls can be lowered on tracks mounted to the posts during inclement weather. *Photo by John M. Lewis*

Photo by John M. Lewis

Photo by John M. Lewis

Photo by John M. Lewis

Photo by John M. Lewis

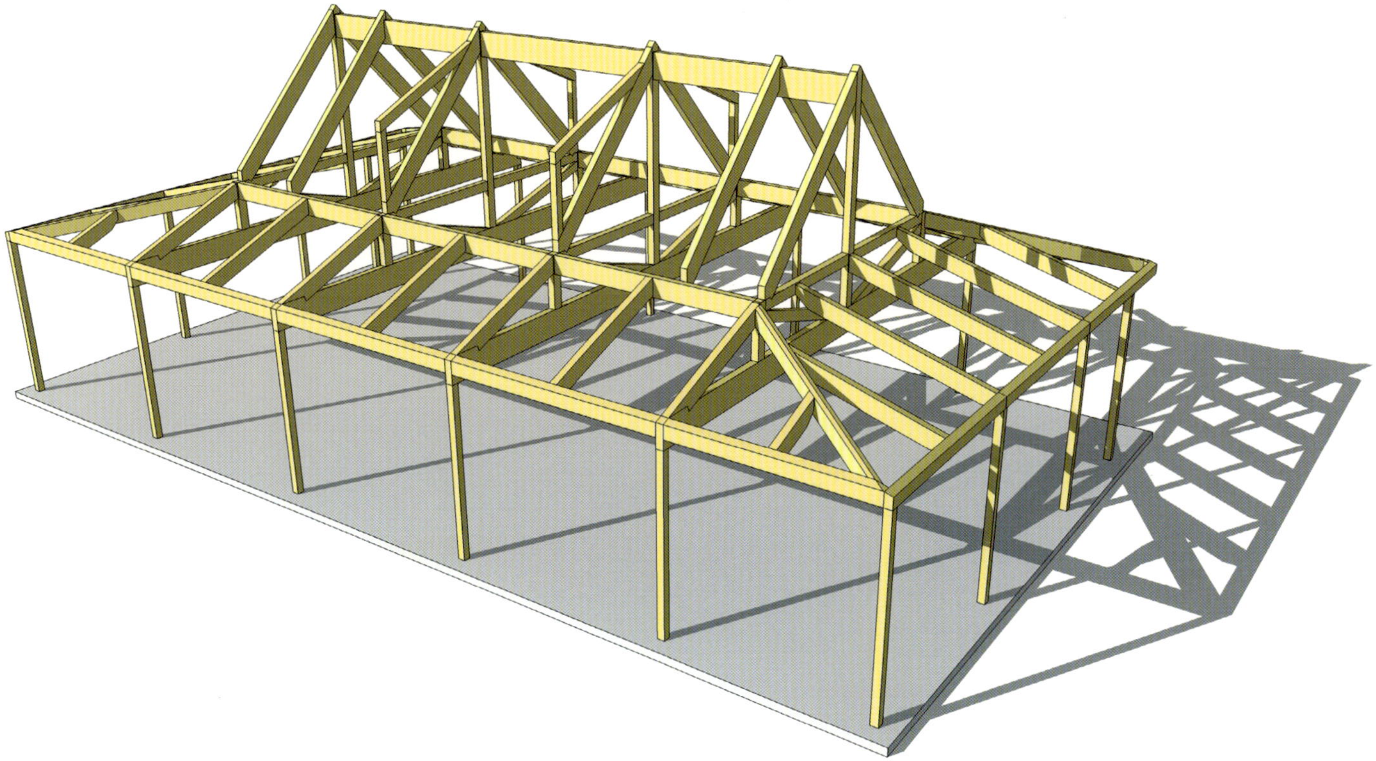

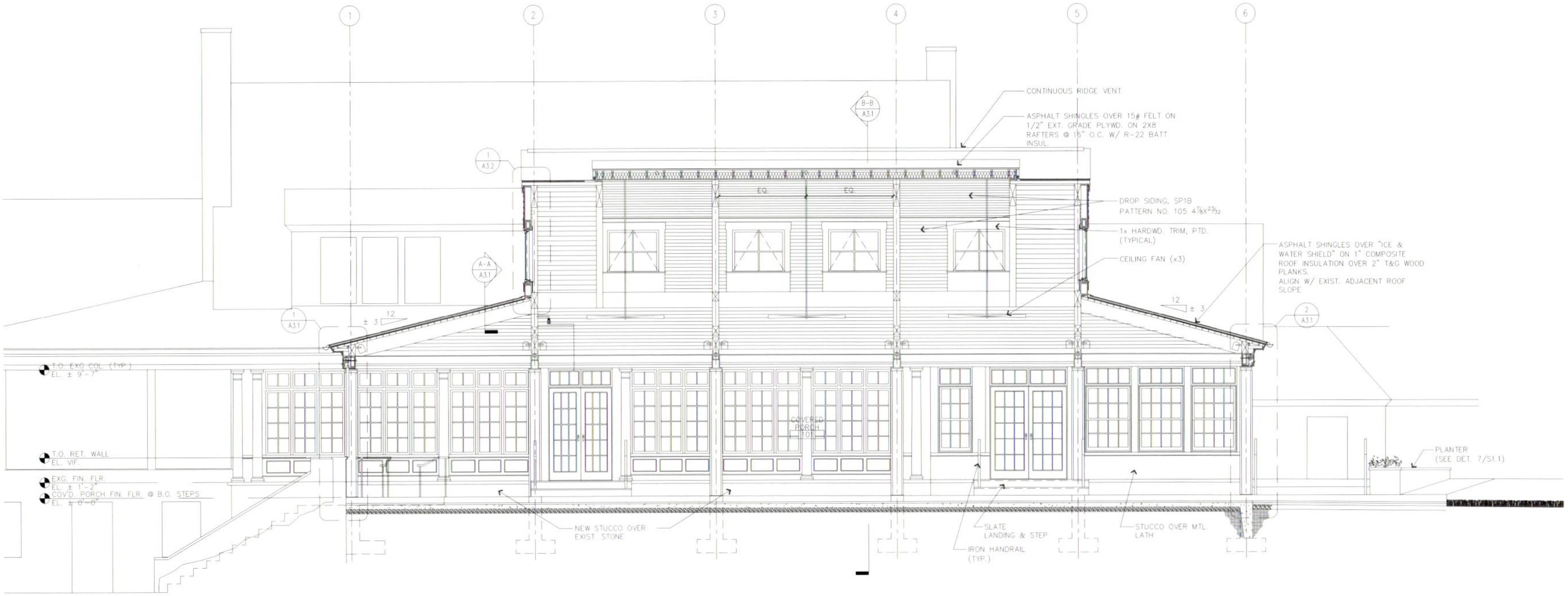

CONTINUOUS RIDGE VENT
ASPHALT SHINGLES OVER 15# FELT ON 1/2" EXT. GRADE PLYWD. ON 2X8 RAFTERS @ 16" O.C. W/ R-22 BATT INSUL.
DROP SIDING, SP1B PATTERN NO. 105 4⅞X23/32
1x HARDWD. TRIM, PTD. (TYPICAL)
CEILING FAN (x3)
ASPHALT SHINGLES OVER "ICE & WATER SHIELD" ON 1" COMPOSITE ROOF INSULATION OVER 2" T&G WOOD PLANKS. ALIGN W/ EXIST. ADJACENT ROOF SLOPE
T.O. EXG COL. (TYP.) EL. ± 9'-7"
T.O. RET. WALL EL. VIF.
EXG. FIN. FLR. EL. ± 1'-2"
COV'D. PORCH FIN. FLR. @ B.O. STEPS EL. ± 0'-0"
COVERED PORCH 101
PLANTER (SEE DET. 7/S1.1)
NEW STUCCO OVER EXIST. STONE
SLATE LANDING & STEP
IRON HANDRAIL (TYP.)
STUCCO OVER MTL. LATH

Great Harbor Yacht Club

Nantucket, Massachusetts, 2008

Owner
Great Harbor Yacht Club,
Nantucket, Massachusetts

Architect
Hart Howerton,
New York

Engineer
Ruff Engineering,
Douglassville, Pennsylvania

General contractor
Stateside Construction Group,
Andover, Massachusetts

With the waiting list for new members at the only yacht club on Nantucket being measured in decades rather than years, several impatient individuals decided to develop and build their own. One of these, Gary McCarthy, had been our first client on the island several years earlier.

More than six years passed from the time McCarthy first asked us to execute timber frame conceptuals from the architectural drawings he had commissioned, until the frame was raised. All of that time had been consumed by permitting, studies, approvals, bureaucratic roadblocks, and legal hurdles.

We introduced structural elements that echo those found on historic wooden vessels, only upside down, as logic would have it. The frame, of stained Douglas fir, required 20,000 board feet and more than 200 timbers.

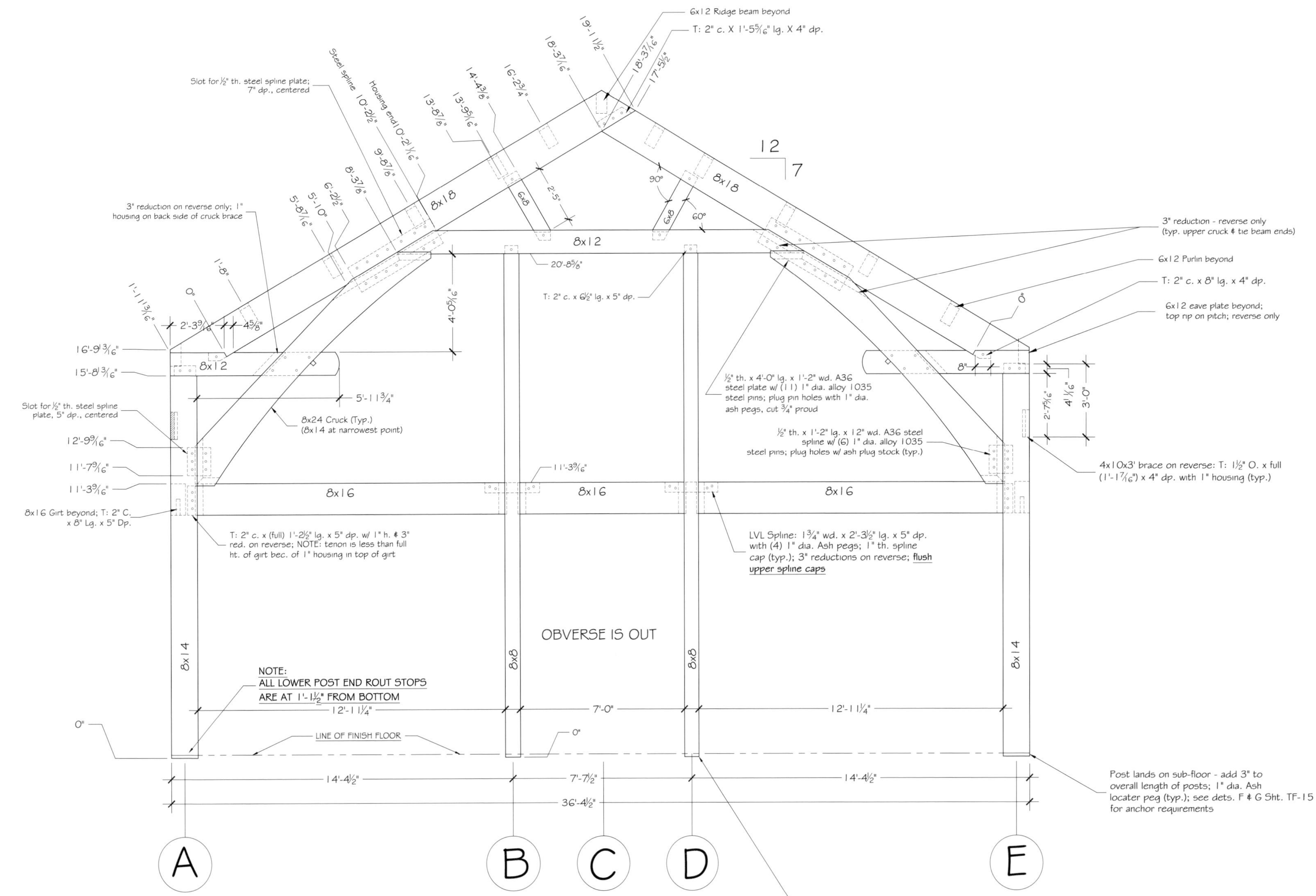

A BENT 1 SECTION - VIEW FROM OUT

NOT TO SCALE

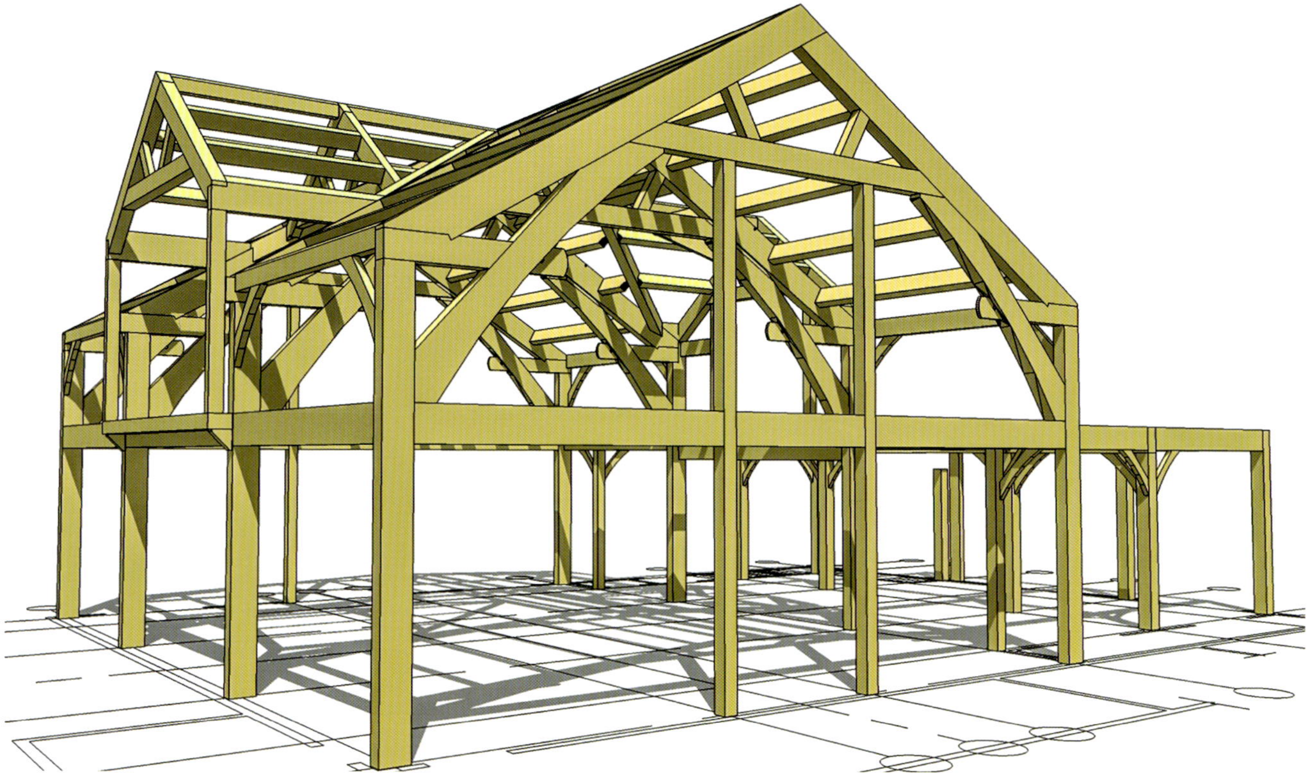

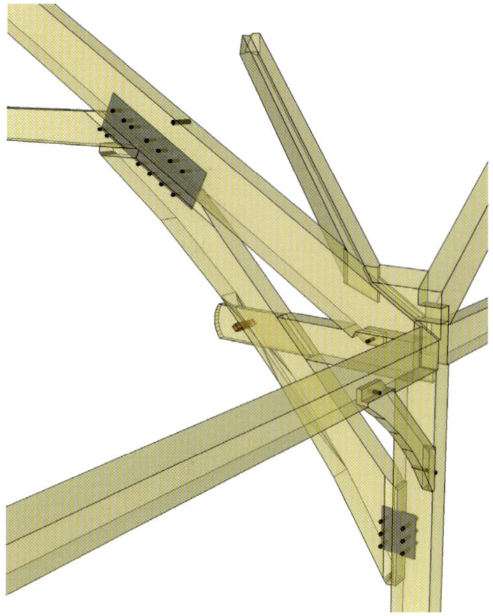

The crucks were connected to the posts and rafters with concealed steel spline plates and steel pins. The steel pins were capped with wood plug material to resemble a traditionally pegged joint.

One of the crucks being carved in the shop at Lancaster County Timber Frames.

Arrowhead Resort Lodge

Pocono Lake, Pennsylvania, 2013

Owner
Arrowhead Lake Community Association,
Pocono Lakes, Pennsylvania

Architect
Facility Design & Development,
Scranton, Pennsylvania

Engineer
D. Remy & Company,
Hayesville, North Carolina

General contractor
Berks Ridge Enterprises,
Harleysville, Pennsylvania

This community lodge in the Pocono Mountains is part of a three-and-a-half-square-mile, privately owned gated community near two lakes (260 acres and 90 acres) and four beaches. The lodge is 17,500 square feet and our work consisted of the central lodge and two wings. The two main longitudinal supporting girts (purlins) in the central lodge consisted of two members, each measuring 8¾ inches thick by 45 inches high by 63 feet long. These pieces were too large to fit into our shop, so we prepared them on-site.

The fourteen trusses that sit on these huge girts have a rather unusual configuration. They are comprised of two closely set queen posts and the lower chords are angled down at the same pitch at which the upper chords angle up. The trusses in the two wings have a horizontal lower chord. The Douglas fir glulam roof system consumed 300 timbers and totaled 55,000 board feet.

Snow was a constant while we were on-site and the temperature was below 0 degrees Fahrenheit each morning. We had to wait to stain the 63-foot timbers until the building was enclosed and heated.

A somewhat unusual inverted truss design, connected with face-mounted steel plates. The trusses rest on twin glulam purlins, each measuring 8¾ inches thick by 45 inches tall. The longest members were more than 60 feet long.

EXIT

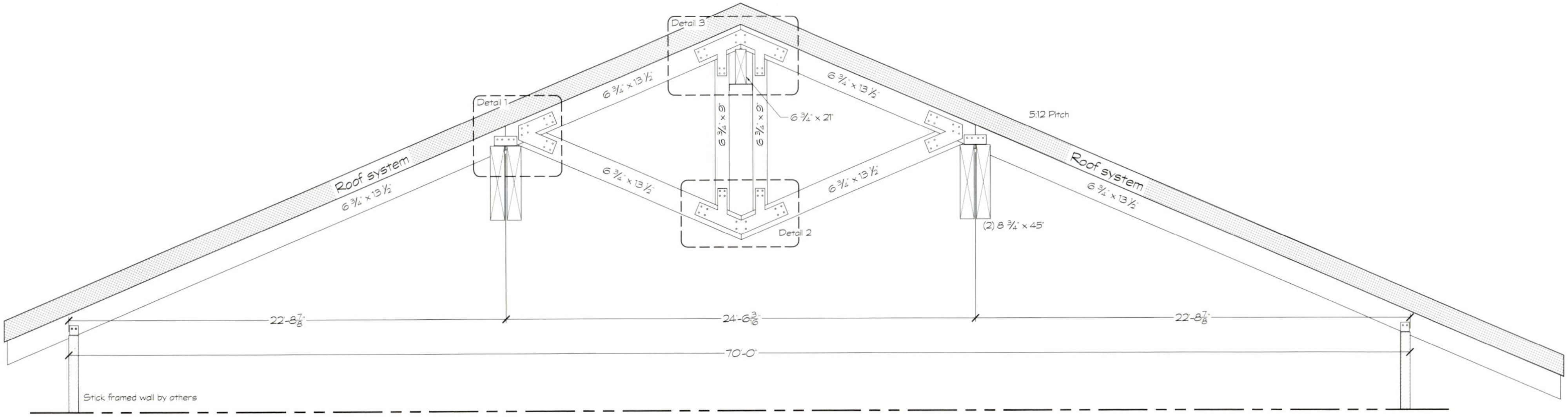
Detail 3
Detail 1
Detail 2
6 3/4" x 13 1/2"
6 3/4" x 9"
6 3/4" x 21"
5:12 Pitch
Roof system
(2) 8 3/4" x 45"
22'-8 7/8"
24'-6 3/16"
70'-0"
Stick framed wall by others

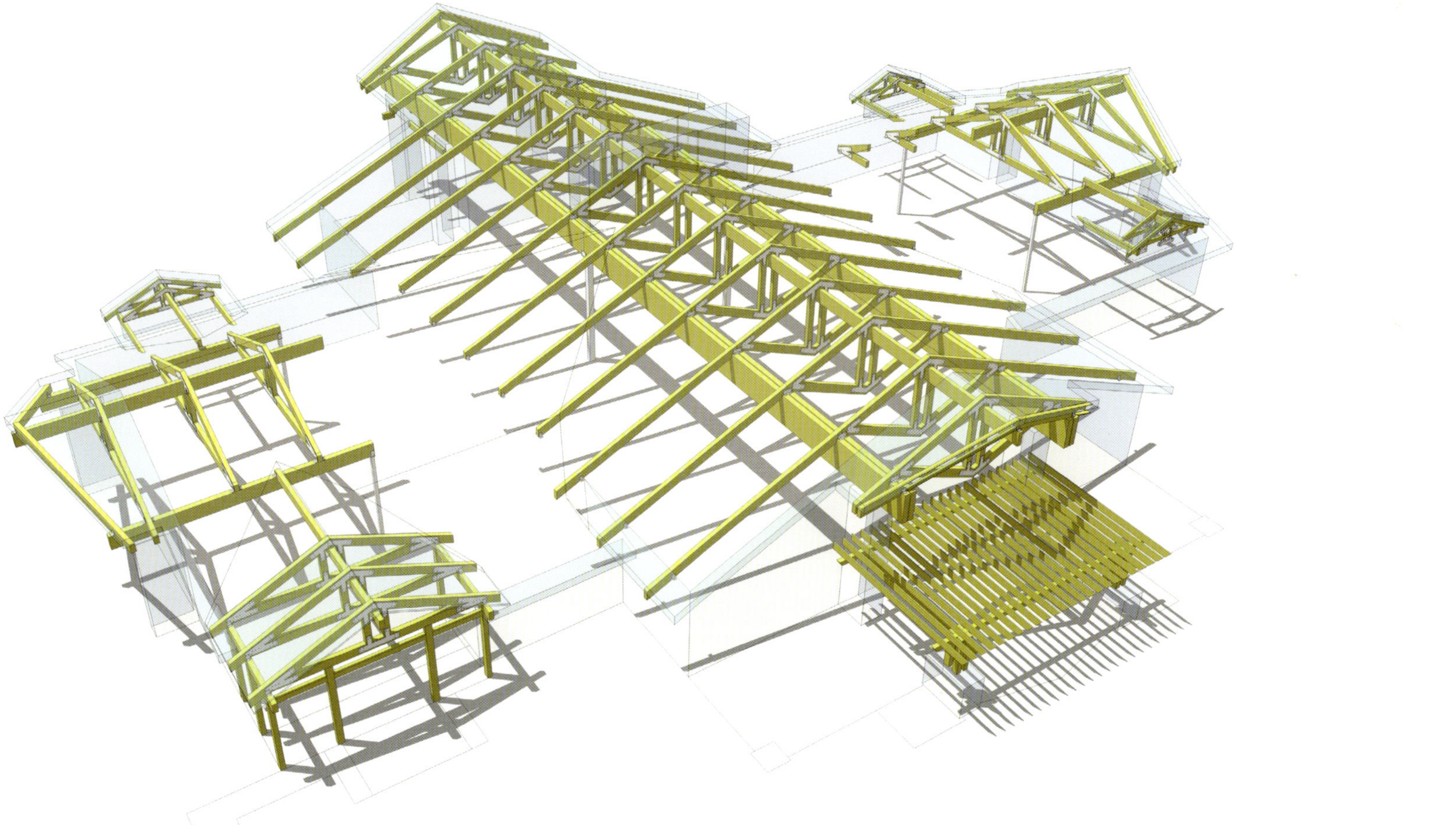

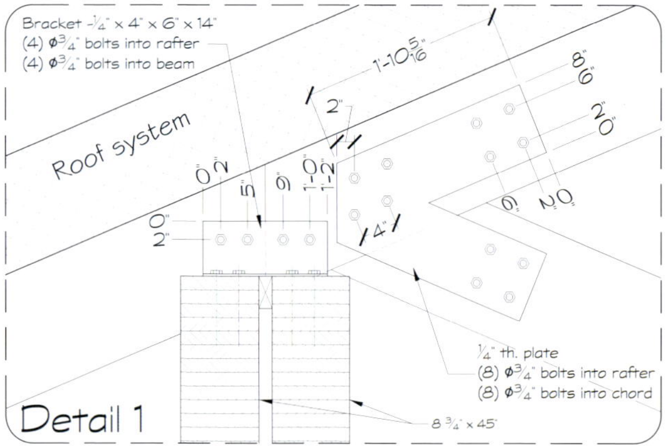

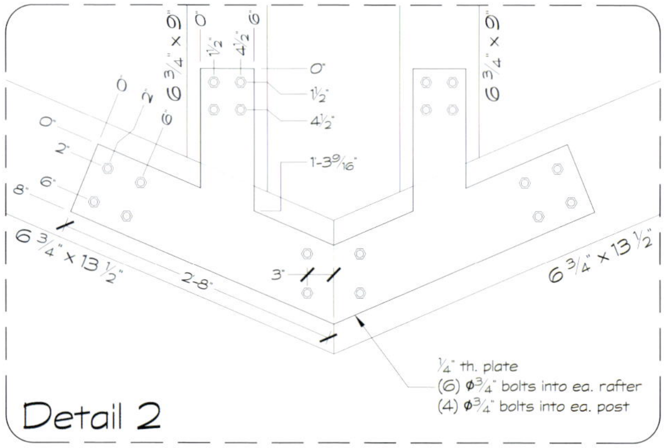

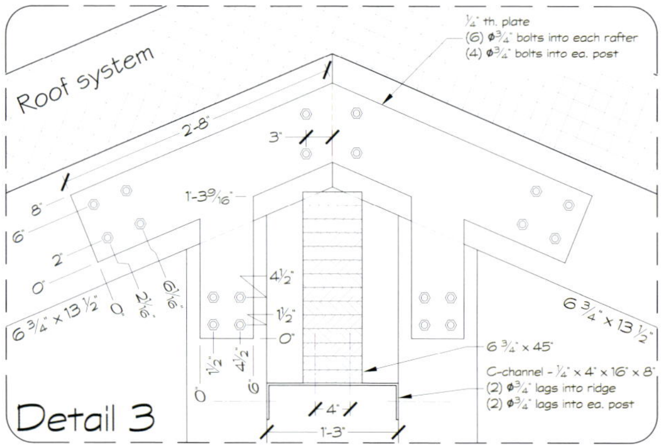

View of the partially completed clubhouse from atop the frozen lake.

Work started each day with the removal of snow from the glulams and the building deck. Even during the installation of the 3-inch-thick laminated tongue and groove roof decking, a nightly snowfall of 3 to 6 inches was to be reckoned with. Temperatures remained well below freezing for the duration of Lancaster County Timber Frames's work.

Hawk Pointe Golf Club

Washington, New Jersey, 2006

Owner
Hawk Pointe Golf Club,
Washington, New Jersey

Architect
JGA Architectural Design,
Pawtucket, Rhode Island

Engineer
Ruff Engineering,
Douglassville, Pennsylvania

General contractor
Critical Path Management,
Hampton, New Jersey

Historically the term porte cochère referred to a covered entrance to a building through which a carriage (or motor car) could pass from the street to an interior courtyard. Today, particularly in the United States, the term can also refer to a roofed structure that extends from a building over an adjacent driveway to shelter those exiting a vehicle.

This porte cochère, at the entrance to a private clubhouse, is comprised of king post trusses attached to two longitudinal plates, which are supported by posts at each corner. The two knee (or wind) braces at each corner post help the structure resist lateral loads. The building's fifty-two Douglas fir solid timbers totaled 6,400 board feet.

Rafter tail end embellishment.

Potomac Shores Recreation Facility

Dumfries, Virginia, 2015

Owner
Harbor Station Communities,
Woodbridge, Virginia

Architect
Hart Howerton,
New York

Engineer
Timber Tech Engineering,
Denver, Pennsylvania

General contractor
Olde Red General Contracting,
Chantilly, Virginia

The warming kitchen in the Social Barn at the Potomac Shores Recreation Facility.

The Social Barn entry lounge.

An emerging trend in master-planned housing developments is the creation of a community hub intended to foster a neighborhood spirit. There is often an attempt to create a sense of organic growth, as if the facilities had been built gradually over a period of many years. This is true of the Recreation Center at Potomac Shores, a planned community several miles south of the Washington, DC, beltway.

The Recreation Center is comprised of four separate structures, each containing some heavy timber construction: the main Recreation Barn, an adjacent Social Barn and Market Pavilion, and a Pool Pavilion a short distance away from these three buildings.

The project architects had originally designed a system of heavy timber trusses and exterior colonnades, some structural and some decorative, fabricated from through-bolted glulams or boxed, simulated heavy timbers. After consulting with the owner's rep and the general contractor, we learned that they had originally wanted a more traditional timber frame look. With the blessing of the team, we developed a traditional timber frame design that also trimmed costs. Although the final design also included many non-structural elements, such as the ceiling beams in the warming kitchen of the Social Barn, some of the heavy timber components were integrated into the buildings' framing designs. No glulams were used in the revised design.

Of the four structures, the Market Pavilion is the only one that might be called a "pure" timber frame: there is no hybridization of construction methods, and wherever possible, only traditional joinery was used. It was necessary to design a post foot connection that would both resist the wind uplift and provide a stout moment connection to resist lateral loads. This connection was a custom-fabricated steel saddle that was directly anchored in the foundation masonry.

The Recreation Barn reception area, with the gym in the background.

The Motion Studio in the Recreation Barn.

The Social Barn roofed porch with timber post and beam colonnade.

The Social Barn viewed from the Recreation Barn entry.

The Pool Pavilion with timber post and beam sitting area.

View of the Social Barn from within the entirely timber-framed Market Pavilion.

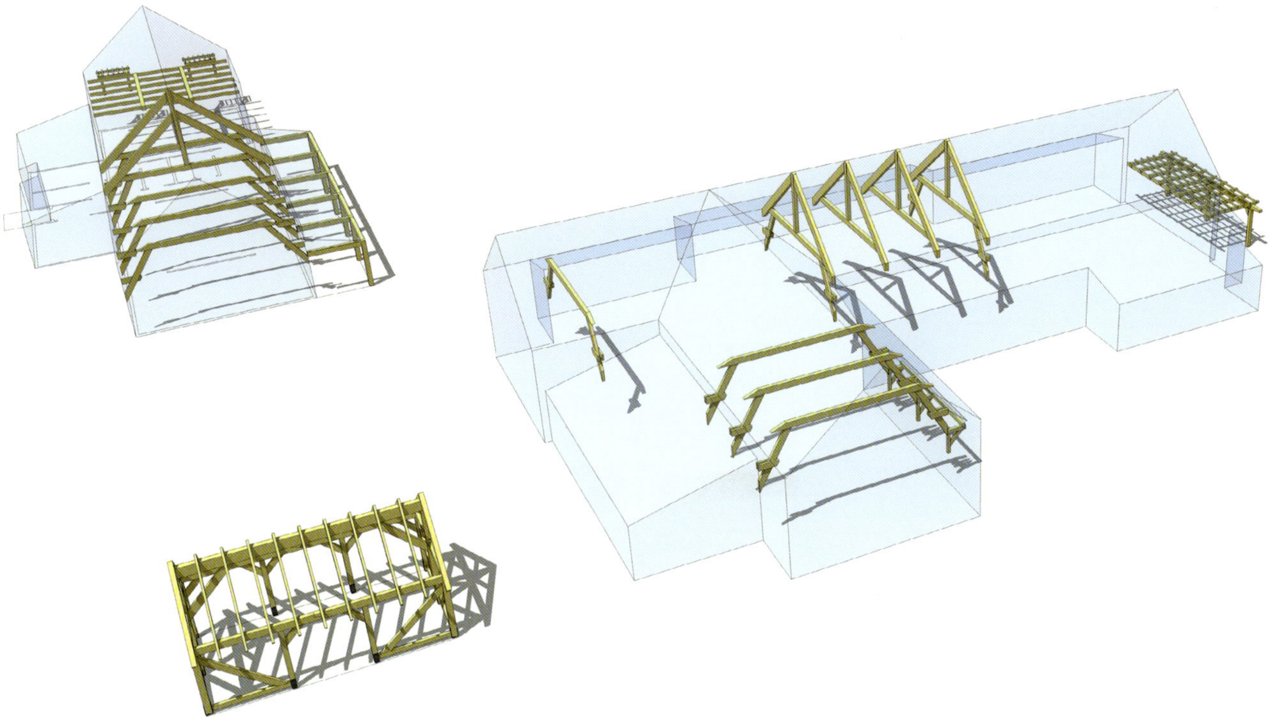

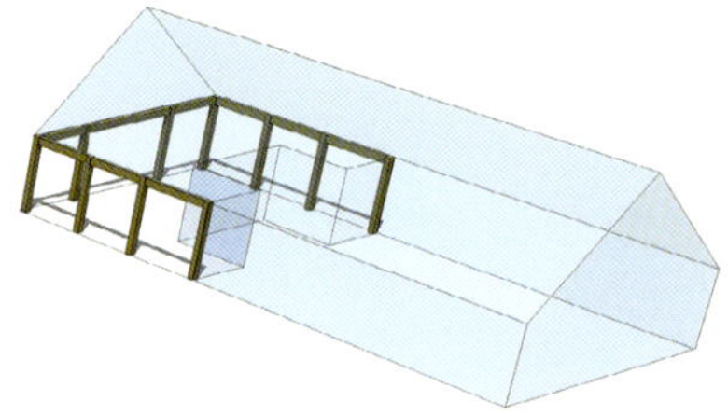

The full scope of the project, with the Social Barn in the upper left, Market Pavilion in the lower left, Recreation Barn at center, and Pool Pavilion in the upper right.

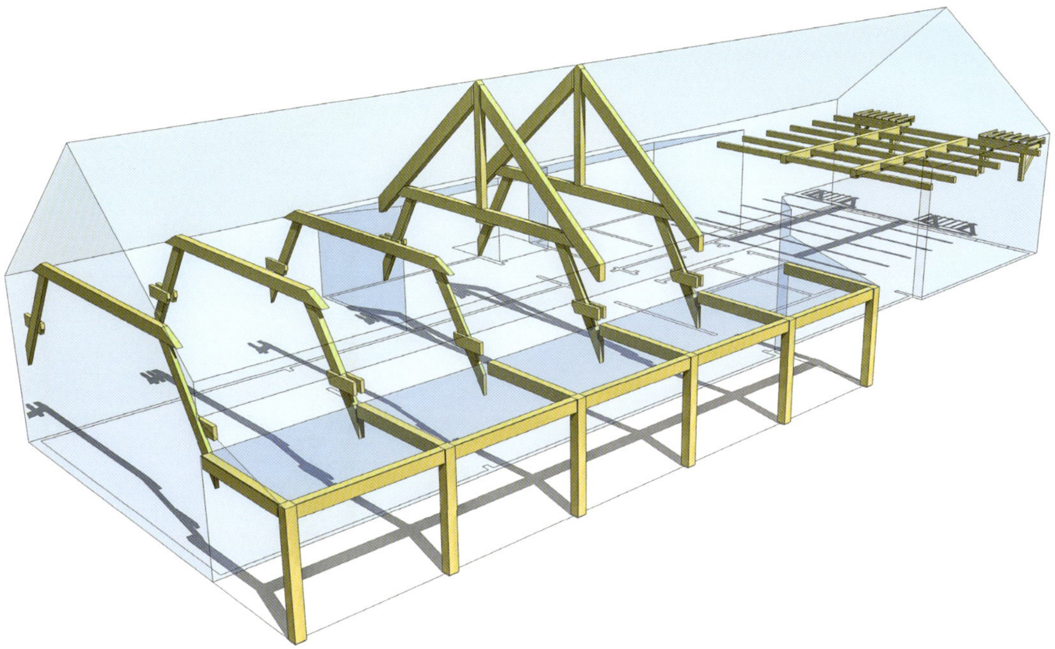

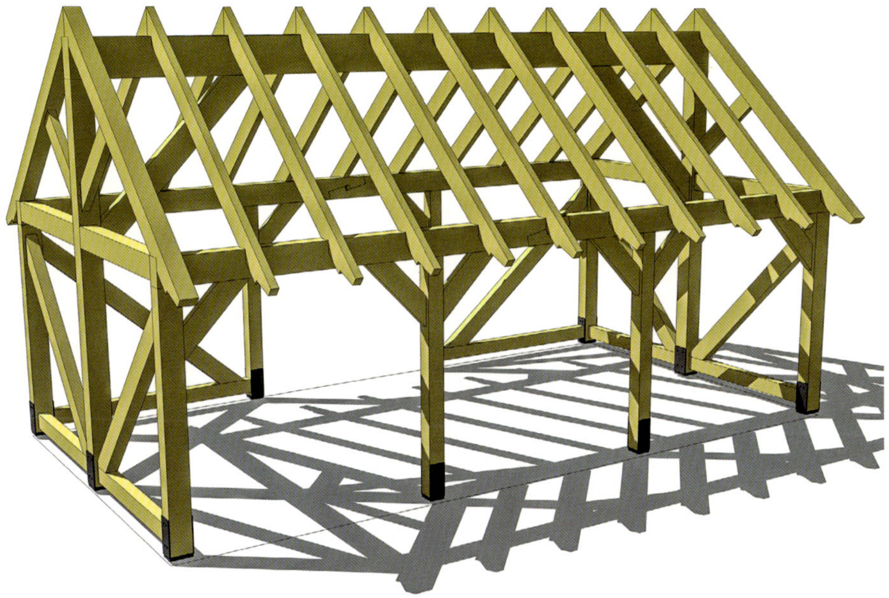

Aerial rendering of the entire recreation facility, from roughly the same vantage point as the conceptual timber frame model.

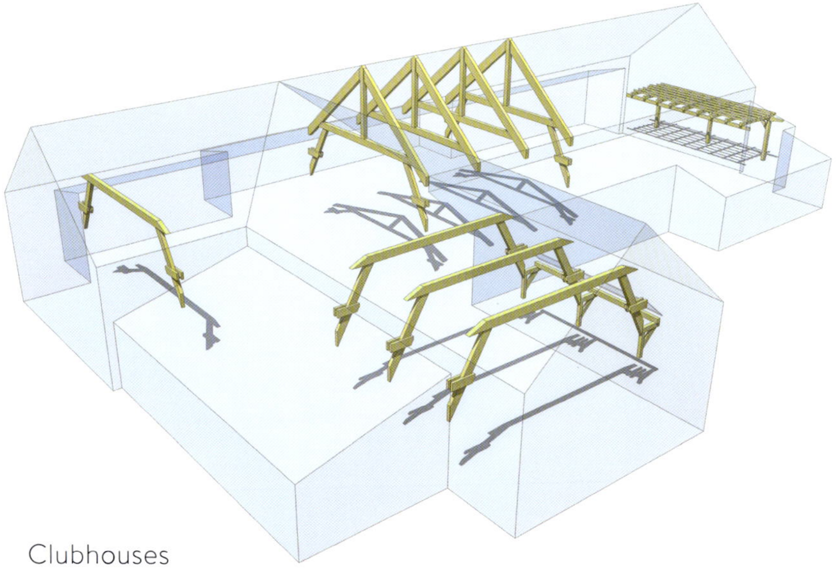

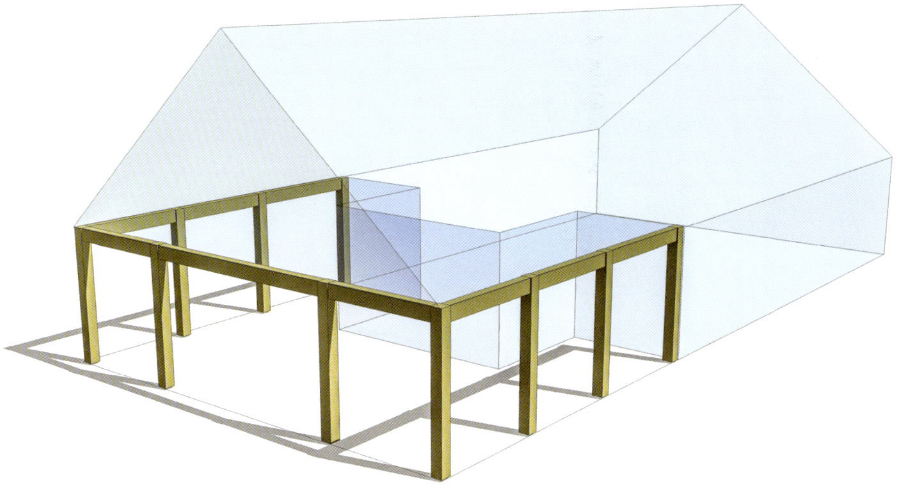

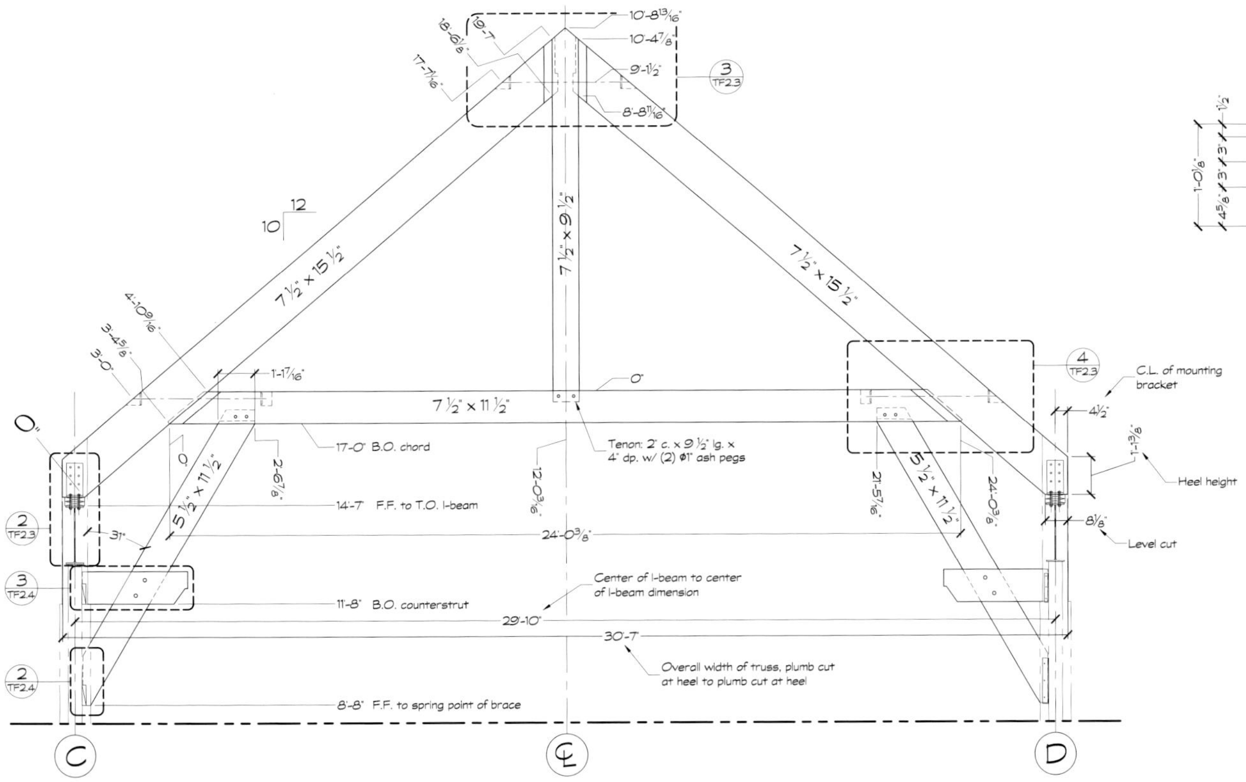

1 TF2.3 REC BARN GYM HEAVY TIMBER TRUSSES @ GRIDLINES 4 & 5 (2 THUS)
1/2" = 1'-0"

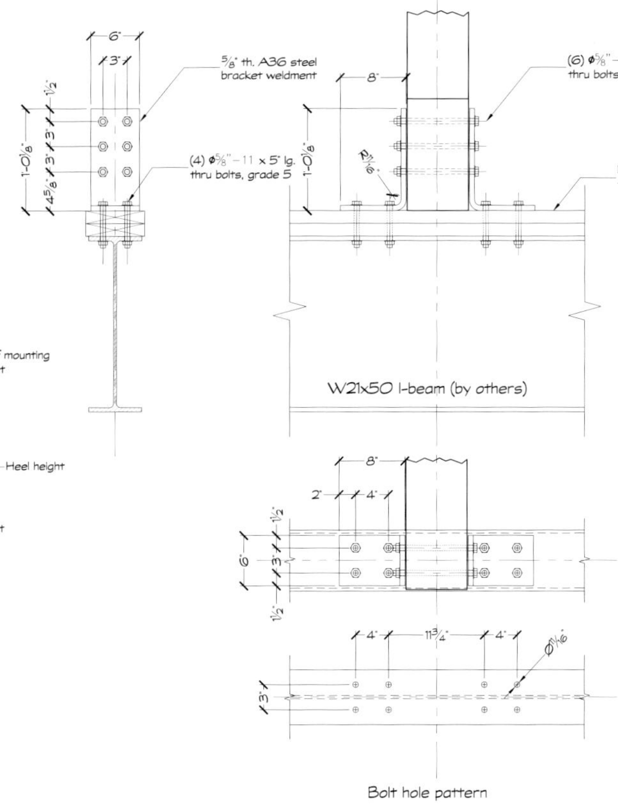

2 TF2.3 TRUSS MOUNTING BRACKETS
1 1/2" = 1'-0"

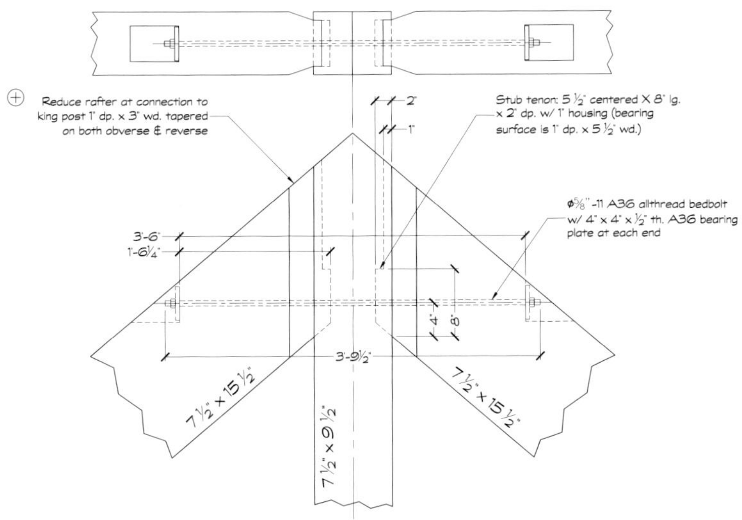

3 TF2.3 BEDBOLT @ TRUSS PEAK
1 1/2" = 1'-0"

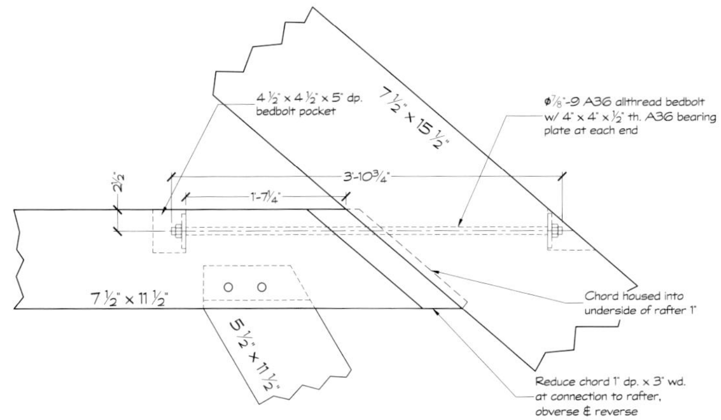

4 TF2.3 COLLAR TIE BED BOLT
1 1/2" = 1'-0"

Classic Car Lodge

Allentown, Pennsylvania, 2014

Photos by Alyssha Eve Czük

Owner
Nicola Bulgari, Rome; A. C. Drive-In Holding, Allentown, Pennsylvania

Architect
Benjamin L. Walbert Architects & Planners, Allentown, Pennsylvania

Engineer
Pennoni, Mechanicsburg, Pennsylvania

General contractor
Shane Patrick Associates, Allentown, Pennsylvania

This private classic car park sits on twenty-one acres of land purchased as separate parcels over the years. When the final purchase, an adjacent drive-in movie theater, was made, the owner indulged his passion for American cars—notably Buicks from the 1940s and '50s—by developing a car park and museum. The owner, Nicola Bulgari of Rome, scion of the jewelry dynasty, discovered Allentown while visiting the car collection of one of his jewelry customers. It was also in Allentown that Bulgari met and hired Keith Flickinger, a master mechanic and renowned restorer who oversees Bulgari's interests in all things automotive.

The latest parcel now contains an almost 100-foot by 200-foot lodge, a restored drive-in theater, a mile of macadam serpentine roads (to exercise the cars), and a 20-acre landscaped park. We used antique white oak timbers to timber frame the lodge, and reclaimed and re-sawn white pine barn siding for the ceiling boards, satisfying the client's desire for an old-world feel. Some 125 of his cars will be housed at the park.

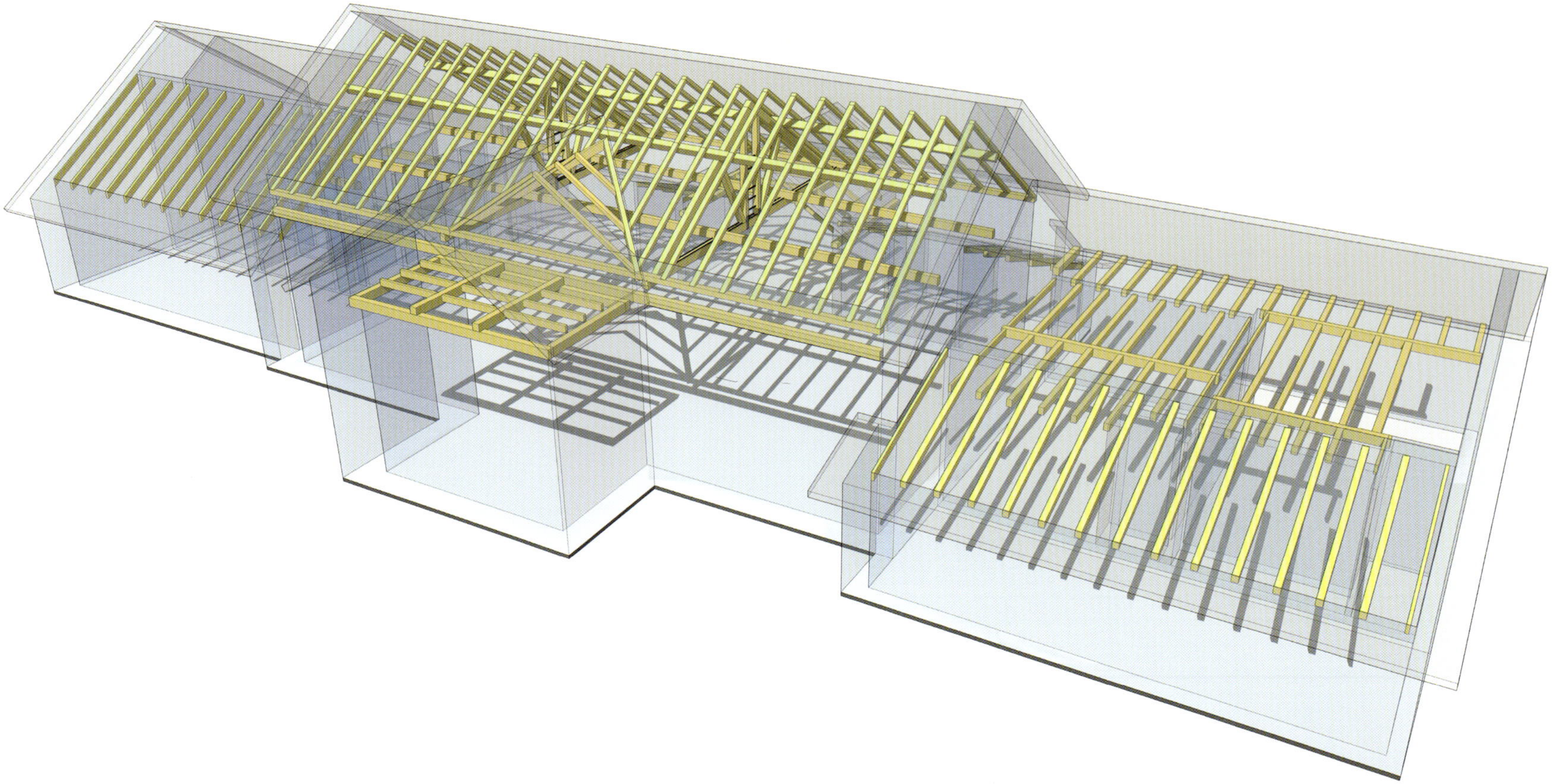

The owner of the classic car park, Nicola Bulgari.

The owner's bedroom, looking down on part of his collection.

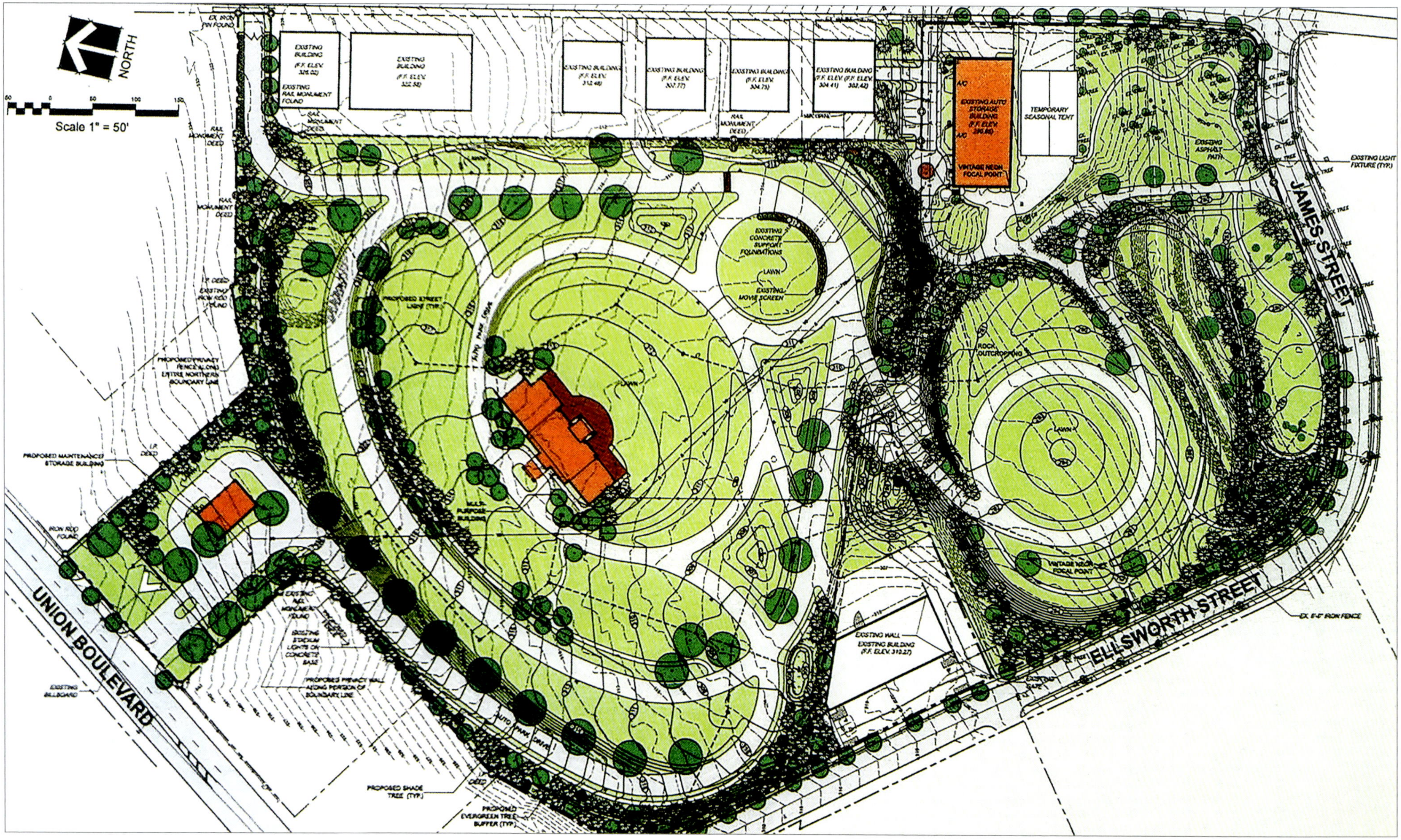

The 100-foot by 200-foot car lodge sits in the middle of the large oval "car exercising" track. A movie projector is housed in the gable facing southeast (upper right in this plan view). An old-fashioned drive-in movie screen is located in the middle of the smaller circular track in the southeast corner of the park. The rectangular buildings along the eastern edge of the compound house parts of the auto collection and shop facilities for restoration and maintenance.

Photo by Alyssha Eve Czük

6

Historic Reconstruction

Any healthy culture strives to preserve the most significant buildings of its past. In the eastern United States, barns, covered bridges, and grist mills are three of the most revered structures of our agrarian roots, and we make great effort to maintain, preserve, restore, and rebuild these icons from our past. The Siegrist Mill Covered Bridge in Lancaster County, Pennsylvania, was rebuilt primarily because of the activism and persistence of local residents who petitioned their local and state governments.

The Fosterfields Living Farm barn reconstruction and the Cooper Grist Mill flume reconstruction were both undertaken under the auspices of the Morris County, New Jersey, parks department. All three projects sought to reconstruct, as closely as possible, the original structures they replaced. Historical reconstruction specialists were employed, and the Secretary of the Interior's Standards for Reconstruction were scrupulously followed every step of the way.

Siegrist Mill Covered Bridge

Lancaster County, Pennsylvania, 2013

Owner
Lancaster County,
Lancaster, Pennsylvania

Engineer
Rettew Associates,
Lancaster, Pennsylvania

General contractor
Bulldog Construction Company,
Coatesville, Pennsylvania

Before it was damaged, the Siegrist Mill Covered Bridge, a 100-foot, free-span Burr Truss structure, was a regularly traveled one-lane bridge. In September 2011, high waters from tropical storm Lee lifted it off its foundation. Its movement downstream was halted by the upturned root system of a large sycamore tree. Using two large cranes, the bridge was hoisted from the creek and set on dry land. There it sat until officials sorted out whether to reconstruct the bridge.

After the decision was made to rebuild it and funding was in place, we removed the roofing, siding, and flooring, dismantled the bridge timber by timber, and shipped the salvageable pieces to our shop. Thirty of the original timbers were saved and 365 new raw timbers were ordered. Many of the salvaged timbers were returned to their original position. Some were subjected to reductions, usually in length, to eliminate rot or damage and were employed in a different manner or location. We carved the reborn bridge at our shop and assembled it at the site along the banks of Chiques Creek, where it had been lifted out of the water nearly eighteen months earlier.

In May 2013, a 300-ton crane positioned the bridge on its new foundation, which was elevated by 2 feet. As was the original, the bridge is sheathed with pine boards and battens and roofed with cedar shakes; the timbers are rough-sawn Douglas fir.

The Siegrist Mill bridge is also known as the Scripture Bridge, due to the hand-painted Bible passage placards that local residents nailed to the undercarriage over the span of 60 years. Though it wasn't part of our contract, we rehabilitated the placards and re-attached them in their original position. The bridge is listed in the World Guide to Covered Bridges as Number 28-36-37 and was added to the National Register of Historic Places in 1980.

Siegrist Mill Covered Bridge History

1885

Original bridge over Chiques Creek built by James C. Carpenter for $1,872

1972

Survives Hurricane Agnes

2011

Lifted from its abutments by rising waters of Tropical Storm Lee

2013

Rebuilt by Lancaster County Timber Frames, working with Bulldog Construction Company. The reconstruction cost $842,000, which included engineering studies, raising abutments by 2 feet, road work, and the bridge reconstruction itself. About eight percent of the original timbers were re-used in the reconstruction.

2013

Tropical Storm Andrea raises water levels to within a foot of the newly raised covered bridge road bed.

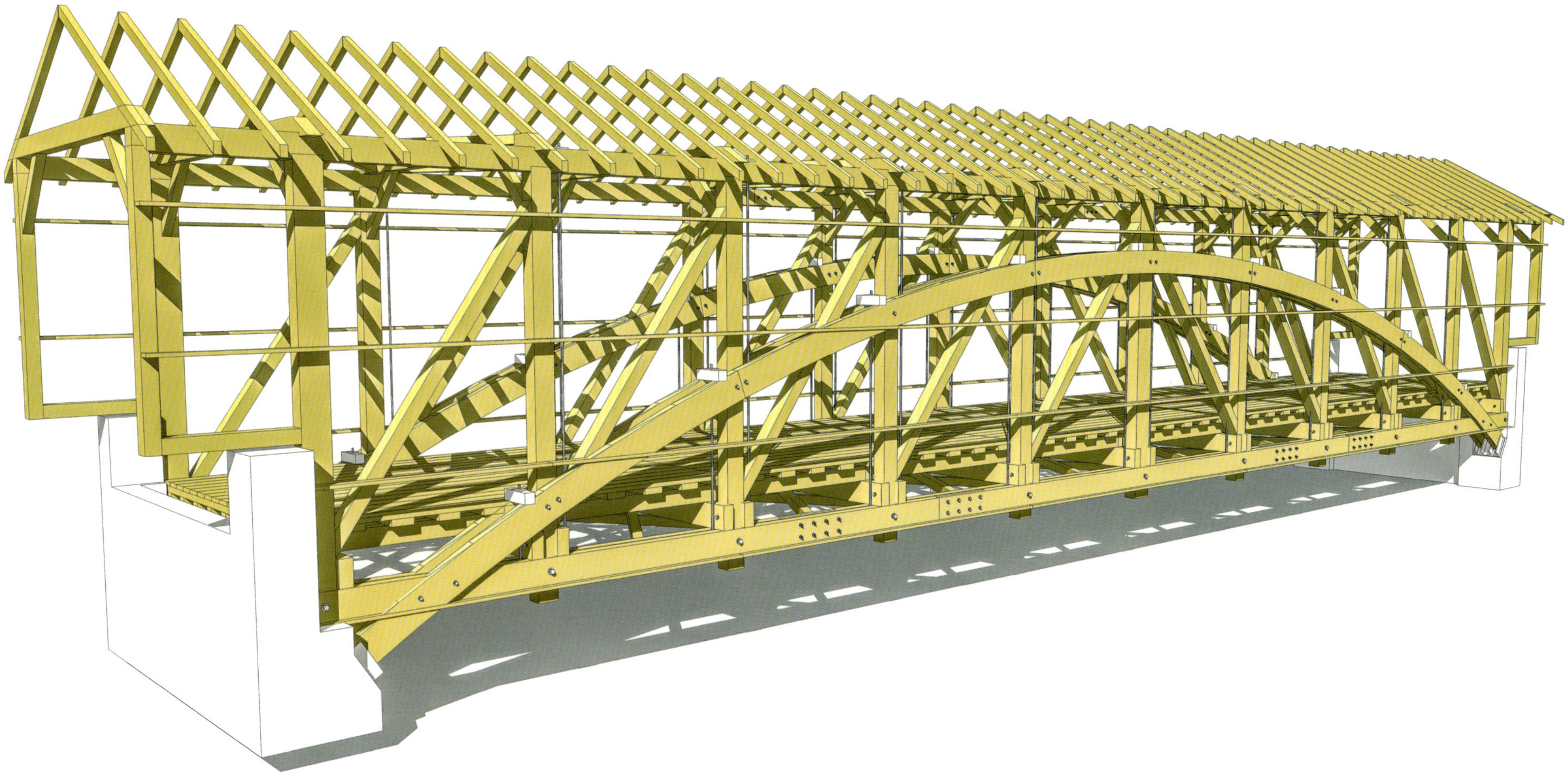

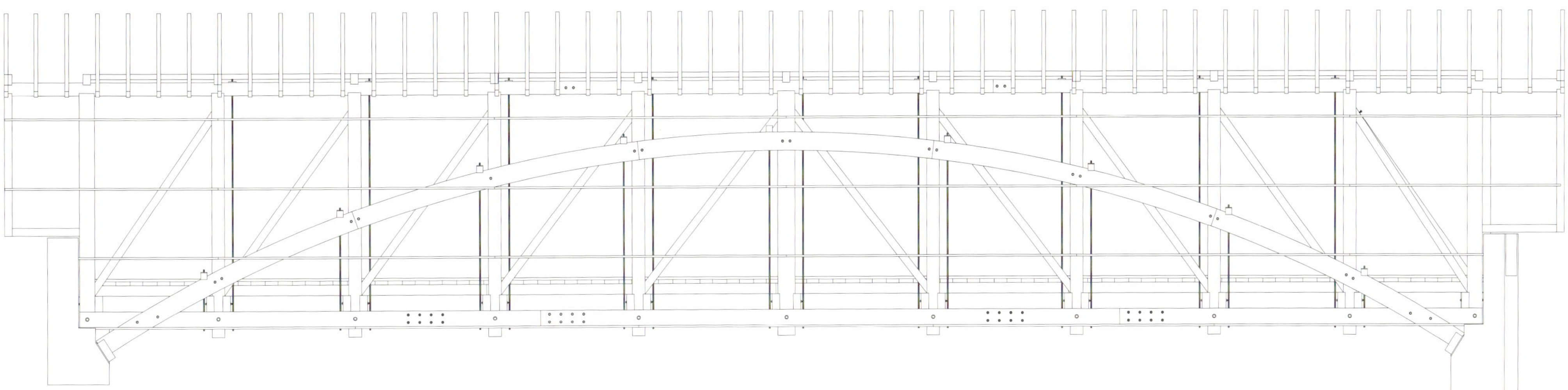

Washed off its abutments by tropical storm Lee in 2011, the bridge came to rest against a stand of trees on the creek bank less than 100 feet downstream.

Two cranes lift the destroyed bridge from the creek.

The destroyed bridge is lowered onto cribbing on the creek bank.

The bridge with roofing, roof framing, and siding removed and awaiting dismantling and transport to the Lancaster County Timber Frames shop for reconstruction.

Checking the pre-loaded camber at mid-span.

LANCASTER COUNTY
TIMBER FRAMES, INC
JLG

Fosterfields Living Historical Farm Barn Reconstruction

Morris County, New Jersey, 2013

Owner
Morris County Parks Commission,
Morris County, New Jersey

Architect
Connolly & Hickey Historical Architects,
Cranford, New Jersey

Engineer
Ruff Engineering,
Douglassville, Pennsylvania

General contractor
Precision Building & Construction,
Bound Brook, New Jersey

Owned and operated by the Morris County Parks Commission, this 200-acre property has been a working farm since 1760. Three of the structures, including a stately Gothic revival house, were built by Gen. Joseph Warren Revere, grandson of Paul Revere. After Gen. Revere's death, the farm was purchased in 1881 by Charles Foster, a wealthy commodities broker. After his death, his daughter, Caroline, oversaw the farm operations until her death at age 102 in 1979. She had lived for ninety-eight years at the farm. Wanting others to experience the rich agricultural and cultural heritage of her farm, Caroline bequeathed the entire property to the park commission. Today, the farm operates much as it did during the period from 1918 to 1927, and is open for tours and demonstrations.

The main barn was built in the 1700s and remodeled in the early 1920s. By 2004, it needed to be rebuilt. It was decided the new barn would be rebuilt using the same species of timber in the same structural configuration as the original. The barn measures 36 feet by 65 feet, and the ensilage and corn crib measure 32 feet by 18 feet. Almost 700 rough-cut white oak timbers were needed, six of which were 36-foot-long 8×8s. The only structural alteration requiring an engineer's seal was the addition of wind braces in the roof plane.

Above are the old ensilage pits at the end of the barn. The ensilage barn, built over the rehabilitated pits, is shown at top right. The corn cribs are accessible from inside this section of the barn.

The restored barn, seen from roughly the same vantage point as the conceptual timber frame model.

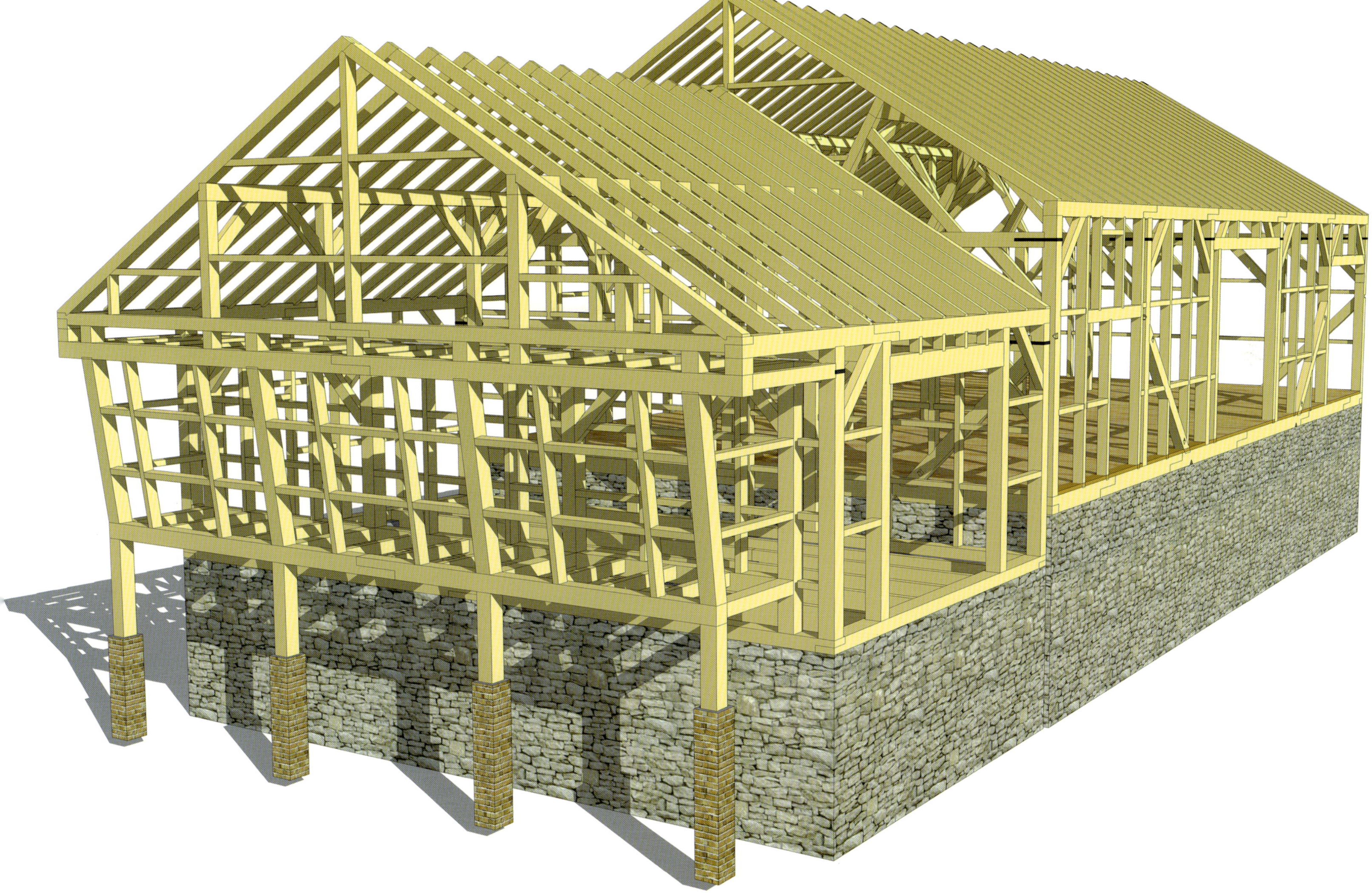

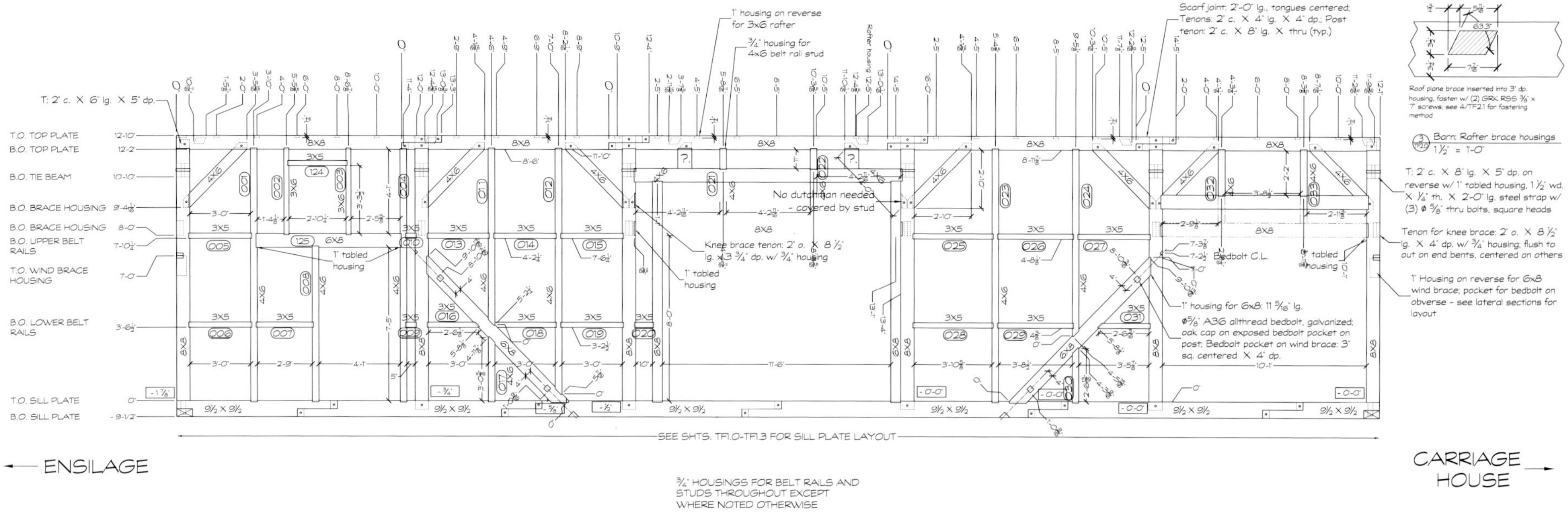

Barn: Gridline A wall section - View from Out/North
3/8" = 1'-0"

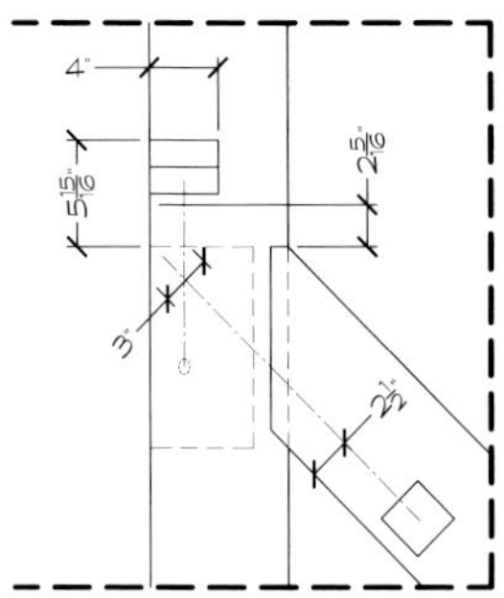

Post 5-I: Wind brace bolt pocket layout
1 1/2" = 1'-0"

NOTE: BOLT POCKET HEIGHTS ON POSTS VARY TO ALLOW BEDBOLTS TO BYPASS EACH OTHER AT CORNERS I-5 AND I-10

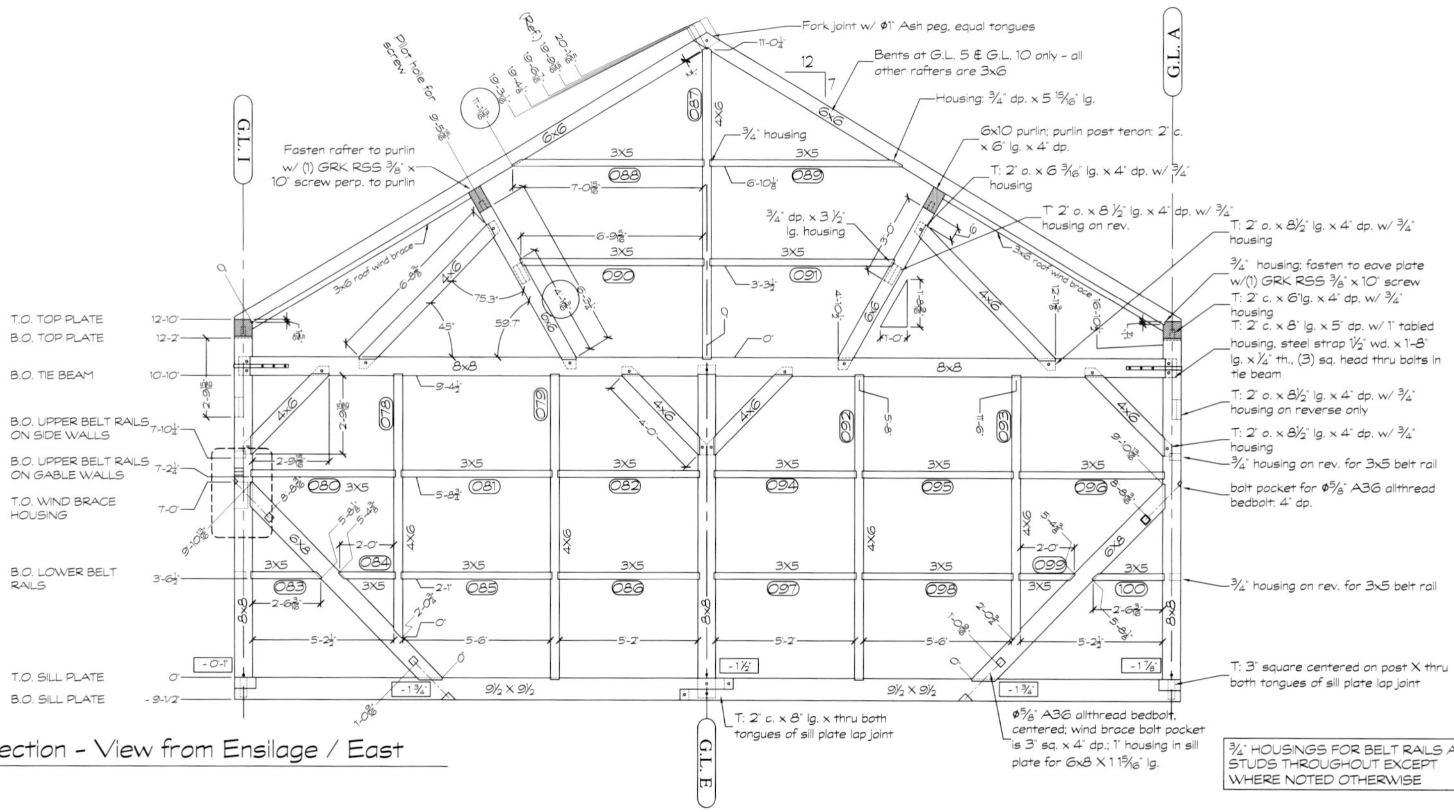

Barn: Gridline 5 wall section - View from Ensilage / East
3/8" = 1'-0"

3/4" HOUSINGS FOR BELT RAILS AND STUDS THROUGHOUT EXCEPT WHERE NOTED OTHERWISE

The barn cupola, fully assembled, in the barnyard, waiting to be lifted into place atop the roof framing.

Sill plate scarf joint being pre-fit in the Lancaster County Timber Frames shop.

Historic Cooper Grist Mill

Morris County, New Jersey, 2013

Owner
Morris County Parks Commission,
Morris County, New Jersey

Engineer
Christie Engineering, PC,
Bedminster Township, New Jersey

General contractor
Charles Mann General Contracting,
Pittstown, New Jersey

The miller, L. Ivins Smith III, looking out the window onto the restored flume on the first day of resumed mill operation. The small window next to the millstone hopper allows the miller to monitor and regulate the flow of water over the waterwheel with a lever attached to a shaft, and thus to slow down or speed up the millstones.

The miller at the ribbon-cutting ceremony for the reopening of the mill. Ground wheat, corn, and other grains are sold to park visitors in the mill store. The miller stands at the gate to the catwalk, which provides access to the flume for inspection.

Morris County, New Jersey, is significant on both the state and national level. George Washington and his Continental Army spent two winters there, and it was known as the military capital of the American Revolution. Thanks to the reconstruction, this barn where Samuel Morse and Alfred Vaile perfected the telegraph and from where they sent the first message, "A patient waiter is no loser," is still standing.

This grist mill is the only fully powered mill in New Jersey that continues to produce flour. A 6½-ton, 16-foot-diameter waterwheel is moved by the water of the Black River. We were in the midst of rebuilding the Fosterfields Living Historial Farm barn a few miles from the grist mill when the Morris County Parks Commission asked that we rebuild the flume that carried the water from the river to the wheel. All structural members are #1 white oak, while the flume lining boards are #1 red cypress.

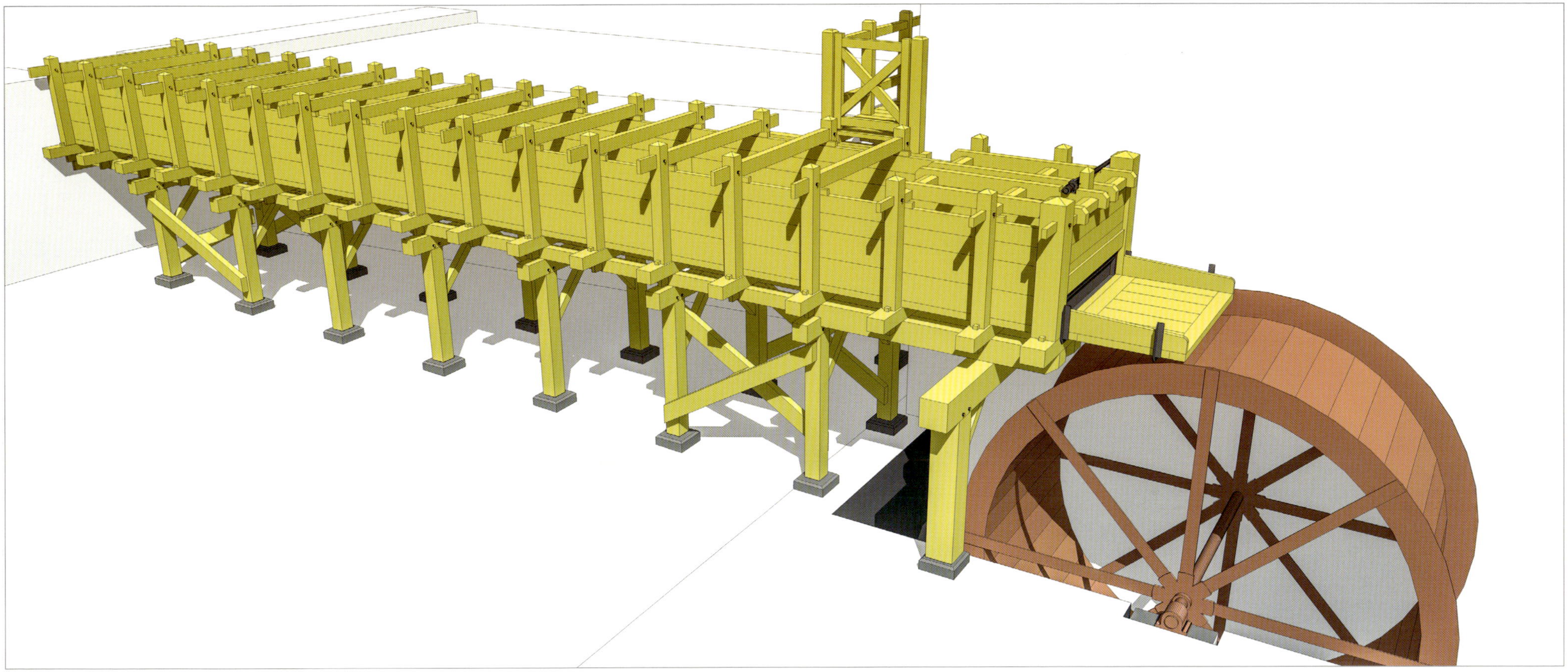

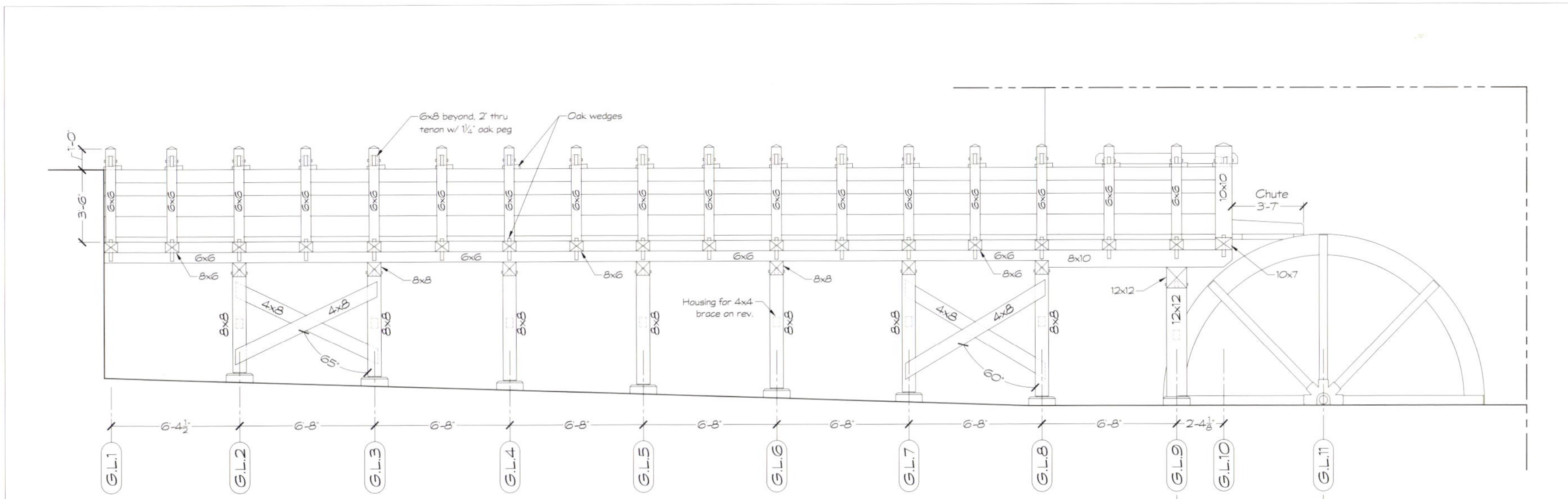

1 TF4 FLUME LONGITUDINAL ELEVATION
3/8" = 1'-0"

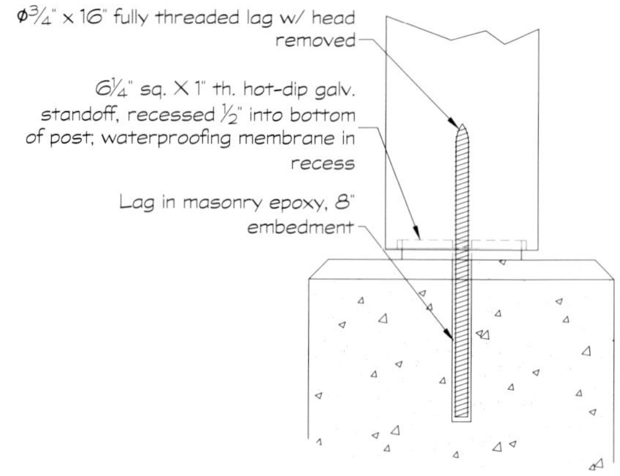

2 TF5 POST FOOT CONNECTION
3" = 1'-0"

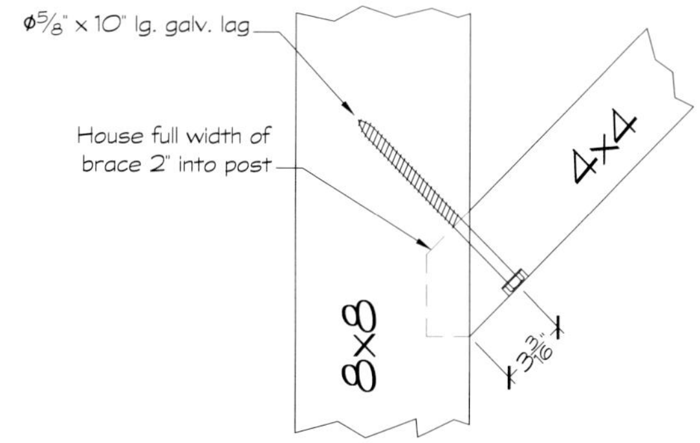

3 TF5 BRACE to POST CONNECTION
3" = 1'-0"

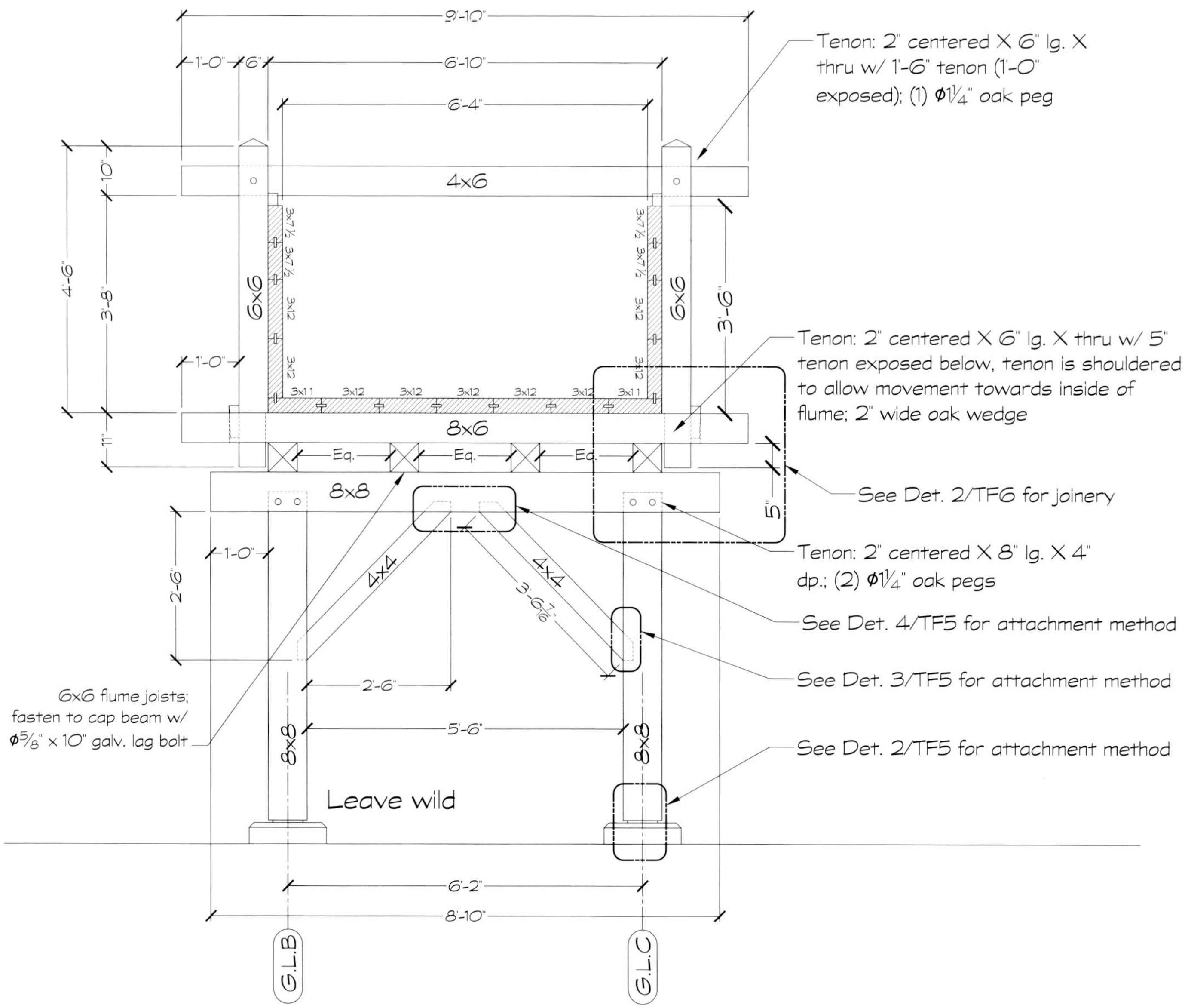

1 TF5 TYPICAL TRESTLE SECTION - Gridlines 1 thru 8
1" = 1'-0"

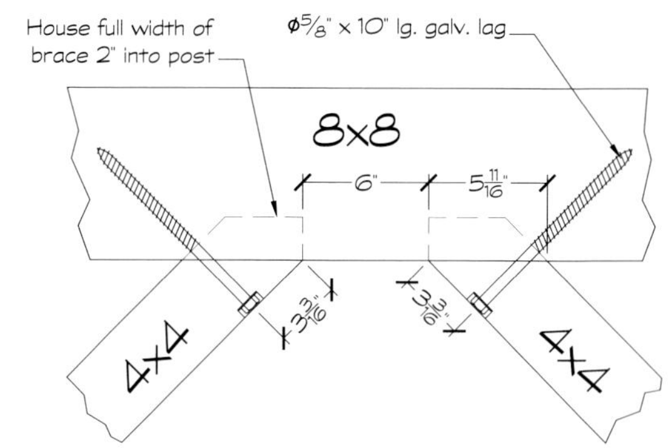

4 TF5 BRACE tp CAP BEAM CONNECTION
3" = 1'-0"

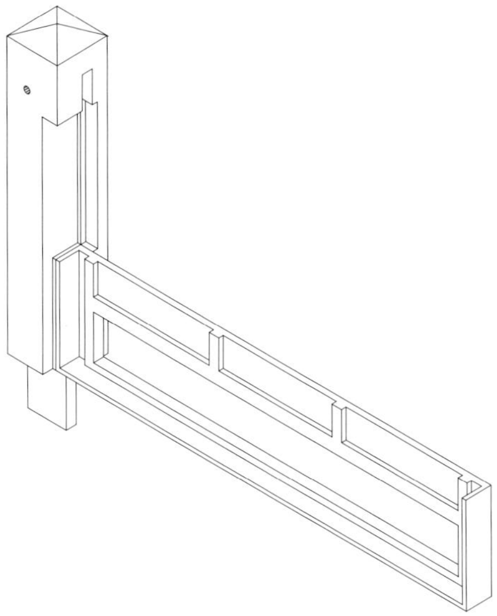

1 TF11 FLUME GATE CASTING 3D VIEW
Not to Scale

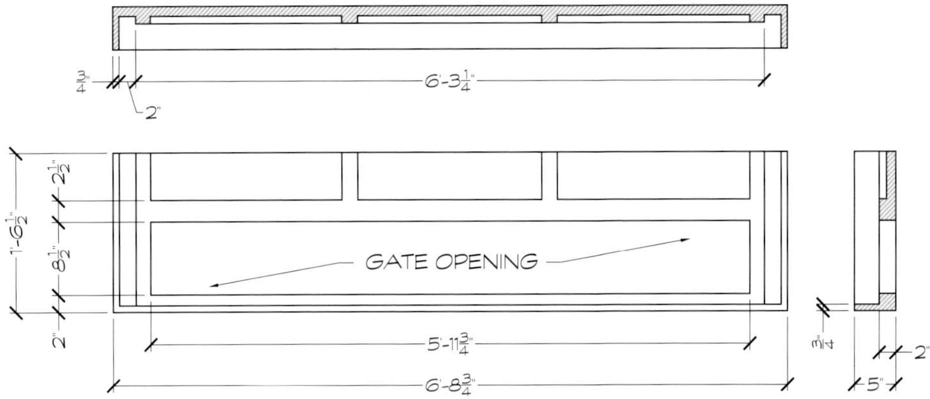

2 TF11 FLUME GATE CASTING
1 1/2" = 1'-0"

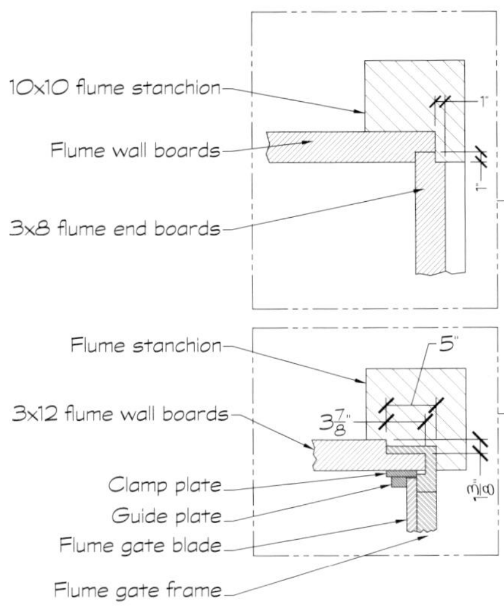

3 TF11 FLUME GATE STANCHION SECTIONS
1 1/2" = 1'-0"

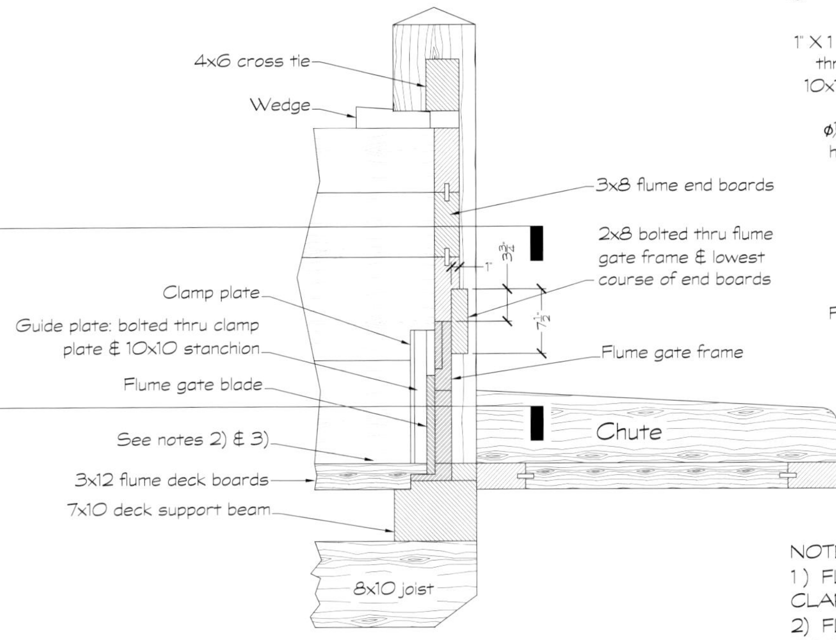

4 TF11 FLUME GATE SECTION
1 1/2" = 1'-0"

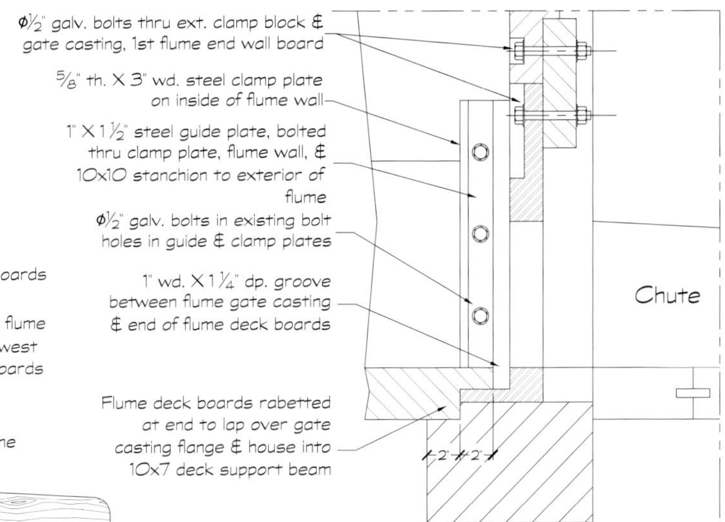

5 TF11 FLUME GATE SECTION
3" = 1'-0"

NOTES:
1) FLUME BLADE LIFTING STANCHION & YOKE NOT SHOWN FOR CLARITY
2) FLUME BLADE SEATS IN GROOVE BETWEEN DECK BOARDS & GATE CASTING FLANGE
3) DECK BOARDS ARE RABBETTED AT ENDS TO LAND ON GATE CASTING FLANGE & IN DECK SUPPORT BEAM HOUSING

NOTES:
- DECK BOARDS ARE 3" TH. CYPRESS
- CHEEK WALL IS 2" TH. CYPRESS
- SPLINES ARE ¾" TH. MARINE PLYWOOD
- USE S.S. SCREWS WHERE NECESSARY

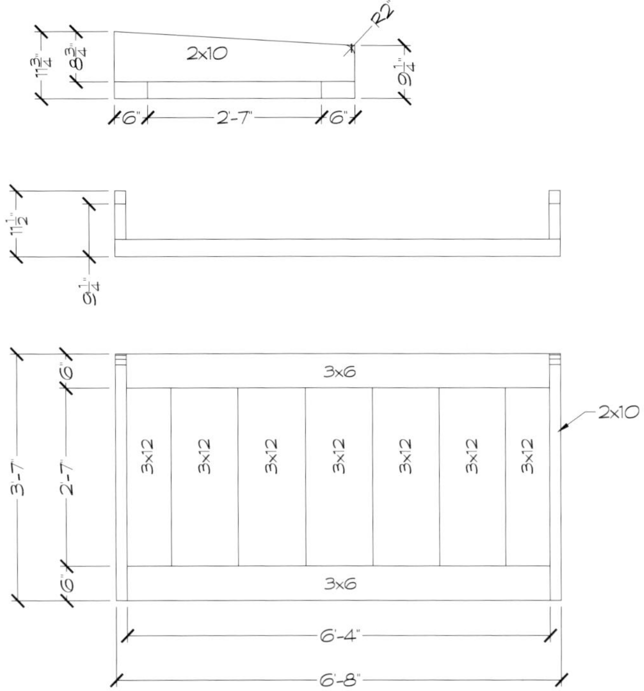

1 TF12 CHUTE
1" = 1'-0"

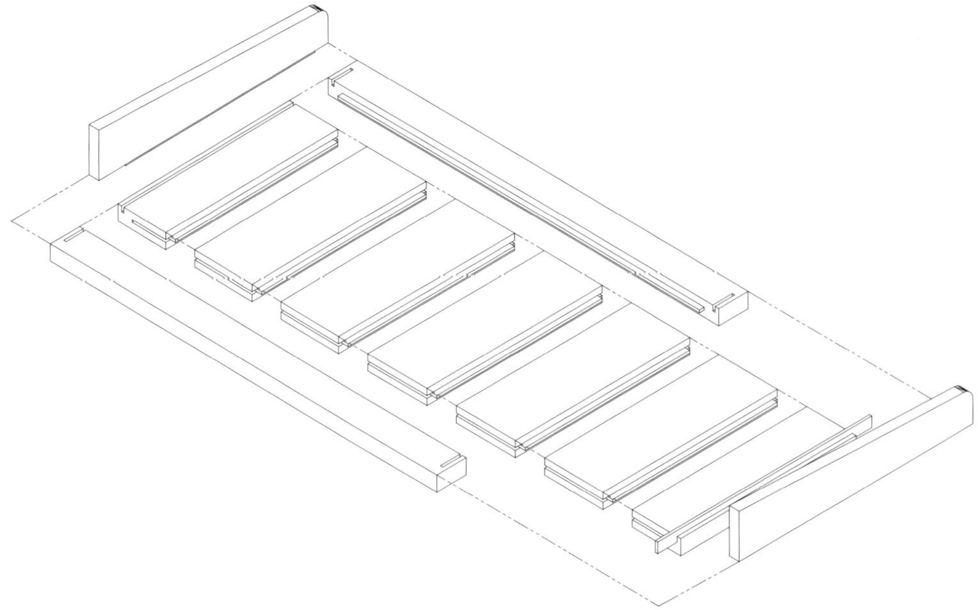

2 TF12 CHUTE EXPLODED VIEW
Not to Scale

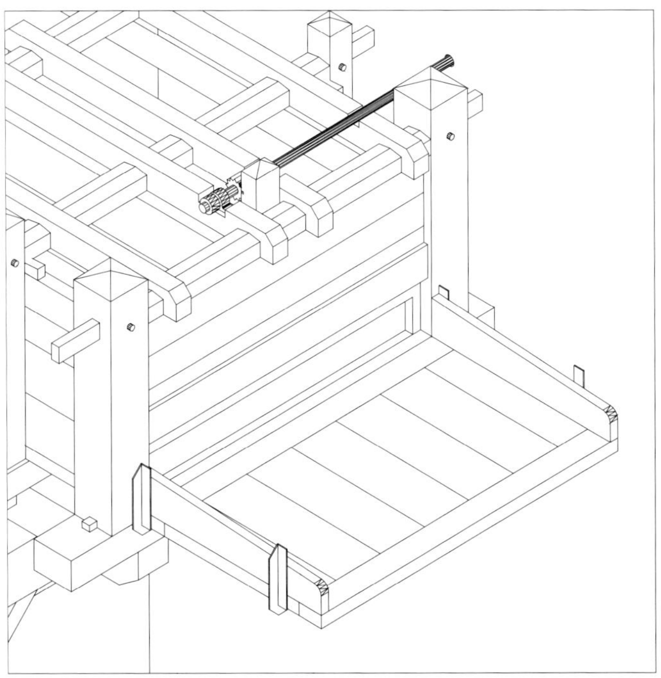

3 TF12 CHUTE EXPLODED VIEW
Not to Scale

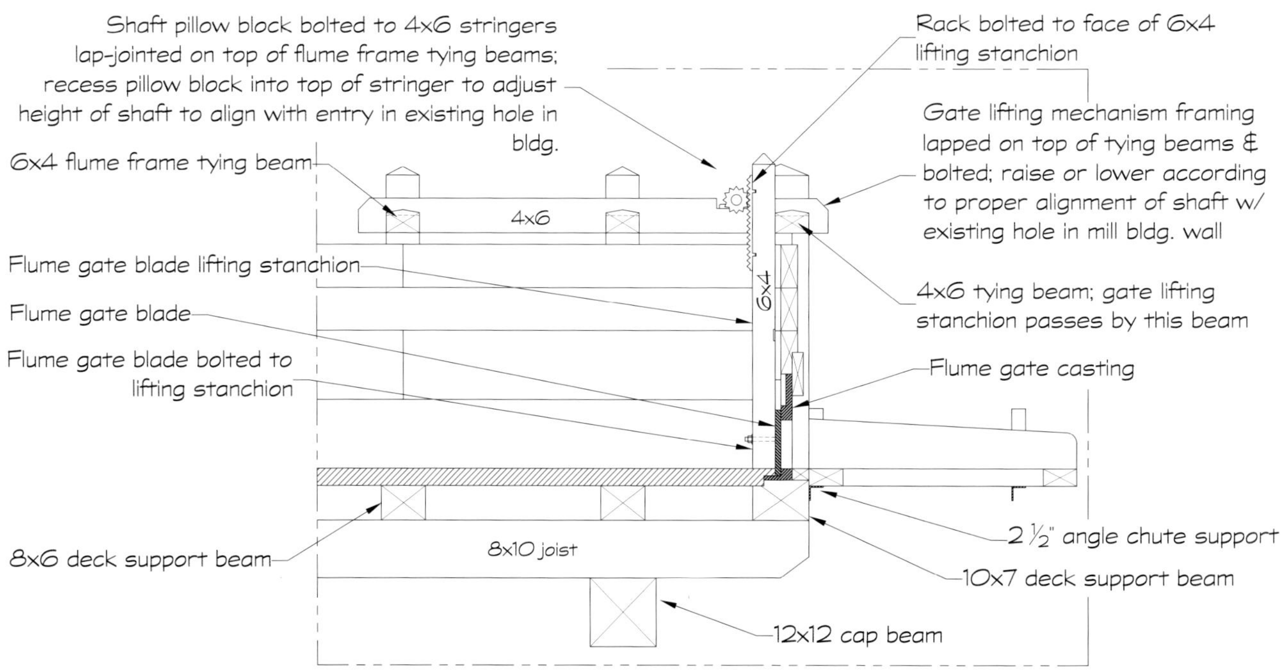

4 TF12 GATE LIFTING MECHANISM & FRAMING
1" = 1'-0"

Partially reconstructed flume.

Wedged stanchion posts. The wedges allow workers to adjust the pressure of the posts holding the side wall panels in place. As the floorboards of the flume expand and contract, the wedges control the tightness of the floorboard fit, and thus the number of leaks in the flume.

Part of the rack and pinion mechanism used to lower and raise the flume gate, the means of controlling the speed of the mill. The shaft penetrated the mill building wall and is connected to a lever that the miller uses to control the flume gate opening.

Retail

Throughout history the transition from the outside world to a sheltered space has been given special attention. Entrances were unambiguous, inviting, and almost always afforded protection from the elements. Heavy timbers declaring, defining, and supporting the entry can warm up an otherwise forbidding façade. In *A Pattern Language* Christopher Alexander writes that " . . . it is hard to overestimate the contribution it [the entrance] makes to a good building." The entrances to Freedom Armory in Glen Rock, Pennsylvania, Kinsey's Outdoors in Mount Joy, Pennsylvania, Kinsley's ShopRite in Brodheadsville, Pennsylvania, and Sauder's Store in Seneca Falls, New York, graphically underscore that axiom.

At the Plain and Fancy Gift Shop in Bird-in-Hand, Pennsylvania, the timber work is carried from the entrance area (a "forebay" in barn parlance) into the entire interior. The King of Prussia Town Center project in King of Prussia, Pennsylvania, was a contemporary mix of entrances, façades, and trellises.

Plain & Fancy Country Store

Bird-in-Hand, Pennsylvania, 1997

Owner
Plain & Fancy Farm Restaurant,
Bird-in-Hand, Pennsylvania

Architect
Paul Risk Associates,
Quarryville, Pennsylvania

Engineer
Geoffrey James Kase, P. E.,
Chester County, Pennsylvania

General contractor
Paul Risk Construction,
Quarryville, Pennsylvania

The covered entry of Plain & Fancy Country Store. This area is under the forebay, the overhanging part of traditional barns that protected stable access on the lowest level.

In 1955 a musical entitled *Plain and Fancy* opened on Broadway. The play concerned a New York couple who traveled to Bird-in-Hand, Pennsylvania, got lost, and had a fascinating encounter with the Amish. That play was the inspiration for the name of this farm restaurant, which opened in 1959. Its 1997 gift shop addition was our company's debut project.

The owners not only wanted the structure to look like a barn, they also wanted to use the construction methods of the historic barns for which Lancaster is known. Most of them had a canted purlin roof system. Each bent—a structural wall segment spaced roughly 16 feet apart along the length of the structure—had two interior queen posts that rose to the roof line, where they were connected with two longitudinal and parallel major purlins. The purlins support the common rafters that sit on them. We used this building technique on the addition. Another common barn-building technique was to nail the vertical siding boards to belt rails—slender timbers that run horizontally and are spaced about 3 feet apart on the barn walls. That system was also used here.

To insulate the wall while maintaining the vertical siding pattern inside and out, we applied rigid foam insulation to the exterior boards. Then 2×4s, running horizontally and in line with the belt rails, were secured through the foam and the first layer of boards, into the belt rails. This procedure yielded a 1½-inch space for electric wiring. The next step was to attach another layer of vertical boards.

Whereas red barns are common in many parts of the United States, in Lancaster County the siding is typically white or weathered gray. To achieve the latter look, the pine siding was left raw. The 400 hemlock timbers that form the structural skeleton of this 9,000-square-foot barn/gift shop have a rough-cut surface. They were lightly sanded and finished with boiled linseed oil.

MEN

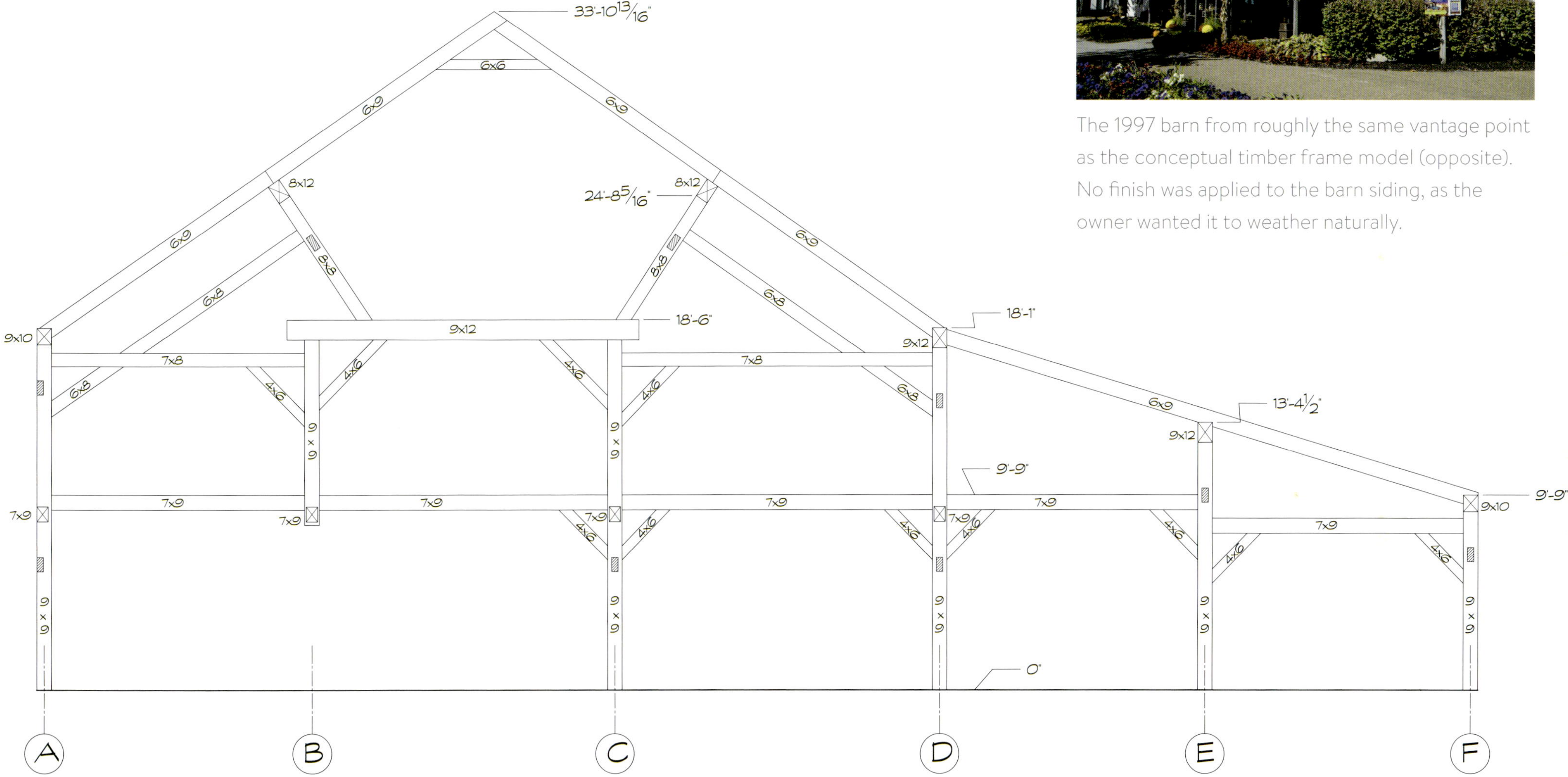

The 1997 barn from roughly the same vantage point as the conceptual timber frame model (opposite). No finish was applied to the barn siding, as the owner wanted it to weather naturally.

Freedom Armory

Glen Rock, Pennsylvania, 2005

Owner
Freedom Armory,
Glen Rock, Pennsylvania

Architect
Hamme Associates Architects
& Engineers, York, Pennsylvania

General contractor
Hogg Construction,
York, Pennsylvania

This project is another example of how the judicious use of timber can exponentially enhance a big box structure. This covered entrance to a gun shop and two-level shooting range required only twenty Douglas fir timbers totaling 1,350 board feet.

View from under the entry canopy to the rolling hills of rural Pennsylvania.

Conceptual model of the timber frame. The timber frame is limited to a single bent and row of posts, with eave plates returning to the face of the building. The roof is conventionally framed on top of the timber frame structure below, and the ceiling is decked with 1×8 white pine tongue and groove boards.

King of Prussia Town Center

King of Prussia, Pennsylvania, 2016

Owner
JBG Rosenfeld Retail Properties,
Chevy Chase, Maryland

Architect
Brown Craig Turner Architects,
Baltimore, Maryland

Engineer
Carroll Engineering,
Hunt Valley, Maryland

General contractor
IMC Construction,
Malvern, Pennsylvania

A scale model of the King of Prussia Town Center, showing several structures provided by Lancaster County Timber Frames. The pavilion is visible at top center, with the bus pergola slightly to its left. Davio's overhanging roof is supported with timber-clad columns, and City Works pergola is shown at lower left. The Fogo de Chão restaurant is surrounded by decorative timber columns and has two projecting canopies that were fully timber framed. Numerous other structures were fabricated and erected by Lancaster County Timber Frames.

King of Prussia Town Center, just northwest of Philadelphia and a mile or so south of Valley Forge National Historical Park, is a 125-acre, mixed-use retail development that opened in October 2016. Our contribution consisted of seventeen distinct heavy timber structures, most of which are located on or around the Main Street area. Some of the structures were made of solid Douglas fir timbers; others were fashioned from Douglas fir glulams.

Notable structures include the REI store, which has a glulam entry canopy connected with steel plates and an exposed tongue and groove roof deck. This building also features three 32-foot-tall heavy timber window assembly frames that were installed into existing masonry with a ½-inch tolerance with a 40-ton crane. The natural three-coat finish on the window assembly frames and the canopy strikes a bold contrast to the large steel siding plates mounted to the exterior, which have been left untreated to create a rusted industrial aesthetic.

Another striking timber structure is the Plaza Pavilion, which features timber "fins" mounted to a geometrically complex steel canopy. This plaza is designed to host community events and outdoor movie screenings on a gigantic suspended television. Near the pavilion is a valet pergola featuring solid-sawn Douglas fir timbers similarly mounted to a cantilevered steel structure, providing shelter for restaurant patrons entering and exiting. Throughout the development, several heavy timber pergolas provide sheltered restaurant dining areas. On the Fogo de Chão pergola, for example, a pattern of heavy timber columns, beams, and canopies coordinate with the exterior lighting and signage to create a warm and inviting atmosphere.

Leaving no detail unturned, almost every dumpster enclosure is dressed with a simple pergola to conceal the contents and maintain the community's polished appearance.

Our intermittent presence on site spanned one year. Approximately 850 timbers, totaling 40,000 board feet, were used.

TOWN SQUARE PL W
ONE WAY

The pavilion, used to shelter a large liquid crystal display for gatherings and events.

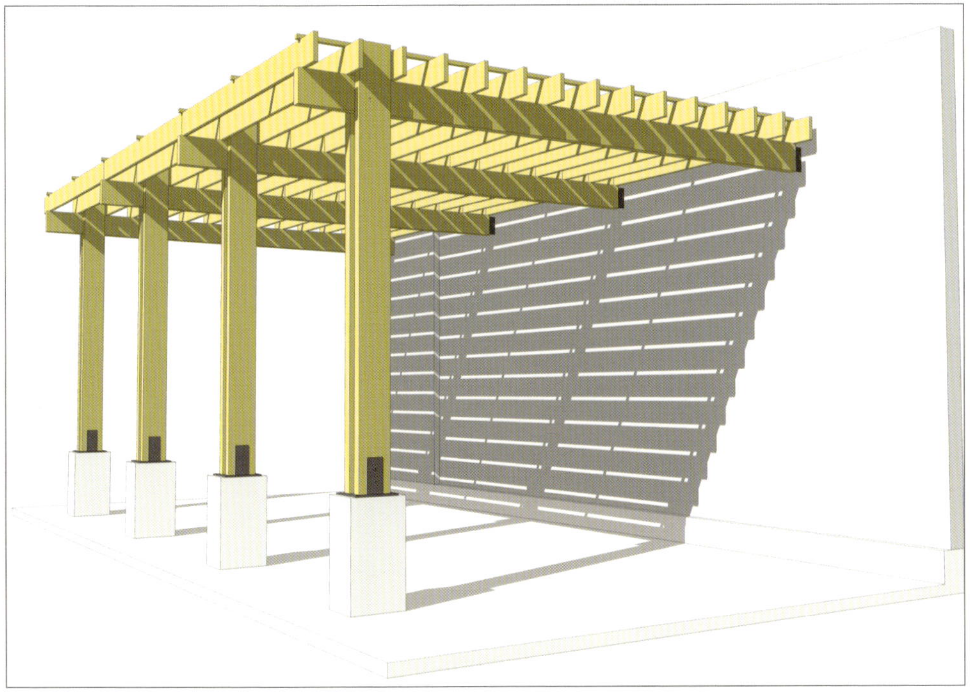

The entry canopy of the REI store at King of Prussia Town Center.

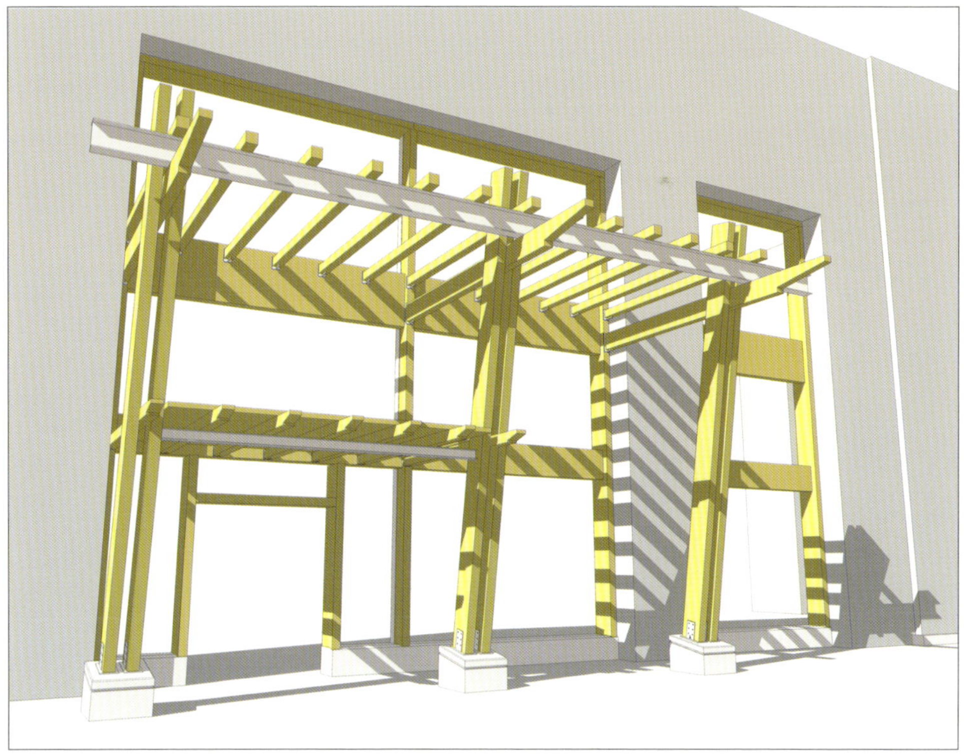

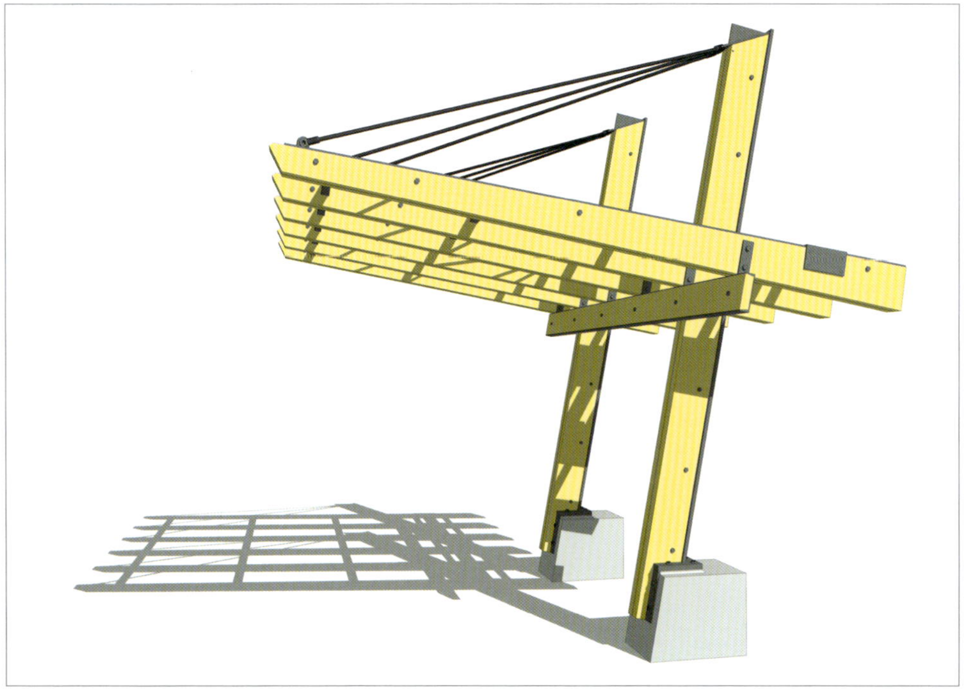

The bus pergola.

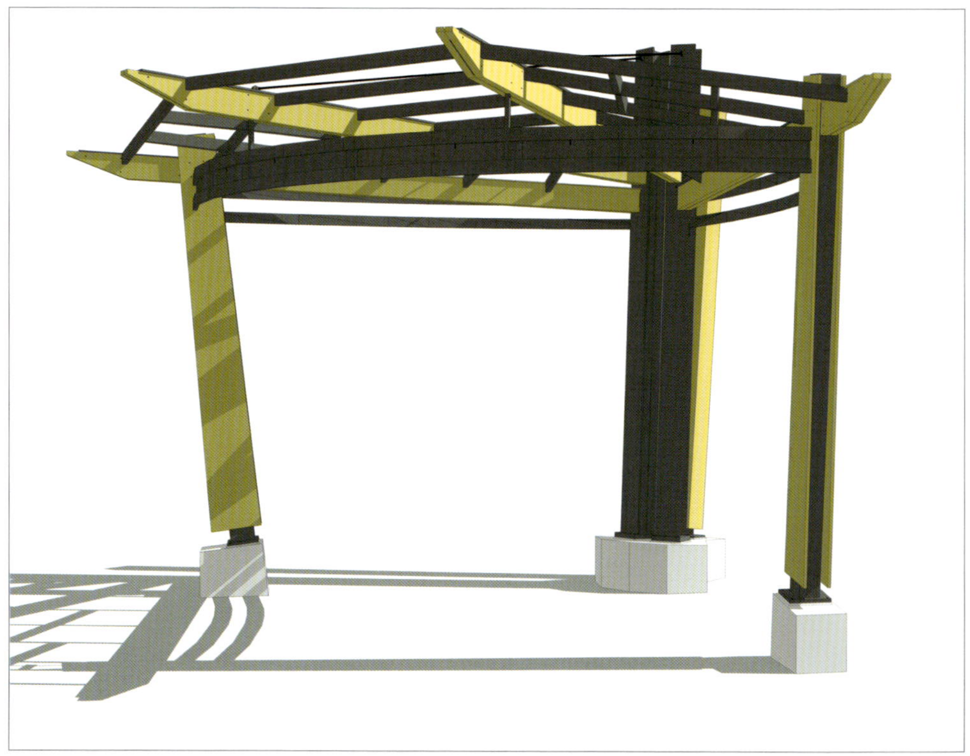

Kinsey's Outdoors

Mount Joy, Pennsylvania, 1999

Owner
Kinsey's Outdoors,
Mount Joy, Pennsylvania

Architect
Cornerstone Design Architects,
Lancaster, Pennsylvania

General contractor
Horst Group,
Lancaster, Pennyslvania

This early project marks our first timber frame covered entrance for a big box store. The architect wanted to create a bold, inviting entrance for a building that, due to budgetary constraints, was otherwise characterless. Twenty timbers totaling 5,250 board feet added much-needed warmth to this entrance.

Over the years we have done many big box timber entrances. This first one, though, demonstrated the inherent warming and welcoming power of heavy timbers, even when sparingly used. That the architecture firm's owner had been a student in a 1970 high school architectural class taught by LCTF's president was icing on the cake.

A timber-framed structure makes the entrance to a big box store obvious.

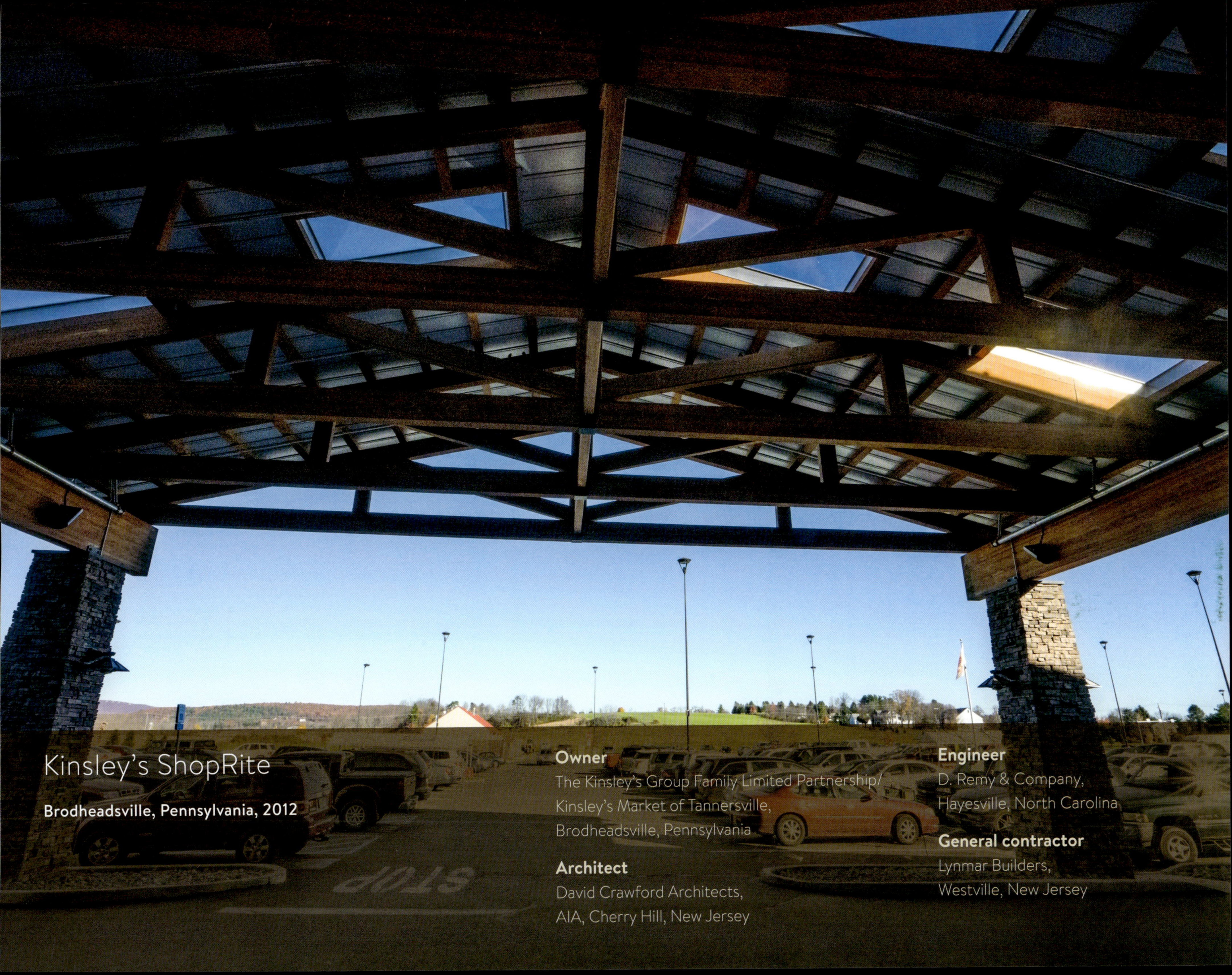

Kinsley's ShopRite

Brodheadsville, Pennsylvania, 2012

Owner
The Kinsley's Group Family Limited Partnership/
Kinsley's Market of Tannersville,
Brodheadsville, Pennsylvania

Architect
David Crawford Architects,
AIA, Cherry Hill, New Jersey

Engineer
D. Remy & Company,
Hayesville, North Carolina

General contractor
Lynmar Builders,
Westville, New Jersey

This project doubled the size of the existing Kinsley's ShopRite. LCTF's involvement included seven exterior timber-framed canopies and an interior timber-framed staircase. More than 700 Douglas fir timbers totaling 42,000 board feet were used for the canopies. Additionally, the 250 timbers used on the staircase totaled 3,500 board feet, excluding the handrails.

The most difficult challenge occurred at a corner at which two of our roof structures converged to form a hip. At that height, the newly constructed wall formed a corner that was 5 degrees short of 90 degrees. As our joinery and roof systems were laid out and cut at our shop predicated on the corner being, in fact, 90 degrees, we had a full additional day's work to sort out and correct the issue. We had taken copious measurements on the building to which our frame would attach and verified the measurements several weeks before installation, but we had neglected to double check that corner angle at the height of convergence.

The entry canopy to the world's largest ShopRite store is more than 100 feet wide.

COLD
BEER
TO
GO
LOTTERY
PLAY
HERE!

ShopRite

PIZZERIA
DINNER
for 2
STOP

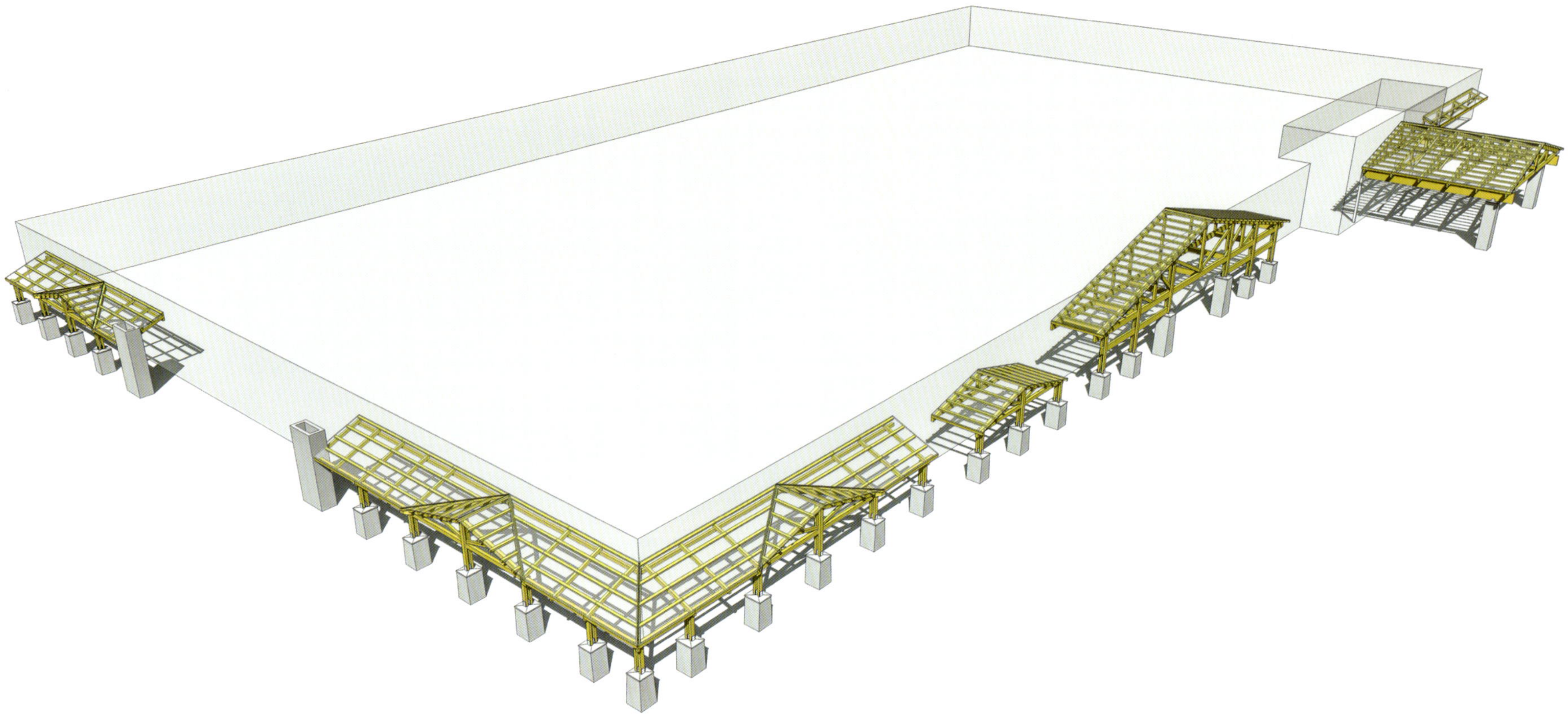

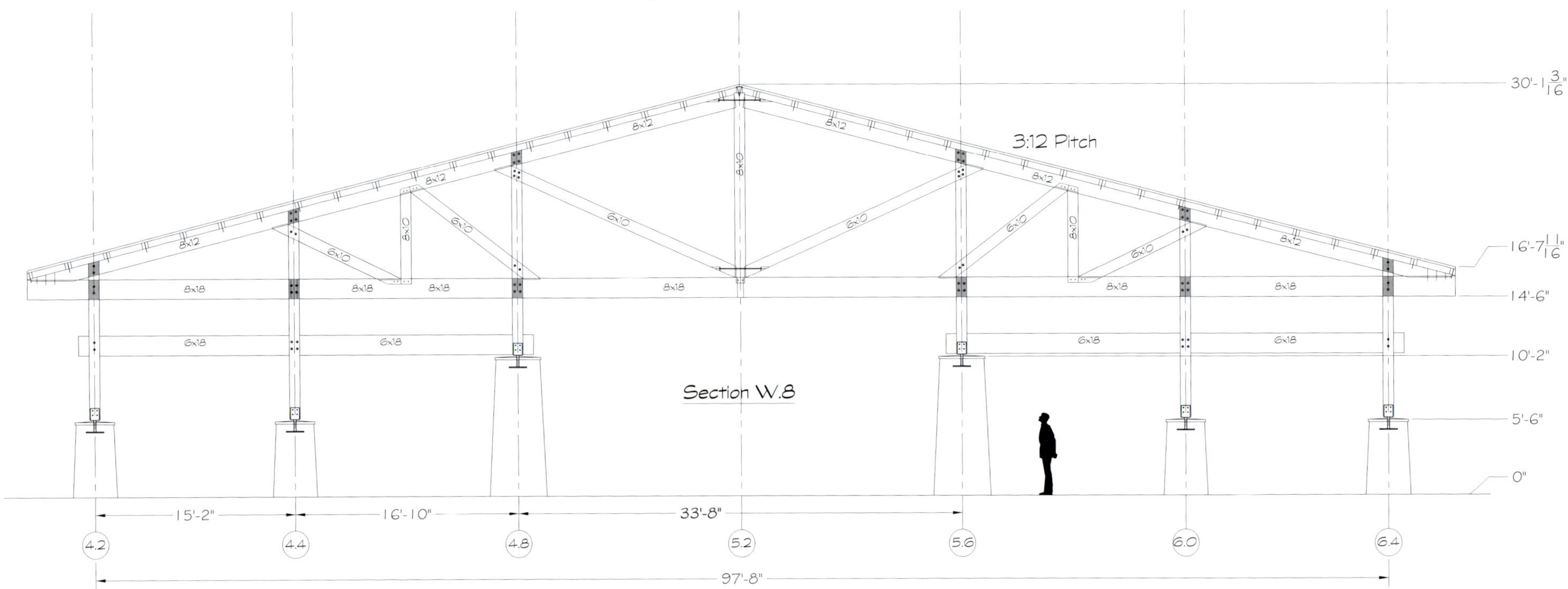

30'-1 3/16"
3:12 Pitch
8x12
8x10
6x10
8x18
6x18
16'-7 11/16"
14'-6"
10'-2"
Section W.8
5'-6"
0"
15'-2"
16'-10"
33'-8"
4.2
4.4
4.8
5.2
5.6
6.0
6.4
97'-8"

The owners wanted a timber-framed staircase to lead from the shopping floor up to the dining mezzanine. A conceptual model of the staircase is shown above left.

Sauder's Store

Seneca Falls, New York, 2014

Owner
Sauder's Store,
Seneca Falls, New York

Architect
Engle Architects,
Lancaster, Pennsylvania

Engineer
Rocky Mountain Log Homes Direct,
Hamilton, Montana

General contractor
Hoover Building Specialists,
Lancaster, Pennsylvania

Sauder's Store, known for its organic family farm produce, opened in 1978. It is owned and operated by Mennonites originally hailing from Lancaster County, Pennsylvania. The owners' ties to that county were so strong that when they decided to add almost 40,000 square feet, they looked toward home for their architect, builder, and timber framer.

Our work consisted of a main port cochère, two gabled porches, two long sidewalk porches, and railings for an interior loft. Wanting a rustic feel and to accent the organic focus of their food, the clients requested peeled logs.

The term post and beam refers to a construction method in which heavy vertical, horizontal, and angled members are joined to form a skeletal structure. The methods of joining can include visible or concealed steel plates, hangers or mechanical fasteners, or mortise and tenon joints carved directly into the wood. This latter method is what defines timber framing. Timber framing is a subset of post and beam. Thus all timber frames are post and beam, but not all post and beam buildings are timber frames.

In timber framing the typical component is a timber that was been sawn and, frequently, also planed, to consistent dimensions along its length, and whose surfaces, or faces, are usually 90 degrees to one another. The more consistent and true a timber, the easier it is to lay out and cut the mortise and tenon joinery.

Logs, on the other hand, raise the ante considerably. Logs can be ordered from the mill either turned—actually turned on a huge lathe to a consistent diameter along their entire length, or peeled—the bark removed. Peeled logs have an organic shape with bumps and dips, and a varying diameter along its length. This project used more than seventy peeled logs and approximately 17,000 board feet of material.

SWISS DELI
SAUDERS
Quality & Savings
COUNTRY CAFE

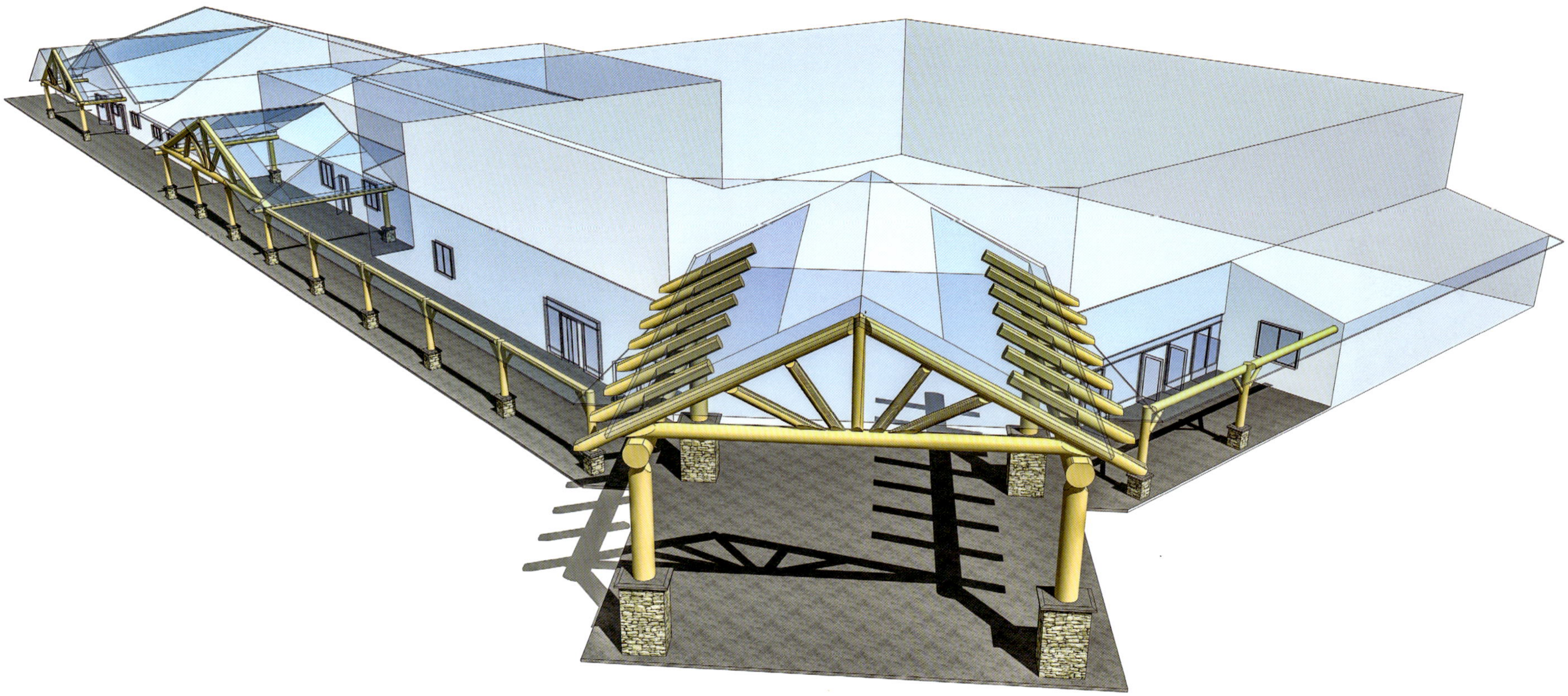

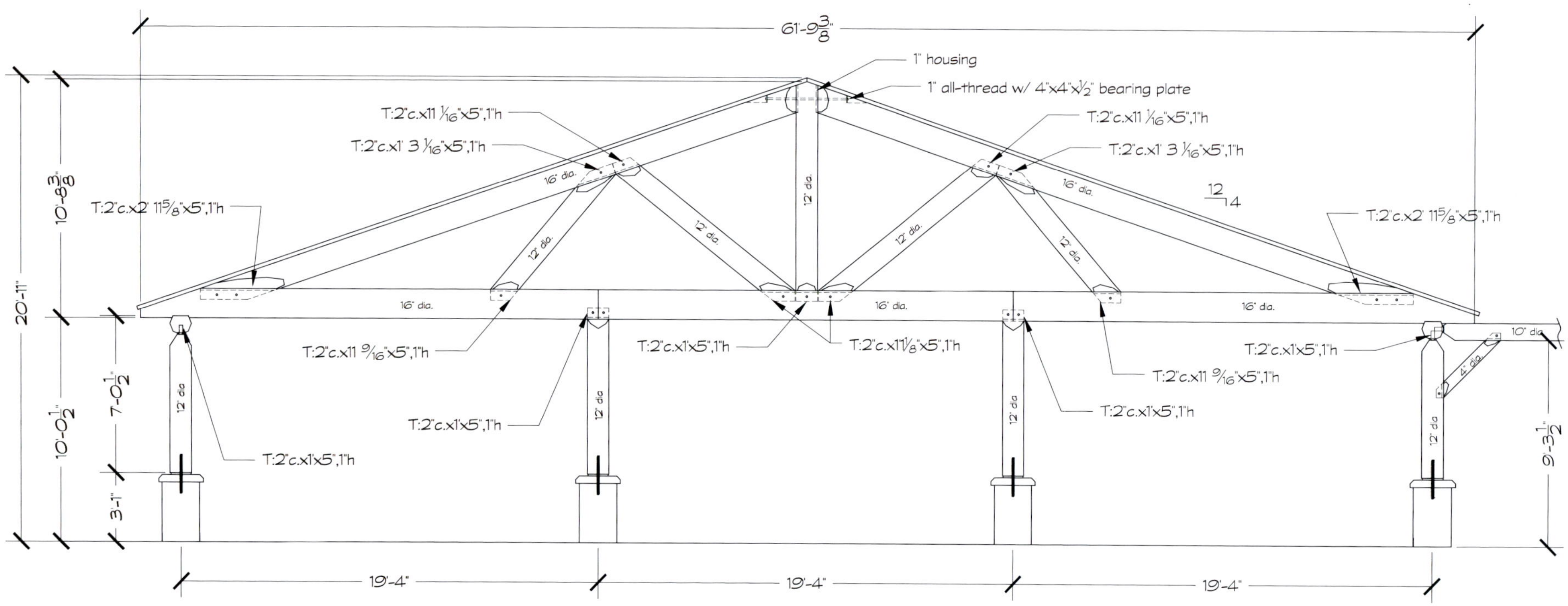
61'-9 3/8"
1" housing
1" all-thread w/ 4"x4"x1/2" bearing plate
T:2"c.x11 1/16"x5",1"h
T:2"c.x1' 3 1/16"x5",1"h
T:2"c.x11 1/16"x5",1"h
T:2"c.x1' 3 1/16"x5",1"h
T:2"c.x2' 11 5/8"x5",1"h
T:2"c.x2' 11 5/8"x5",1"h
12
14
16" dia.
12" dia.
10" dia.
4" dia.
T:2"c.x11 9/16"x5",1"h
T:2"c.x1'x5",1"h
T:2"c.x11 1/8"x5",1"h
T:2"c.x1'x5",1"h
T:2"c.x11 9/16"x5",1"h
T:2"c.x1'x5",1"h
T:2"c.x1'x5",1"h
T:2"c.x1'x5",1"h
20'-11"
10'-8 3/8"
10'-0 1/2"
7'-0 1/2"
3'-1"
9'-3 1/2"
19'-4"
19'-4"
19'-4"

Carving the 36-inch-diameter logs that serve as eave plates in the porte cochère on site. Most of the work was done with chain saws.

"Flying" a truss member into position.

Notes

1. The most commonly cited source for this information is Vitruvius, *De Architectura*, known today as *The Ten Books on Architecture* and available in various translations. Book IV, Chapter 2 ("On the details of the orders") and Chapter 3 ("On the Doric order") contain the most explicit analysis of the origin of many features of classical Greek temple architecture.

2. Much of the following discussion of the physiological effects of exposure to nature, both inside and outside the built environment, follows quite closely the review of the literature helpfully provided in David Robert Fell's doctoral dissertation *Wood in the Human Environment: Restorative Properties of Wood in the Built Indoor Environment* (University of British Columbia, 2010). Where accessible, a number of his original sources were also consulted, and some of these are given in the Bibliography. The various claims made for the health benefits of plants and wood in the interior built environment are offered here more as an informal summary than as scientific discussion.

3. As described in Curry 2014.

Bibliography

Alexander, Christopher, et al. *A Pattern Language: Towns, Buildings, Construction*. New York: Oxford University Press, 1977.

Augustin, Sally, et al. "Wood as a Restorative Material in Healthcare Environments." *FPInnovations Publications* (June 2015): https://fpinnovations.ca/media/publications/Documents/health-report.pdf.

Curry, Andrew. "The Neolithic Toolkit: How Experimental Archaeology is Showing that Europe's First Farmers Were Also Its First Carpenters." *Archaeology* (October 14, 2014): http://www.archaeology.org/issues/152-1411/features/2591-germany-recreating-neolithic-toolkit.

Fell, David Robert. "Wood in the Human Environment: Restorative Properties of Wood in the Built Indoor Environment." Doctoral dissertation, University of British Columbia, Vancouver, 2010. Retrieved from https://open.library.ubc.ca/cIRcle/collections/ubctheses/24/items/1.0071305.

Forest & Wood Products Australia. "Wood: Housing, Health, Humanity." April 9, 2015. http://makeitwood.org/documents/doc-1253-wood--housing--health--humanity-report-2015-03-00-final.pdf.

Kellert, Stephen P., et al. *Biophilic Design: The Theory, Science, and Practice of Bringing Buildings to Life*. Hoboken, NJ: John Wiley & Sons, 2008.

Kopec, Dak. *Environmental Psychology for Design*. New York: Fairchild Publications, 2006. First edition.

Masuda, M., and N. Yamamoto. "The Wood Ratio in Interior Space and the Psychological Images (II)." *Bulletin of Kyoto University Forests* (1988): 60.

Masuda, M., and N. Yamamoto. "The Wood Ratio in Interior Space and the Psychological Images (II)." *Bulletin of Kyoto University Forests* (1990): 62.

Nakamura, M., et al. "Visual Factors Influencing Psychological Images of Woods and Stones." *Bulletin of the Kyoto University Forests* 40 (1994): 364–376.

Nyrud, Anders Q. "Psychological Effects of Indoor Wood Use, Empirical Evidence and Possible Applications in Care Environments." *Norsk Treteknisk Institutt* (2012). https://www.kyamk.fi/.../Wood%20Academy/HealthBenefits2013%202013-04-25.pdf.

Rice, Jennifer, et al. "Appearance Wood Products and Psychological Well-Being." *Wood and Fiber Science*, (October 2006): http://www.woodworks.org/wp-content/uploads/Appearance-Wood-Products-and-Psychological-Well-Being.pdf.

Sakuragawa, S., et al. "Influence of Wood Wall Panels on Physiological and Psychological Responses." *Journal of Wood Science–The Japan Wood Research Society* 51 (2005): 136–140.

Shibata, S., and N. Suzuki. "Effects of Foliage Plants on Task Performance and Mood." *Journal of Environmental Psychology* 22 (2002): 265–272.

timber+DESIGN magazine. "Wood Psychology: Make It More Visible and Improve Well-Being." (July 7, 2014): http://www.timberdesignmag.com/articles/wood-psychology/.

Tsunetsugu, Y., et al. "The Visual Effects of Wooden Interiors in Actual-size Living Rooms on the Autonomic Nervous Activities." *Journal of Physiological Anthropology* 21(6) (2002): 297–300.

Tsunetsugu, Y., et al. "Physiological Effects in Humans Induced by the Visual Stimulation of Room Interiors with Different Wood Quantities." *Journal of Wood Science–The Japan Wood Research Society* 53 (2007): 11–16.

Vitruvius. *The Ten Books on Architecture*. Translated by Morris Hickey Morgan. New York: Dover Publications, 1960.

Wilson, Edward O. *Biophilia*. Boston: Harvard University Press, 1984. Revised edition.

Wright, Frank Lloyd. "In the Cause of Architecture, IV: The Meaning of Materials–Wood." *Architectural Record*, May 1928.

Zaya, Anthony F., and Tim Diener. *Timber Frame Hybrids: Enduring Traditions, Boundless Possibilities*. Atglen, PA: Schiffer Publishing Ltd., 2008.

Rhode Island native **Anthony Zaya** is president and co-founder of Lancaster County Timber Frames, Inc. He holds a master's degree in industrial arts and has taught architectural drawing at the secondary and college levels. He has been a designer for Apeco Corporation, freelance writer, consultant to government agencies involved in K-9 work, and contributing editor at *DogSport* magazine. Tony has been timber framing since 1986 and has published numerous articles on the subject. On Sunday afternoons he rides his vintage 1968 Suzuki Titan motorcycle over the winding roads of Lancaster County. He lives with his wife, Barb Byler, in Lititz, Pennsylvania.

Tim Diener has worked in a wide variety of fields, from fine arts to foreign language translation and teaching, manufacturing, and academia. Raised in Southeast Asia, he lived in Germany for many years while a student of Arabic, and taught, translated, wrote, and edited during his several years in Japan. Tim holds a bachelor of fine arts degree in sculpture from Tyler School of Art of Temple University and a master's degree in Japanese history from Cornell University.